Learning Carbon

Learning Carbon

Apple Computer, Inc.

O'REILLY®

Beijing · Cambridge · Farnham · Köln · Paris · Sebastopol · Taipei · Tokyo

Learning Carbon
by Apple Computer, Inc.

Published by O'Reilly & Associates, Inc., 101 Morris Street, Sebastopol, CA 95472.

Editor: Troy Mott

Production Editor: Sarah Jane Shangraw

Cover Designer: Pam Spremulli

Printing History:

>   May 2001:   First Edition.

ISBN: 0-596-00161-4
[M]   [6/01*]

Table of Contents

Preface

If you want to get up to speed quickly on using Carbon to create Mac OS X applications, this is the book for you. It shows how to put together a Carbon application that does all the things commonly found in an application, such as handling windows, responding to menu commands and controls in the interface, printing documents, and opening and saving files. The application you'll create in this book isn't one of those boring computational programs that figure prime numbers or compute factorials. Instead, you'll put together something that could be of practical value as we enter the third millennium—a moon travel planner.

This book is not an exhaustive guide to writing Carbon applications. We've limited the topics and scope of coverage to those we think are most important for programmers new to Carbon. We've provided a road map to all the Carbon managers and services (Chapter 1, *Introduction to Carbon*) and an introduction to a few advanced topics—scripting, tab controls, threads, and multiprocessing (Chapter 14, *Beyond Moon Travel: Advanced Topics*). So once you are finished with this book, you'll be prepared to write a Carbon application on your own.

Why Carbon?

If you're writing an application that will run exclusively on Mac OS X, there are several ways you can do it. You can use Cocoa, Carbon, or Java. So why use Carbon? If you know a procedural language, such as C, you'll feel right at home with Carbon. You'll be able to draw upon your knowledge and experience of procedural programming languages. You might even find that in new applications you create with Carbon, you can reuse code you've already written.

Although the Carbon programming interface uses the C language, you can write Carbon applications in many different languages, including object oriented languages such as C++. Apple provides both C and C++ compilers for use with Carbon, and third-party tools are available for writing Carbon applications in Pascal, BASIC, Fortran, and other languages.

If you are more familiar with object-oriented programming, you should take a look at *Learning Cocoa* (O'Reilly & Associates). Java programmers may want to read *Inside Mac OS X: Java Development for Mac OS X*, available from Apple's Java Developer Documentation web site:

> *http://developer.apple.com/techpubs/java/*

Who Might Find This Book Helpful

Anyone who has some experience programming with the C language (extensive programming experience is not required) and a rudimentary understanding of computer science concepts should find the book helpful and fun. This book is a good starting point for students, individual programmers, small developers, and anyone who has an interest in, or curiosity about, Mac OS X.

You don't need to be familiar with the Mac OS, or any platform for that matter. As long as you've knocked out a few small programs using C, you should do just fine with Carbon.

What You Need

This book takes a hands-on approach. To get the most out of it, you need to use this book along with Apple's development tools—Project Builder and Interface Builder. You'll need the following to complete this tutorial:

- A computer that's running Mac OS X.

- Project Builder and Interface Builder, available on the Mac OS X Developer CD, which is included with every copy of Mac OS X.

- Files and images to complete the Moon Travel Planner application you'll build in this book. You can find information on how to download these materials by going to this O'Reilly web site (where you'll also find all of the numbered code examples from this book): *http://www.oreilly.com/catalog/learncarbon/*.

What's Up Ahead

This book is designed as a tutorial. Each chapter builds upon the previous one. You should start at the beginning and proceed sequentially. Chapters are designed so you can stop at the end of each one, then pick up with the next at a later time.

This book will take you, step by step, through the design and building of a simple Carbon application (Moon Travel Planner). After finishing this book, you should be comfortable enough with basic Carbon concepts and the workings of Project Builder and Interface Builder to start writing your own Carbon applications.

The topics in upcoming chapters are as follows:

- Chapter 1, *Introduction to Carbon*, provides an overview of Carbon, Mac OS X, and the Carbon programming interfaces and tells what's involved in building a Carbon application.

- Chapter 2, *Specifying a Carbon Application: Moon Travel Planner*, discusses the process of specifying a simple application, Moon Travel Planner, and its user interface.

- Chapter 3, *Project Builder Projects*, introduces Project Builder and describes how to build a minimalist application (essentially the prototypical "Hello World" application without the "Hello World" part). It also introduces the concept of bundles and application packaging.

- Chapter 4, *Interface Builder: Nibs and Windows*, introduces Interface Builder and shows how to use it to create a simple window.

- Chapter 5, *Interface Builder: Tools and Controls*, expands on Chapter 4, letting you add buttons and other controls to the simple window.

- Chapter 6, *Carbon Events*, introduces the Carbon event-handling model and shows you how to create a basic event handler.

- Chapter 7, *Interface Builder: Menus*, shows you how to use Interface Builder to create menus for your application.

- Chapter 8, *Text and Localization*, shows you how to organize a project to support localization and how to handle text that is displayed in a window.

- Chapter 9, *Printing*, introduces the basics of printing in Carbon and shows you how to print a window containing text.

- Chapter 10, *Property Lists*, introduces property lists, which are a generic way to store information needed by your application. It also describes how to design and implement an About window so that it displays information from a property list.

- Chapter 11, *Files*, shows you how to store and retrieve data in a file.

- Chapter 12, *Providing Help*, describes help facilities, namely help books and help tags, available to your application and shows how to implement them.

- Chapter 13, *Desktop Icons*, shows how to create an icon for your application and how to identify your application (and any files it creates) to the Finder application.

- Chapter 14, *Beyond Moon Travel: Advanced Topics*, describes some additional features that may be useful for your applications.

- Appendix A, *Additional Resources*, provides information on Carbon-related resources and where to find them. If a book or document is mentioned in a chapter, you'll find out how to get it here.

- Appendix B, *Carbon Event Classes and Kinds*, describes the event constants you'll need when you create an application that uses the Carbon Event Manager.

- Appendix C, *Parameter Names and Types for Common Event Kinds*, provides a detailed set of tables that list constants you'll need to retrieve parameter values associated with Carbon events.

Side Trips and Terms

Although this book is a primer, not an encyclopedia, there are times when we'll provide supplemental material. You can skip over this material and still complete the tutorial, or you can read the supplemental information if you'd like a better understanding of a topic or why certain choices were made. Supplemental material is set off in a box that looks like this:

Look in these sections for supplemental information and tips.

Information we think you need to know to avoid problems or to make the code work properly is set off in a box that looks like this:

Look in these sections for important information and warnings.

Constant width is used to indicate command-line computer output and code examples, as well as filenames, directories and pathnames, functions, constants, variables, and flow-control statements like repeat.

Italics are used to introduce new terms and to indicate URLs.

Constant width bold is used to indicate user input.

You can find information on how to get books or other documents mentioned in a chapter in Appendix A.

Code

Throughout this book, we've put a number or letter on the right side of any line of code we explain. Numbered explanations appear below a listing, as shown by the following:

```
myCartoonRef = GetStandardCartoon (myCartoonID);          //1
status = FloatCartoon (myCartoonRef, myWindow);           //2
```

1. The Cartoon Manager function GetStandardCartoon returns a reference to the cartoon character specified by myCartoonID. A cartoon ID is a unique 8-bit value you assign to the cartoon character when you create it.

2. The Cartoon Manager function FloatCartoon floats a cartoon character across a window. It returns a status of 0 if the character successfully gets to the other side.

Where appropriate, we'll identify the name of the Carbon manager or technology to which a function belongs. If you want to find out more about the function and its manager or technology, see Chapter 1 or Carbon Help (available in the Project Builder Help menu).

In some cases we do not provide error checking so you can more easily see the code that's central to a function.

The Environment Could Change

NASA has had to make a few mid-course corrections on occasion, and we may too! The authors have made every effort to make sure the information in this book is accurate. We've had technical reviews, we've compiled all the code, and we've thoroughly tested all the steps. The book is based on the first official release of Mac OS X, Project Builder version 1.0, and Interface Builder version 2.0. If you use this book with a later release of any of these products, the user interface and features may be different from those shown in the book.

You should not use this book with the Public Beta version of Mac OS X, Project Builder, or Interface Builder, all of which are substantially changed (and improved!) with the official release of Mac OS X.

How to Contact Us

You can write to:

O'Reilly & Associates, Inc.
101 Morris Street
Sebastopol, CA 95472
1-800-998-9938 (in the U. S. or Canada)
1-707-829-0515 (international/local)
1-707-829-0104 (FAX)

You can also send us messages electronically. To be put on the mailing list or request a catalog, send email to:

info@oreilly.com

To ask technical questions or comment on the book, send email to:

bookquestions@oreilly.com

We have a web site for the book, where we'll list examples, errata, and any plans for future editions. You can access this page at:

http://www.oreilly.com/catalog/learncarbon/

For more information about this book and others, see the O'Reilly web site:

http://www.oreilly.com

1

Introduction to Carbon

The element carbon is an essential building block for life on earth. For C programmers, Apple's Carbon is the essential building block for applications on Mac OS X. With Carbon, you not only gain the benefits of Mac OS X, but you do so while using some of the simplest traditional C interfaces available. This combination makes it easier than ever to create world-class applications for a world-class operating system.

Carbon and Mac OS X

Carbon is the collection of C programming interfaces for Mac OS X, Apple's next-generation operating system.

 A programming interface is the set of functions and data structures defined by one piece of software, such as an operating system service, for use by client software, such as applications and device drivers. For example, you would access one programming interface to enable your application to print and another to manipulate your application's menus.

Carbon was originally designed to support the evolution of the Mac OS. Apple updated and reimplemented programming interfaces written for earlier versions of the Mac OS to take advantage of new features and enhancements in Mac OS X. Mac OS X brings many modern operating-system features to the Macintosh, including:

- **Protected memory.** Each application lives in its own address space, which prevents errant applications from crashing the system or other applications.

- **Preemptive multitasking.** Each application is guaranteed processing time, resulting in a more responsive user experience.

- **Dynamic resource allocation.** Your application can allocate memory and other shared resources based on actual needs rather than predetermined values, such as fixed memory allocations.

- **Aqua look and feel.** Apple's new user interface is available only to applications that run natively on Mac OS X. Aqua provides a feast of visual effects—active buttons pulse, icons dance, windows spring to life—and showcases the sharpest graphics ever seen on a personal computer.

 Carbon is especially useful for developers who need to update older Mac OS code to run on Mac OS X. This book doesn't cover this porting process, but if you're interested, see *Inside Carbon: Carbon Porting Guide* (listed in Appendix A, *Additional Resources*).

In addition to updating older features, Mac OS X adopts some industry-standard practices and introduces brand new technologies. To support these features for C-language programmers, Apple added new programming interfaces to the venerable Mac OS. The collection of updated and new programming interfaces is called *Carbon*.

As shown in Figure 1-1, Carbon is one of several application environments available on Mac OS X.

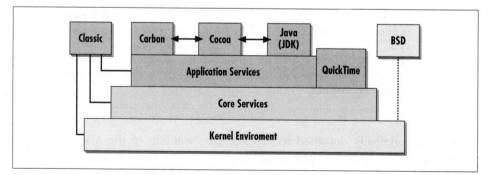

Figure 1-1. Carbon in relation to other Mac OS X environments

These other environments include:

- **Cocoa.** The object-oriented interface for writing Mac OS X applications in Objective-C or Java

- **Classic.** A compatibility environment for applications written for systems prior to Mac OS X. These applications do not gain all the advantages of Mac OS X

- **Java.** A JDK-compliant virtual machine for running pure Java applications

These environments depend on the same application and core services for their operation, and the underlying services rely on Darwin (Apple's open-source core operating system) and the Mach kernel.

Each environment (including the optional BSD command-line environment) has advantages and disadvantages, but for C and C++ programmers, Carbon is the best choice.

What's in Carbon?

Carbon contains thousands of functions, data structures, and constants, but don't worry, this book uses only a small number of these. Related functions and data structures are organized into functional groups, usually referred to as managers or services. For example, the Window Manager contains functions and data structures that let you create, remove, and otherwise manipulate application windows.

In this book you'll use functions from only a handful of these managers and services, most of which are commonly used in all Carbon applications. These interfaces cover the following functionality:

- **User interface creation and manipulation.** That is, handling windows, menus, and other common graphical user interface (GUI) elements.

- **Event handling.** How to find out when something happens and what to do when it does.

- **Basic string manipulation.** How to put together text you want to display in a window.

- **Basic graphics rendering.** How to display the text and windows on a screen.

- **Printing.** How to print the text in a window.

- **Saving and opening files.**

- **Help.** How to implement a simple online help system and how to add informative "help tags" to buttons and other controls.

- **Storing and accessing resources.** Mac OS X has a "bundle" feature that lets you store all the files an application needs in one easily accessible package.

You'll probably be surprised to see how few functions you need from each manager or service to implement basic functionality. That's what's great about Carbon on Mac OS X. The operating system and the development tools you'll use—Project Builder and Interface Builder—do most of the grunt work for you. For example, you might think you'd have to write a lot of complicated code to allow a user to drag a window around the screen. In actuality, you get this for free: the operating system automatically makes the appropriate calls for you and makes sure the dragged window behaves properly. Of course, if you need to control every aspect of an action or want to add custom features, Carbon lets you do that too. However, if you're willing to accept the standard behavior—and there is little reason not to—for most user interface elements, you'll have far less code to write.

Building Carbon Applications

Because Carbon is just a collection of C programming interfaces, you can use just about any Macintosh C development environment that supports PowerPC to build Carbon applications. However, there are some limitations. For example, Carbon developers can create applications in two different executable formats:

- **Mach-O.** This is the native executable format on Mac OS X. Mach-O-based executables can run only on Mac OS X.

- **PEF.** The Preferred Executable Format (PEF) binary was the native executable format for PowerPC Mac OS systems before Mac OS X. With some work, PEF executables can run on Mac OS X as well as some earlier systems. Note that PEF applications are sometimes called CFM-based applications because the Code Fragment Manager is the mechanism for preparing and executing such files.

Older environments, such as Apple's MPW, can produce only PEF executables; while others, such as Metrowerks CodeWarrior, let you build either PEF or Mach-O versions. Which tool you use depends on what platforms you are targeting.

The tutorials in this book will use Project Builder and Interface Builder, which are Apple's development tools for building Mach-O-based applications on Mac OS X. Both tools have been written with Carbon in mind, and they come free with Mac OS X, making them excellent choices for new developers.

Project Builder and Interface Builder work in conjunction with each other to make building applications easier than ever:

- **Project Builder.** The main development environment; it lets you create and assemble the components of your application. Being a user-friendly development environment, Project Builder gives you many standard application features for free, such as support for basic event handling.

- **Interface Builder.** A WYSIWYG tool that lets you lay out user interfaces in a simple, intuitive manner. These interface templates are stored as a .nib file, which your application can then access to create its windows, menus, and other elements.

The Carbon Factory Tour

Because Carbon contains many, many programming interfaces, it can be quite daunting to a new developer. While this book provides a good start, at some point you will need to begin fending for yourself. What interfaces you will require depends on the type of applications you want to write, but as is often the case, some are more commonly used than others. This section divides up the Carbon interfaces according to usage (from fundamental to esoteric) and gives some useful information about each one. To learn more about a particular interface, you can use the Carbon Help feature integrated into Project Builder (to be described later in this book). You can also consult the technical documentation on the Apple developer web site.

The Starter Kit

This section covers the interfaces most likely to be called by a Macintosh application (and covers those that can be found in this book). These managers and services provide basic user interface functionality as well as fundamental features, such as the ability to save and print files. You can build basic but fully functional Carbon applications using the interfaces described here.

 If Carbon were an interface to build automobiles, the Starter Kit interfaces would define the engine, wheels, brakes and other essential components, as well as the user interface (dashboard, steering wheel, gas and brake pedals, and so on).

The Toolbox interfaces

The following interfaces are grouped together because they generally work together to create and manage the user interfaces. In most cases, Interface Builder and the Interface Builder Services interface can handle the creation and control of the basic user interface. However, to accomplish more esoteric tasks, you may need to call additional functions in one of these so-called Human Interface Toolbox interfaces:

- **The Appearance Manager.** Coordinates the look of the standard Mac OS human interface and allows for the adaptation of custom human interface elements to a coordinated appearance. The Appearance Manager provides the underlying support for themes, which unify the appearance of human interface objects in your application, including alert icons, controls, background colors, dialogs, menus, and windows.

- **The Control Manager.** Lets you create and manipulate controls, which are user interface elements belonging to a window. Buttons, scroll bars, and sliders are examples of controls.

- **The Dialog Manager.** Lets you create and manipulate dialogs, which are windows that either prompt you for input or display information. Although the Window Manager can give you much of the same functionality, the Dialog Manager is a simpler interface for managing these specific types of windows.

- **The Menu Manager.** Lets you create and manipulate menus.

- **The Window Manager.** Lets you create and manipulate windows, which are the user's primary means of interacting with your software.

- **Interface Builder Services.** Lets your code access the user interface elements created with Interface Builder and stored in a nib file. Obviously, if you aren't using Interface Builder, you don't need this interface.

Aqua

Aqua is not an interface, but you need to follow the Aqua guidelines when designing and laying out your user interface. While the Carbon programming interfaces are flexible enough to let you do just about anything with your user interface, that doesn't mean you should. Just as adherence to common rules and customs when designing steering wheels and dashboards makes driving more pleasant and less confusing, following the Aqua guidelines lets your application provide the best possible experience for your users.

Behind the curtain

The following interfaces work behind the scenes, as it were, to provide the basic functionality that you expect from most applications:

- **The Carbon Event Manager.** Controls the event model for Macintosh applications. Note that Carbon also contains an older event-handling system (simply called the Event Manager), which is included only to assist legacy applications moving to Mac OS X.

- **The Carbon Printing Manager.** Lets you print from Macintosh applications.

- **Navigation Services.** Creates a standard user interface for opening and saving documents.

- **The File Manager.** Lets you read and write data to storage media (hard drives, Zip drives, and so on).

- **Bundle Services.** Lets you access data stored in a bundle file hierarchy, which is the standard method of packaging applications in Mac OS X.

- **The Resource Manager.** Lets you access information in a bundle hierarchy stored as an old-style Mac OS resource (that is, in a data fork-based file with the .rsrc extension). The Resource Manager complements Bundle Services in allowing access to images, text, and other resources stored in a bundle.

- **String Services.** Allows basic manipulation of Unicode strings.

- **The Multilingual Text Engine (MLTE).** Provides basic text display and formatting features. Because it is Unicode-based, MLTE can easily handle other languages and script systems.

- **QuickDraw.** Carbon's interface for drawing 2D graphics to the screen.

- **The Memory Manager.** Allows you to allocate and release temporary memory for your application.

The Expansion Pack

This section lists interfaces that are desirable, but not necessary for most applications. Full-featured commercial applications usually adopt a number of these interfaces.

 Continuing the automobile metaphor, these interfaces would add useful features that may be essential in some cases, such as power-steering, windshield wipers, and air conditioning.

- **The Scrap Manager.** Lets the user copy items to and from the Clipboard for cut-and-paste operations.

- **The Drag Manager.** Used for implementing drag and drop between applications. For example, the user can select text in one application and then, rather than copying and pasting, simply drag the text into the window of another application.

- **The Font Manager.** Lets you manipulate the fonts that your application uses to display or print text. For example, if you want your application to support a Font menu, you probably need the Font Manager.

- **Icon Services.** Provides a simplified way to present icons in your application. Instead of storing every type of icon you need with your application, you can obtain commonly used icons through Icon Services. Doing so minimizes the amount of work you have to do and increases system efficiency.

- **The Folder Manager.** Lets you find, create, and otherwise manipulate folders.

- **The Alias Manager.** Lets you create and resolve aliases to files and folders. An alias is a small "copy" of an application, folder, or file that points to the original.

- **The Open Scripting Architecture.** Describes the interfaces to control or automate the actions of one or more applications. You use the Apple Event Manager portion to interpret and react to events received from other applications, and AppleScript is the scripting language that you use to describe what actions to take. For example, if your application might be used in an automated workflow, where multiple applications manipulate a file in turn, you should make your application Apple Event savvy so it can act upon commands sent to it from an external script.

 The Apple Event Manager is different from the Carbon Event Manager. While there is some overlap in their capabilities, Carbon events are typically received from the user interface or operating system, while Apple events come from scripts or other applications.

- **Core Foundation.** A collection of interfaces that can simplify common needs of applications. Bundle Services and String Services (already described in the section "The Starter Kit") are Core Foundation services. Other Core Foundation interfaces handle plug-ins, preferences, and so on. The complete list of Core Foundation interfaces is as follows:

  — Base Services

  — Bundle Services

  — Collection Services

  — Plug-In Services

  — Preference Services

  — Property List Services

  — String Services

  — URL Services

— Utility Services

— XML Services

- **QuickDraw Text.** Lets you draw simple text with more control than MLTE can give you. For more complex text manipulations, look into Apple Type Services for Unicode Imaging (ATSUI).

- **The Gestalt Manager.** Lets your application determine specific information about the system or its interfaces. For example, you can call the Gestalt Manager to determine what version of a particular technology is installed. Doing so lets you avoid calling functions that may not be available on a particular computer.

- **Multiprocessing Services.** Lets you create preemptively scheduled execution tasks (threads) in your application. If your application might want to perform several actions simultaneously (such as downloading files or performing background calculations), you should consider adopting Multiprocessing Services. Tasks created with this interface will automatically take advantage of multiple processors, if present.

- **The Thread Manager.** Lets you create cooperatively scheduled threads in your application. This interface is generally not as useful as Multiprocessing Services. However, if you need a certain amount of control over when your threads execute, you should consider the Thread Manager.

- **The Display Manager.** Provides a way to manipulate multiple monitor locations and resolutions from your application. If your application needs the kind of control that the Monitors pane of System Preferences gives users, then consider adopting the Display Manager.

Specialty Interfaces

These are more esoteric interfaces that you generally would not use unless you were interested in creating specific types of applications. Some provide specialized features, while others expand on basic functionality (such as text manipulation). You use these interfaces to create highly sophisticated applications that take full advantage of the system software.

For automobiles, these features would be for specific types of cars: turbocharging and tight suspensions for sports cars, flatbeds and towhooks for trucks, leather seats and soft suspensions for luxury cars, and so on.

QuickTime

QuickTime is Apple's multimedia programming interface. You use QuickTime to create and play file-based or streaming movies, virtual reality environments, sounds, and music files. The Carbon developer documentation site groups Quick-Time into the following categories:

- Image Compression Manager
- (QuickTime) media handlers
- Movie Toolbox
- QuickTime Components
- QuickTime Media Layer
- QuickTime Music Architecture
- QuickTime streaming
- QuickTime VR
- Sound Manager

As you can see, the QuickTime programming interface is huge and somewhat daunting. However, a good place to start exploring is the book *Discovering Quick-Time*, published by Morgan-Kaufmann (see Appendix A).

Color, images, and print production

These interfaces are for applications that create and manipulate images, such as a photo retouching program:

- The Color Picker Manager lets you bring up a simple user interface for choosing colors, which can be useful for paint programs as well as any application that allows the user to customize colors.
- ColorSync is an Apple technology that ensures consistent color calibration across different applications and hardware. For example, when using ColorSync, users can be sure that the particular shade of green they see on their monitor is as close as possible to what they will get when the local print house prints their brochure.
- Picture Utilities are used to obtain information about a graphic image, such as the colors used, its resolution, and any comments that may be included.

3D graphics

For high-quality 3D graphics, the interface of choice is OpenGL. Okay, in actuality this is an industry-standard interface and not part of Carbon, but it is fully compatible with Carbon (just make sure you link to the OpenGL framework when you build). You can use OpenGL's 3D rendering capabilities for everything from medical imaging to virtual reality to incredibly photorealistic games.

HTML

To display HTML text and images, you can use the HTML Rendering Library. Essentially, this interface allows you to render text and images in a window as if it were in a browser. It provides support for such design elements as border and scroll bars, as well as for navigation using URL links.

Speech

These interfaces let your application speak text or recognize speech:

- The Speech Recognition Manager lets your application recognize spoken commands. For example, you can navigate between windows, open files, or run scripts solely through voice commands. It can be especially useful to activate commands that would normally require navigating deeply nested menus or multiple dialogs.

- The Speech Synthesis Manager lets your application speak lines of text using a number of different voices. Note that the speech recognition and speech synthesis interfaces use the same English dictionary, which allows them to work in conjunction with each other. For example, you could use the Speech Synthesis Manager to determine how to pronounce a word, so the Speech Recognition Manager can recognize it more easily.

Text and international services

Most of these interfaces are only for developers writing text-intensive applications or those that handle multiple text encodings. For basic text input and display, the Multilingual Text Engine provides a much simpler interface for most of the same functionality.

- ATSUI is the interface for drawing Unicode text. It allows precise control over all aspects of the text, from kerning to ligatures to bidirectionality.

- The ATS types interface defines data types used by ATSUI and other text interfaces.

- Date, Time, and Measurement Utilities contain functions to obtain and manipulate date, time, location, and other values that may need to be localized for different countries or regions.

- The Dictionary Manager provides an easy interface to access dictionary files. For example, if your application contained a spell checker, it could use this interface to look up words in a dictionary file. Similarly, text input methods that require looking up words in a file could also use this interface.

- The International Resources contain structures and constants that are used for localizing text to different countries or regions. In most cases, you won't need to access this interface yourself, because other text interfaces will access it for you.

- The Text Services Manager provides support for text input methods. For example, some non-Western text cannot be typed directly into a document, but first must be entered into a second window, using multiple keystrokes.

- FontSync allows you to synchronize fonts available on different computers or printers to prevent font mismatches. For example, two fonts on different computers may have the same name but not be identical. FontSync can attempt to match fonts based on content rather than name, thus minimizing the possibility of a mismatch when a text file is moved from one computer to another.

- The Language Analysis Manager allows your application to manage language analysis engines (stored as plug-ins). These engines are typically used with text input methods to isolate meaningful words or characters. For example, for Japanese text input you may use a language analysis engine to interpret the keystrokes the user enters, so you can display the Kanji characters that match their meaning.

- The Script Manager allows you to handle older Mac OS script systems (or text encodings), providing support for text input and display processing. On Mac OS X you will usually be handling Unicode text, so you probably won't need this interface.

- The Text Encoding Conversion Manager allows you to change text from one encoding to another. This conversion can be useful for text going to or from the Internet, where many different text encodings exist. For example, to read text streamed over a network from a Windows computer, you may need to convert it from the Windows text encoding to the corresponding one for Macintosh computers. Similarly, if you are handling input methods or file systems that only support the older Mac OS encodings, you can use the Text Encoding Converter to convert between them and Unicode.

- Text Utilities let you perform basic manipulation of non-Unicode text strings. If Mac OS X is your primary platform, you will likely be using Unicode strings, which means you should investigate the Unicode Utilities or Core Foundation String Services instead.

- Unicode Utilities let you perform basic manipulation of Unicode strings. Note that Core Foundation String Services provide similar functionality and are more portable across Mac OS X execution environments.

Internet and networking

If your application uses or enables network access, you will need to call functions from the following managers or services:

- Internet Config, which is used to access Internet networking preferences from a global repository on a user's machine. For example, Internet Config stores the user's default browser selection, so if another application needs to launch a browser (when a URL is clicked), it can easily determine which one to activate.

- Open Transport is Carbon's low-level networking interface. Typically you need this interface only if you are implementing network protocols (such as TCP/IP) in your application or driver.

- Network Services Location Manager, which provides an easy way to find network services on a local network.

- URL Access Manager, which provides an easy interface for uploading and downloading files to and from a given URL.

Security

If you want your application to provide security measures available on the Macintosh, you should consider these interfaces:

- Security Services is the interface you use to add such security features as certificates and encryption/decryption to your application.

- The Keychain Manager manages the keychain, which is an encrypted repository for all of a user's passwords. By using the keychain, a user need remember only the password that unlocks the keychain. Once the keychain is unlocked, the user can access transparently all the services or applications whose passwords are stored in the keychain. If your application prompts the user for passwords to access particular services or features, you can use the Keychain Manager to access or store these passwords in the keychain.

Low-level tweaking

If your application needs to access or control specific low-level functionality, you should consider these interfaces. Note, however, that Mac OS X is designed to shield applications from low-level workings of the system. To that end, you should use one of these interfaces only if you are sure you need its particular functionality:

- I/O Kit is the Mac OS X interface for hardware. While not considered part of the Carbon programming interface, if you are writing driver-level code that needs to talk directly to hardware (such as a video card), you need to use I/O Kit. Most applications don't need this level of control and should not be at all dependent on hardware.

- The Power Manager allows you to control power management features. For example, a screen saver program could use this interface to put the Power-Book to sleep after a given time. Other applications may want to monitor the battery status of the PowerBook.

- Memory Management Utilities are used for specialized low-level memory operations, such as direct memory access (DMA) and those that take place at the interrupt level. Many of the functions in this interface aren't even supported in Carbon, and it is unlikely that you will need to use the ones that are.

Utility Interfaces

This section covers utility interfaces that may be useful, depending on the application. These managers and services aren't particularly related to any technology or functionality:

 If Carbon were for cars, these interfaces would add possibly useful features, such as headlight wipers, cup holders, curb feelers, and GPS units.

- **Error Handler.** Lets you trap and display certain system errors. It's mostly used by system software, and you will probably never need to use it.

- **Time Manager.** Lets you set timers to perform periodic actions or to have actions occur at a particular time. Although timers in the Carbon Event Manager can provide some of the same functionality, the Time Manager is useful for cases where you need something to happen outside of your usual event loops.

- **Finder.** This interface contains a number of structures that are useful for giving information to the Finder.

- **Debugger Services.** Contains functions that can assist you in debugging your application. In most cases, however, you should begin with the debugging facilities available with Project Builder before using this interface.

- **Mathematical and Logical Utilities.** Exactly what you think it is.

- **Pascal String Utilities.** More or less what you think it is. In most cases you will be using Unicode Strings on Mac OS X, but if you need to manipulate Pascal strings, this is where to go.

Legacy Interfaces

This section covers Carbon interfaces that are mostly of historical interest. These interfaces were included to assist developers porting legacy Mac OS code to Mac OS X. For new developers, these interfaces may be useful only to gain perspective on the evolution of Macintosh system software. In most cases, the functionality of these managers is covered in a newer interface.

 If Carbon were for cars, these interfaces would add older features such as hubcaps, ashtrays, carburetors, and whitewall tires.

- **Event Manager.** Originally written to handle the older cooperative multitasking event model. The Carbon Event Manager is both more efficient and easier to implement.

- **Process Manager.** Also written for the older cooperative multitasking environment.

- **Code Fragment Manager.** Written to allow the system and applications to prepare and execute Preferred Executable Format (PEF) binaries, the native executable file format for PowerPC Macintosh computers. While Mac OS X supports PEF binaries, the native executable file format is called Mach-O.

- **Component Manager.** Older Mac OS programs often loaded special format plug-ins using the Component Manager. On Mac OS X, you should use the Plug-In Services interface in Core Foundation.

- **Collection Manager.** This interface let you create abstract data types to store related information together. On Mac OS X, you should use the Core Foundation interface Collection Services instead.

- **Device Manager.** Older Mac OS programs accessed hardware through the Device Manager. On Mac OS X, you should use the I/O Kit instead.

- **List Manager.** Formerly used to create columned lists of data (similar to the list view option in a Finder window), you should now use the data browser functions and data types that have been added to the Control Manager.

- **TextEdit.** An interface to perform basic text manipulation. Its replacement, the Multilingual Text Engine, offers significant additional features, such as Unicode support.

- **Palette Manager.** This interface allowed to you specify the contents of palettes, which let you specify the colors to use to render an image. For example, if a picture contained mostly dark colors, grays and blues, you could index the palette to use only those colors, eliminating those that didn't appear (yellows, bright red). Using a fixed selection of colors allowed you to reduce the size of the image, because not as much information was needed to render it. The Palette Manager was useful in the days when, due to memory constraints, many computers could display only a limited number of colors.

- **Notification Manager.** This interface allowed applications in the background to notify the user (for example, after finishing a lengthy calculation). Because the Carbon Event Manager defines events that cover the same functionality, you should use that interface instead.

- **Mixed Mode Manager.** Originally designed to allow PowerPC code to call emulated 68K code (and vice versa), the Mixed Mode Manager is now used to allow CFM-based PEF code to call Mac OS X's native Mach-O code and vice versa. Because you are already building Mach-O-based applications with Project Builder, however, you don't need this interface.

- **Low Memory Accessors.** These functions allowed you to access useful system information (such as the location of the mouse) stored as global variables in so-called "low memory." This practice of accessing low memory directly was questionable even then, and certainly not suggested now. In almost all cases, better, safer functions exist in other interfaces for obtaining the same information.

- **SCSI Manager.** Originally written to communicate with SCSI devices. On Mac OS X you should use the I/O Kit instead.

Recap

We introduced Carbon, the C programming interface that lets you take advantage of features in Mac OS X, such as preemptive multitasking and protected memory. Carbon is a synthesis of old and new Mac OS technologies. Although there are many interfaces in Carbon, in most cases only a subset is essential for all applications. Others may be useful only for specialized needs or to support the porting of legacy applications. Of the numerous development environments available to build Carbon applications, this book will use Project Builder and Interface Builder, which are specifically designed for building applications on Mac OS X.

Next, we will design the application, a moon travel planning guide, that we will use to illustrate major Carbon programming concepts and methods.

2

Specifying a Carbon Application: Moon Travel Planner

Specifying a Carbon application is similar to specifying any application. You need to define the goal of the application, sketch out the interface, define the behavior of the interface, and outline the implementation details. Before you start creating the application, it's helpful to sort out what needs to be done in Interface Builder and what complementary things need to be done in Project Builder. Although you'll find yourself switching back and forth between the two development tools, once you get the hang of it, you'll see it's fairly easy and fast to create an application with a great looking interface.

You'll create a sample specification that shows:

- Aspects of the interface that need to be created in Interface Builder and what needs to be done in Project Builder to support the interface

- Other code that needs to be written in C using Project Builder

- Items that should be created as a localizable file or other resource

- Tasks taken care of by the operating system

You'll create the Moon Travel Planner application that's specified in this chapter throughout the course of the book. Once you define the goals of the sample application, the specification progresses according to what the user will see in the interface.

Windows and menus are the two basic elements users see in any interface. So you'll sketch out each window and menu, describe its behavior, and outline the implementation details. This chapter includes cross references to the chapters in which you'll actually implement the details.

The Moon Travel Planner Window

You'll need a window to give the user an idea, in practical terms, of how far away the moon is from the earth. Let's call it the Moon Travel Planner window. You'll let the user compute the travel time to the moon for various modes of transportation. Figure 2-1 shows a sketch of what the main window of the application should look like. You'll use this sketch as a model when you actually create the interface.

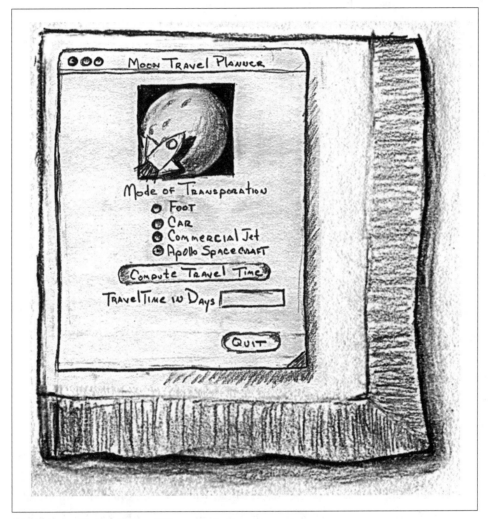

Figure 2-1. The Moon Travel Planner window

Behavior

The Moon Travel Planner window will display an image of the moon, a list of modes of transportation, a field that shows computed travel time, and two buttons. One button will compute travel time, and the other will quit the application. The window's title bar will display the words "Moon Travel Planner."

The window opens when the application launches and closes when the application quits. The user will be able to minimize the window so its icon displays in the Dock. The user should be able to quit the program by clicking the Quit button.

The *Dock* is a feature of Mac OS X that appears at the bottom of the monitor. The Dock displays an icon for each open application and minimized document, as well as web site links and commonly used items, such as System Preferences and Trash. It's designed to help combat onscreen clutter and to aid in organizing work.

When the user clicks the minimize button on a window, the window shrinks and moves to the Dock. If the user clicks the miniaturized window in the Dock, the window expands to full size.

The window should be movable, but it won't be resizable. It will become inactive when other windows are open.

When the pointer is placed over the graphic in the window, a help tag appears.

Implementation

For the Moon Travel Planner, you'll need to use Interface Builder to:

- Define the window size, background, and title. See Chapter 4, *Interface Builder: Nibs and Windows*, for details.

- Add controls, a text field, and static text fields (labels); adjust the layout of the window and controls; assign a command to the Compute Travel Time and Quit buttons; assign control ID information to the radio button group and the text field that shows the time it takes to travel to the moon. See Chapter 5, *Interface Builder: Tools and Controls*, for details.

- Add an image resource of the moon to the window. See Chapter 5 for details.

- Define a help tag for the graphic in the window. See Chapter 12, *Providing Help*, for details.

In Project Builder, you'll need to:

- Add code to the main function to create the window from the nib file. See Chapter 3, *Project Builder Projects*, for details.

- Write a function that reads the radio button settings, computes travel time, and writes the value to the travel time text field; write a handler that responds to the Compute Travel Time command and calls your function for computing travel time. See Chapter 6, *Carbon Events*, for details.

- Add a PICT resource file that contains an image of the moon to the Moon Travel Planner project. See Chapter 5 for details.

- Initialize the help tags. See Chapter 12 for details.

For the image of the moon that you use in Chapter 5 you can use an image we provide (see the Preface for details on getting materials needed to build the Moon Travel Planner application), or use a graphics application to create an image of the moon and save it as a PICT resource file.

What you won't need to do:

- Implement the Quit command assigned to the Quit button. The operating system does that.

- Write code to minimize or move the window. The operating system takes care of that as well.

The Menu Bar

You'll need to use these standard Mac OS X menus: Application, File, Window, and Help. In the application menu, you'll use the About and Quit menu items, but you'll customize the About menu item for the Moon Travel Planner application.

There are five items in the File menu you'll need: Open, Close, Save As, Page Setup, and Print. The only kind of file the Moon Travel Planner will open is a special file you'll create that contains an itinerary. So you'll need to customize Open so it says Open Itinerary, and Save As so it says Save Itinerary As.

The Minimize item is the only item you'll need in the Window menu. You'll need one item in the Help menu—Moon Travel Planner Help.

You'll also need an application-specific menu you'll call Moon. The Moon menu needs two commands—one to open a window that shows information about the moon as a travel destination, and another to compute travel time. The sketch in Figure 2-2 shows the application-specific menu and menu items you'll need.

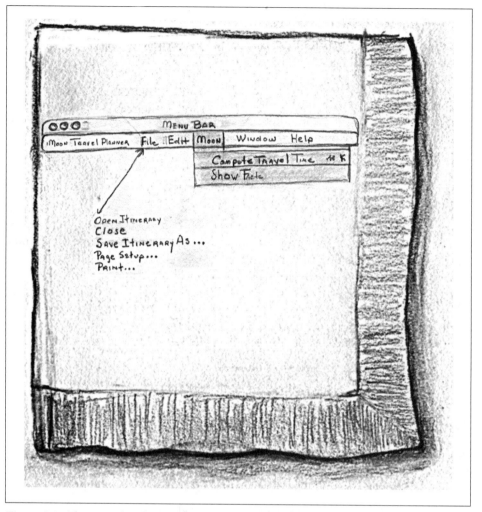

Figure 2-2. The menu bar for the Moon Travel Planner application

Behavior

When a user presses a menu name, the menu should open and stay open as long as the user holds down the mouse button. When the user selects a menu item, a command will be issued and something will happen. Table 2-1 lists the menus and menu items you'll use in the Moon Travel Planner application and the action each should take.

Table 2-1. Menus, Menu Items, and Actions

Menu	Menu Item	Action
Application	About Moon Travel Planner	Opens a window that shows version information.
	Quit	Quits the application.
File	Open Itinerary	Opens a dialog that lets the user choose an itinerary file, then opens the file chosen by the user.
	Close	Closes the window that's in the front.
	Save Itinerary As	If an itinerary window is open and active, opens a dialog that lets the user specify a new filename and where to save the file. The contents of the window are saved to the new file and the itinerary window remains open.
	Page Setup	Opens a dialog that lets the user choose page setup options.
	Print	Opens a dialog that lets the user choose printing options. Then, prints the contents of the window that shows information about the moon as a travel destination.
Window	Minimize	Shrinks the frontmost window and places it in the Dock.
Moon	Compute Travel Time	If the main window is open and active, reads the radio button settings, computes the travel time, and writes the value to the travel time text field.
	Show Facts	Opens a window that shows information about the moon as a travel destination
Help	Moon Travel Planner Help	Opens the Apple Help Viewer to the main page of the help book.

Implementation

In Interface Builder, you'll need to:

*   Add an application-specific menu and items; modify the names of standard menu items; assign commands to menu items that don't have built-in commands; make sure unneeded menu items are either removed or dimmed. See Chapter 7, *Interface Builder: Menus* for details.

In Project Builder, you'll need to:

- Add code to the main function that creates the menu bar from the nib file. See Chapter 3 for details.

- Write a function that opens the About window; include code in a handler that responds to the About Moon Travel Planner command and calls your function to open the window. See Chapter 10, *Property Lists*, for details.

- Write functions that open, close, and save itinerary files with a new name; include code in a handler that responds to the Open Itinerary, Close, and Save Itinerary As commands and calls the appropriate function. See Chapter 11, *Files*, for details.

- Write functions that set up and print the window that shows information about the moon as a travel destination; include code in a handler that responds to the Page Setup and Print commands and calls one of your functions to set up or print the file. See Chapter 9, *Printing*, for details.

- Include code in a handler that responds to the Show Facts command and calls the function to show the window. See Chapter 8, *Text and Localization*.

- Write code in a handler that responds to the Compute Travel Time command and calls the function to compute travel time. See Chapter 6.

What you won't need to do:

- Create any standard menu items. Interface Builder provides a menu bar that already has all the standard items.

- Write any code to open menus. The operating system does that.

- Assign commands to the Quit and Help menu items. They are assigned commands by the operating system.

- Write code to implement the Quit command. The operating system takes care of that.

The About Window

You'll need an About window to display version information for the application. *Inside Mac OS X: Aqua Human Interface Guidelines* (listed in Appendix A, *Additional Resources*) contains specific guidelines for what should be in an About window, so you'll need to follow those. Figure 2-3 shows the minimum items you need to display—the application icon and version and copyright information for the application.

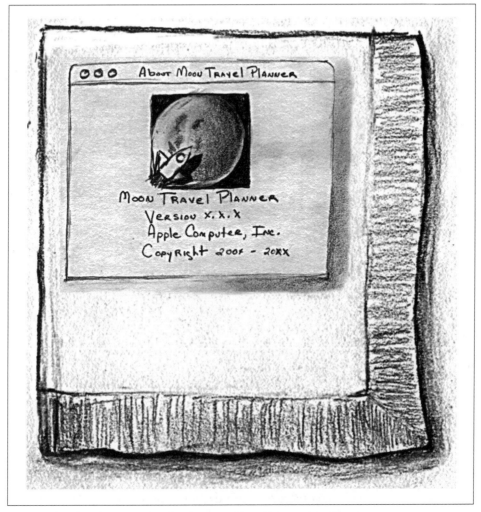

Figure 2-3. The About window for the Moon Travel Planner application

Behavior

The window will open when the user chooses About Moon Travel Planner from the Moon Travel Planner application menu. Its title bar should display the words "About Moon Travel Planner." The user will be able to close the window. The user won't be able to modify or copy the text or change the size of the window.

Implementation

In Interface Builder, you'll need to:

- Create the window; define the window size, background, and title; add a static text field; adjust layout of the window; add an image resource for the application icon to the window. See Chapter 5 for details.

In Project Builder, you'll need to:

- Add code to the main function to create the window from the Interface Builder file. See Chapter 6 for details.

- Add version and application information to the project. See Chapter 10, for details.

- Add an application icon file to your project. See Chapter 13, *Desktop Icons*, for details.

- Write a handler that closes the About window when the user clicks the close button. See Chapter 10 for details.

You'll also need to use Icon Composer to create an icon suite for your application. See Chapter 13 for details.

The Facts for the Traveler Window

You'll need a window to display some interesting facts for the prospective moon traveler. Figure 2-4 shows a sketch of what you'll create in the Moon Travel Planner application. You'll display the facts in a window that has an attractive border.

Behavior

The window will open when the user chooses Show Facts from the Moon menu. The window's title bar should display the words "Facts for the Traveler." The user will be able to close and minimize the window. The user won't be able to modify or copy the text displayed in the window or to resize the window. The window should be movable and will become inactive when the user makes the main or itinerary window active.

Implementation

Except where indicated, everything you need to implement the Facts for the Traveler window is described later, in Chapter 8. In Interface Builder, you'll need to:

- Create the window; define the window size, background, and title.

Figure 2-4. The Facts for the Traveler window for the Moon Travel Planner application

- Add a text field; assign an ID and signature to the text field; adjust the layout of the window.

In Project Builder, you'll need to:

- Create content to display in the text field.
- Add code to the main function to create the window from the nib file.
- Write a function that gets the ID and signature of the text field, reads text from a localizable file, and displays the text in the text field.

- Write a handler that closes the window when the user clicks the close button and one that responds to the Page Setup and Print commands by calling your functions for page setup and printing.

- Write functions to handle the Page Setup and Print commands. See Chapter 9 for details.

You won't need to write code to minimize the window. The operating system takes care of that.

The Itinerary Window

No travel planning application would be complete without providing the user with a few suggested itineraries. You'll need to create a window so the Moon Travel Planner application can display an itinerary of suggested activities for the moon tourist. Figure 2-5 shows an idea for one itinerary. You'll use a plain document window to display the contents of itinerary files provided with the Moon Travel Planner application.

Behavior

The itinerary window opens when the user chooses an itinerary file from Open Itinerary under the File menu. It closes when the user clicks the Close button or chooses Close from the File menu. The user should save the itinerary under a new name.

Implementation

Everything you need to implement for the itinerary window is described later, in Chapter 11. In Interface Builder, you'll need to:

- Create an itinerary window in a new Interface Builder file.

In Project Builder, you'll need to:

- Write functions to create the window from the Interface Builder file and dispose of it when it is no longer needed.

- Write functions to allow the user to open and close an itinerary file and to save the file under a different name.

You won't need to write code to minimize the window. The operating system takes care of that.

Recap

We've sketched the interface for the Moon Travel Planner application, detailed its behavior, and listed what you need to do to create the specified application. As

Figure 2-5. The Itinerary window for the Moon Travel Planner application

you create the Moon Travel Planner in the rest of this book, you'll use this specification as your blueprint. You will rely on two tools—Interface Builder to create the interface and Project Builder to create the code. As you can see from the implementation details, when you create objects in Interface Builder you often need to do complementary tasks in Project Builder, such as write the supporting code for a menu command.

With specification in hand, you are ready to build the Moon Travel Planner application. You'll start in Chapter 3 by creating a skeletal application using Project Builder. Once you've had an opportunity to use Project Builder, you'll move on and create the interface using Interface Builder.

3

Project Builder Projects

Project Builder is an application that manages software development projects. It's Apple's integrated development environment (IDE) for Mac OS X, which provides a project browser, a full-featured code editor, language-savvy symbol recognition, advanced project-searching capabilities, documentation access, build and debugging support, and other features that can streamline the development process. With it, you can create such Mac OS X software projects as:

- An application, which is a *bundle* that contains all the resources necessary to launch the application, including the application's executable files. A bundle is a folder packaged to look like a single file.

- *Frameworks*, which are bundles that contain a dynamic shared library and all the resources that go with that library, such as header files, images, and documentation.

- *Kernel extensions*, which are bundles the operating system loads into the kernel environment.

- *Libraries*, which are code and resources that can't execute on their own, but that export functions and global variables for others to use; usually linked to an application when the application runs instead of when it's compiled.

- *Plug-ins*, which are bundles that contain executable code and associated resources that must be loaded into a running application.

This chapter shows you how to create one type of software project—a Carbon application. You'll use the Carbon programming interfaces and the C language from within Project Builder's development environment to:

- Look at the components of a Carbon application project

- Examine the code you get "for free" with the Carbon application template

- See how Project Builder organizes a project

- Find out what's in an application bundle

- Take a look at the tools for building, debugging, and running

- Find out how to access documentation from within Project Builder

- Create, build, and run a new Carbon application

A Carbon Application Project

Before you start building your own application, let's take a tour of Project Builder. When Project Builder opens a new project for a Carbon application, you'll see a window similar to what's shown in Figure 3-1. The area near the top of the window contains buttons for building, cleaning (that is, deleting the current build products and intermediate products), running, and debugging. The Run and Debug buttons remain dimmed until you build a project.

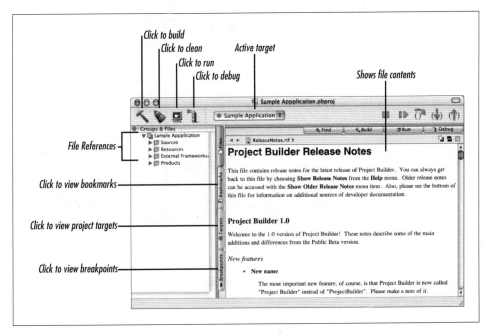

Figure 3-1. A new project window for a Carbon application

The left side of Figure 3-1—Groups & Files—shows a list of file references. The right side of the figure shows the contents of the most recent Project Builder release notes. The vertical tabs let you switch between views of the project's files, bookmarks you save, and targets (should your project have more than one target). Let's look a bit more closely at file references and targets.

File References

File references refer to the source files, resource files, libraries, and frameworks in your project. The important thing to remember is that, although the Groups & Files list shown in Figure 3-2 may look like a directory listing, the items in the list are references to files or folders on your hard disk; they are not the files or folders themselves.

Project Builder organizes the project's file references into four groups: Sources, Resources, External Frameworks and Libraries, and Products. You can move a file reference into any group you want. You can also add your own groups. Groups are there solely for your convenience and do not affect Project Builder's ability to find or compile the files. It's easier to manage large projects if you keep related files together. Let's take a closer look at what each group normally contains.

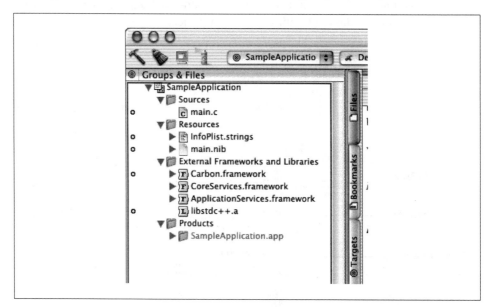

Figure 3-2. Groups and files in a Project Builder project

Sources

These are files that contain the application's source code and are compiled to produce object code. In Project Builder, it's recommended that you list header files in the project window and include them in the Sources group. The project in Figure 3-2 contains only one source file: `main.c`. We'll take a close look at the `main.c` source file Project Builder provides in the section "Main.c: A Skeletal Application."

Resources

These are files that contain resources or that can be compiled to produce resources. The project shown in Figure 3-2 contains two: `InfoPlist.strings`, which contains a list of properties associated with the application, and `main.nib`, which contains the application's interface-based resources. Both the `main.nib` and `InfoPlist.strings` files can be localized. You'll read more about localization in Chapter 8, *Text and Localization.*

 Resources refer to a wide variety of bits and pieces that are needed to run the program, including strings, menus, dialogs, icons and other images, sounds, and much more. Resources are separated out from the program code, so that you can change the resources without having to change the code. For one thing, this makes it easier to design an application with various languages and cultures in mind.

External frameworks and libraries

In Mac OS X, a framework is a shared library that's bundled with its header files and resources. This project shown in Figure 3-2 contains three frameworks and a library. A Carbon project always contains the Carbon framework. If you click the disclosure triangle next to a framework, you can see a list of its header files.

Products

The Products group includes anything produced when you build your project. The Sample Application shown in Figure 3-2 has one product—`SampleApplication.app`. It's an application that runs on Mac OS X. Notice `SampleApplication.app` appears dimmed in the figure. That's because either the project has been "cleaned" (that is, built products have been removed by clicking the Clean button shown in Figure 3-1) or the project hasn't been built yet.

The `SampleApplication.app` product is an application bundle. We'll take a look at a typical bundle in the section "Application Bundles."

Targets

Targets provide a way for you to organize project files so you can build a variety of products. Think of the files, resources, libraries, and frameworks in your project as a list of ingredients and the project targets as courses in a meal. Some targets use some ingredients, and some may use all the ingredients. All targets share some ingredients with other targets.

For example, a project for a client-server software package can contain targets for:

- A client application

- A server application

- A private framework that both applications use

- Command-line tools that you can use instead of the application's menu commands

Although the command-line tools might use most of the same source files the client application uses, the tools might not use the resources needed to build the interface. The client application would use the same framework used by the server, but the client application would use different source files and resources to create the client interface.

When you create a project, you add all the files you need for all your targets. When you set up a new target, you identify which files in the project should be used to build that target.

The complete list of an application's targets is in the Targets pane. You can view the Targets list by clicking the vertical Targets tab shown in Figure 3-3. (The sample application shown in the figure has only one target.) When you view a target, the right side of the project window displays four tabs: Files & Build Phases, Build Settings, Application Settings, and Executables. These tabs provide access to panes in which you can customize settings for a target. For example, in the Files & Build Phases pane, you can specify whether a header file should be private or public; in the Application Settings pane, you can enter the name of the file that contains the target's icons; and so forth.

Project Builder provides most of the defaults you need, such as the location of the Carbon framework and the name of your source files. But there are some settings, such as Application Settings, that you will need to modify for your application. We'll show you how to do that in Chapter 10, *Property Lists.*

Main.c: A Skeletal Application

When Project Builder creates a new Carbon project, it provides a main.c file and a main.nib file. The main.c file contains C code that will actually compile and run. The main.nib file is an Interface Builder file that contains a default menu bar and window. (You'll read more about nib files in Chapter 4, *Interface Builder: Nibs and Windows.*) The code in the main.c file will read the main.nib file and create a simple interface for the skeletal application. Let's take a closer look at the main.c file shown in Figure 3-4.

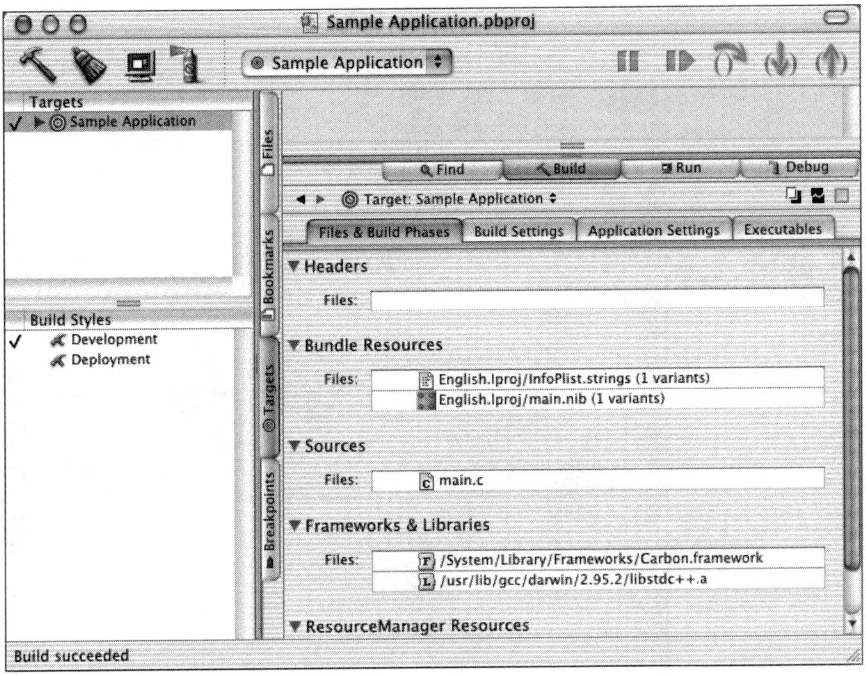

Figure 3-3. The Targets list for an application with only one target

Example 3-1 shows the lines of code from the main function, but without the embedded comments shown in Figure 3-4. Below the listing you'll find an explanation of each numbered line of code. Where appropriate, we'll identify the name of the Carbon manager or service to which each function belongs.

Example 3-1: The Key Lines of Code from the Main Function

```
err = CreateNibReference (CFSTR ("main"), &nibRef);              //1
require_noerr (err, CantGetNibRef);                             //2
err = SetMenuBarFromNib (nibRef, CFSTR("MainMenu"));           //3
require_noerr (err, CantSetMenuBar);
err = CreateWindowFromNib (nibRef, CFSTR ("MainWindow"), &window);
require_noerr (err, CantCreateWindow);
DisposeNibReference (nibRef);                                   //4
ShowWindow (window);                                            //5
RunApplicationEventLoop ();                                     //6
```

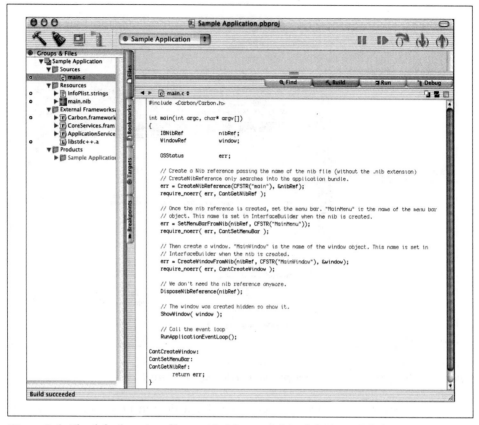

Figure 3-4. The default main.c file provided for a nib-based Carbon application

Here's what the statements do:

1. The Interface Builder Services function `CreateNibReference` creates a reference to a nib file. You must supply two parameters. The first is a `CFString` that represents the name of the nib file, but without the nib extension. A nib file is an Interface Builder file that contains information on how the operating system should construct the interface. You'll read more about these in Chapter 4. The string `"main"` is used here because `main.nib` is the name of the nib file. It must be converted to a `CFString` using the Core Foundation function `CFSTR`. You'll use this function throughout the book to convert a string to a `CFString`.

   The second parameter is a pointer to an `IBNibRef` data type-a nib reference returned by the `CreateNibReference` function. This sample application will later pass the nib reference to other functions that use information from the nib file to construct the menu bar and windows used in the application.

A Core Foundation string (CFString) represents an array of Unicode characters (UniChar) along with a count of the number of characters. Unicode-based strings in Core Foundation provide a solid basis for internationalizing the software you develop. Unicode makes it possible to develop and localize a single version of an application for users who speak most of the world's written languages, including Russian (Cyrillic), Hebrew, Arabic, Chinese, and Japanese. Although conceptually CFString objects store strings as arrays of Unicode characters, in practice they often store them more efficiently. The memory a CFString object requires is typically about the same as or even less than that required by a simple UniChar array.

2. The macro require_noerr checks for an error condition. It takes two parameters—one of type OSStatus, used to return result codes from a function, and a label. If an error is returned, the program jumps to the label. Note that all labels used in the main function are located near the end of the function. So jumping to a label causes the application to quit before it fully launches. You should use this macro to check for "show stopping" errors. If you can't create all or part of the interface, you shouldn't continue to launch the application.

3. The Interface Builder Services functions SetMenuBarFromNib and CreateWindowFromNib set up the menu bar and main window based on the information in the nib file. Each takes a nib reference as the first parameter—it's the nib reference returned by CreateNibReference. You must pass a CFString as the second parameter to denote which interface object from the nib file you want to create. CreateWindowFromNib takes a window reference as the third parameter. On return, the function provides a reference to the window it created from the nib file. You'll need the window reference to show, hide, read, and write to the window.

4. The Interface Builder Services function DisposeNibReference disposes of the reference to the nib file. It doesn't affect the object already created from the reference.

5. The Window Manager function ShowWindow displays the main window. You need to call this function because the function CreateWindowFromNib by default creates a window as hidden.

6. The Carbon Event Manager function RunApplicationEventLoop runs the main event loop. If anything happens in the application, the Carbon Event Manager hands it to your application to take care of or takes care of the event itself, if the event is a standard event like quit. The function RunApplicationEventLoop doesn't return until the application quits. You'll learn more about events and the Carbon Event Manager in Chapter 6, *Carbon Events*.

Things May Not Be Where You Think They Are

Recall that Project Builder shows file references, not the files themselves. This means that the groups and files you see in the Project Builder window may not reflect the actual location and grouping of the files on your hard disk. From the Finder, a project's files and how they are grouped look a bit different from the view you see in Project Builder. Compare the Finder view in Figure 3-5 with the Files & Groups list in Figure 3-2. Here are some additional explanations about the items you see in the Finder view:

SampleApplication.pbproj

> This is a bundle that Project Builder uses to keeps track of the project's files and targets along with project and user-specific settings.

English.lproj

> This folder contains resources that are localized into English. You can have lproj folders for other languages, in which case the folder is named with the English name for the language, such as French.lproj or Japanese.lproj.

build

> Project Builder uses this folder to store build products, including intermediate projects, project headers, and executable files. You won't see this folder until you build the application.

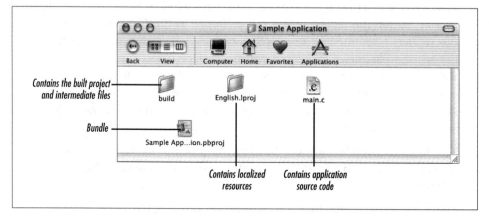

Figure 3-5. The Finder view of a Project Builder project

Notice that Carbon.framework isn't in the project directory. It's in /System/Library/Frameworks. However, as you saw in Figure 3-2, the project contains a reference to it.

The critical point here is that you can regroup files in the Project Builder window, but if you move the files on disk, you'll break the file references. (A broken file reference appears red in Project Builder.) To fix a broken reference, do the following:

1. Choose Show Info from the Project menu.

2. Choose Set Path from the Change Path pop-up menu. A navigation dialog appears.

3. Navigate to the new location of the file or folder whose location you changed.

4. Click Open, then click Change.

Application Bundles

An application bundle is the file package you distribute to users. Now that you know a little about a Carbon application project, it's time to "look under the hood" of a built application to see how Project Builder packages it. Packaging assures that everything your application needs—the executable file, resources, help files, libraries, and plug-ins—is in one location. It also assures that users cannot accidentally break an application by renaming its components, moving them, or otherwise manipulating them in the Finder.

An application bundle can contain any of the following:

- Images, sounds, or other files used by the application
- Localized character strings
- Localized versions of nib files
- Multiple executable versions of an application

An application bundle appears to the user as if it were a file. To see the contents of an application bundle, you can Control-click the application's icon and choose Show Package Contents (as shown in Figure 3-6) from the menu that appears.

These are the items Project Builder puts in the application bundle when you build the application (see Figure 3-7):

- `Info.plist`. The information property list contains information about the bundle. You'll read more about this in Chapter 10.
- `MacOS`. Contains the application's executable files. It's possible to have multiple executable files if you are providing versions for multiple platforms (such as for Mac OS 9 and Mac OS X).

Figure 3-6. An application bundle looks like a file; Control-click the icon to open it

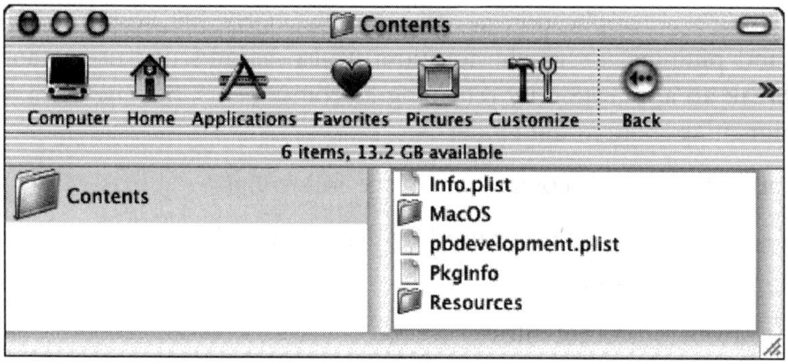

Figure 3-7. The contents of an application bundle

- `pbdevelopment.plist`. Contains information Project Builder uses when it builds your project. This file is created only for development builds. A deployment build does not have this file.

- `PkgInfo`. Contains the bundle type and creator codes for your application.

- `Resources`. All the resources an application needs are in this folder.

Building and Running a Project

The Build and Run buttons at the top of the project window let you build a project and then run the resulting application. When you click the Build button, a pane slides down from the top of your project window. Figure 3-8 shows an example of a build window. The top part displays error messages and warnings (if any), and the bottom part displays the build log. When the build finishes, a message appears at the bottom of the project window. Hopefully, the message is "Build succeeded."

Compiling and linking messages are displayed in the area shown in Figure 3-8. These messages provide a record of the input to, and output from, the tools that Project Builder calls upon to build the targets you set up in your project.

It's pretty optimistic to think you'll create an application that runs successfully every time. Fortunately Project Builder has an easy-to-use debugger for those occasions when the program functions incorrectly. We'll show you how to use the debugger in the next section.

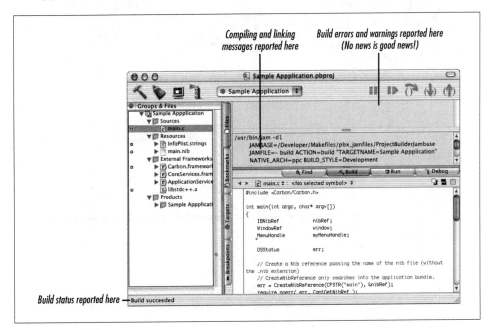

Figure 3-8. A typical build window

Debugging a Project

Project Builder's debugger is easy to activate—just click the Debug button (the bug spray can called out in Figure 3-1). Before you start the debugger, you may want to set some breakpoints so you can examine the state of the running code at points you suspect to be a problem.

To set a breakpoint, scroll to the part of the code in which you want a breakpoint, then click in the margin beside the statement. A marker appears next to the statement, as shown in Figure 3-9. To get rid of a breakpoint, you simply drag the marker out of the margin.

When the debugger runs, the Debug pane slides down (see Figure 3-9). Project Builder runs the application until the first breakpoint, or until the program crashes or is interrupted. When the application stops at the breakpoint, you'll see the currently executed statement highlighted with a red arrow pointing at it. Above the code, you can examine the application's variables and current values.

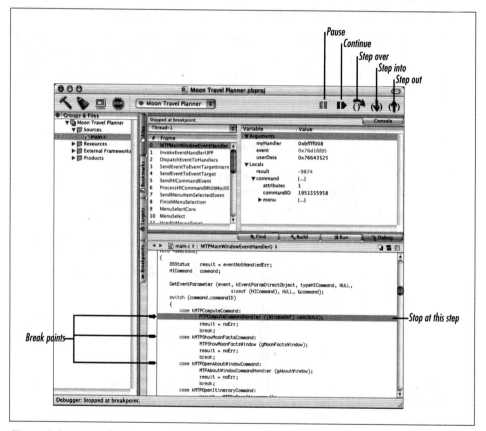

Figure 3-9. An application running in the debugger

You can control the debugger with the buttons located at the far right of the toolbar, as shown in Figure 3-9:

- Pause temporarily stops the application and displays the currently executing statement.

- Continue starts a paused application.

- Step Over executes the next statement within the same function.

- Step Into executes the next statement, but jumps to the first line in the next function if its source code is available.

- Step Out executes until you exit the current function.

The threads pop-up menu in the debugger pane lets you choose among threads in your application. A *thread* is an independent execution path within your application. (Threads are discussed in more detail in Chapter 14, *Beyond Moon Travel: Advanced Topics*.) The list below the pop-up menu displays the thread's call chain in the Frames list. If your application has only one thread, other threads you see are system threads that handle interapplication communication and the debugger.

The Variable list shown in Figure 3-9 displays the values of the local and global variables associated with the selected frame.

Onscreen Documentation

When you use Project Builder, you have access to a wealth of documentation. You can access a variety of help from the Help menu in Project Builder, shown in Figure 3-10. Choosing an item from the Help menu opens Help Viewer to the appropriate set of help or to Project Builder release notes. Searching for specific details in help is as simple as typing words or phrases in the field at the top of the Help Viewer application and clicking the Ask button. The search engine returns a list of "hits" (links), ranked by relevance, that you can browse through.

A search always focuses on the set of documentation you have open. Thus a search when you are perusing Carbon Help confines the results to Carbon documentation. If the results yield nothing of interest, you can easily expand the search to Apple's complete set of Mac OS X developer documents.

Let's look at Apple's Carbon documentation. To open the Carbon Developer Documentation page, click Carbon Help in the Project Builder Help menu. At the upper-left corner of this page you'll find a list of Developer Guides installed on your system. Some of these guides are in HTML format, some are in PDF format, and some are in both. A book in HTML format opens in Help Viewer; a book in PDF format opens in the Preview application or Acrobat Reader (if you've downloaded it from Adobe).

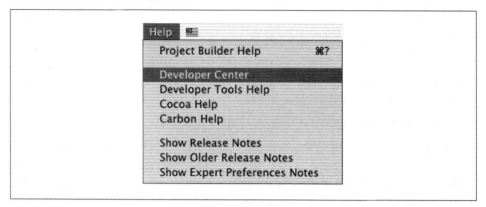

Figure 3-10. The Help menu in Project Builder

In addition to the Developer Guides, the Carbon Developer Documentation page supplies links to detailed documentation for the programming interfaces described in Chapter 1, *Introduction to Carbon*.

The Carbon documentation includes a clipboard feature that allows you to copy declarations and sample code from a Help Viewer page to your project. Figure 3-11 shows the reference documentation for the `ShowWindow` function, with a Clipboard button to the right of the function declaration. Click the Clipboard button to copy a declaration or code example from a Help Viewer page to the system's Clipboard. Then, in Project Builder, move the insertion point to the desired place in your code and choose Paste from the Edit menu.

Moon Travel Planner: Creating a Project

Let's get some practice with Project Builder by creating a project from a Carbon application template, then building and running it. You'll create a new project for the Moon Travel Planner application we specified in Chapter 2, *Specifying a Carbon Application: Moon Travel Planner*. When you're done, you'll have an application that displays an empty window and lets you quit.

To create the Moon Travel Planner project, do the following:

1. Double-click the Project Builder icon located in Mac OS X in the directory `/Developer/Applications`. The first time you open Project Builder, the Project Builder Assistant opens. You'll need to complete the setup process before you can proceed with the next step.

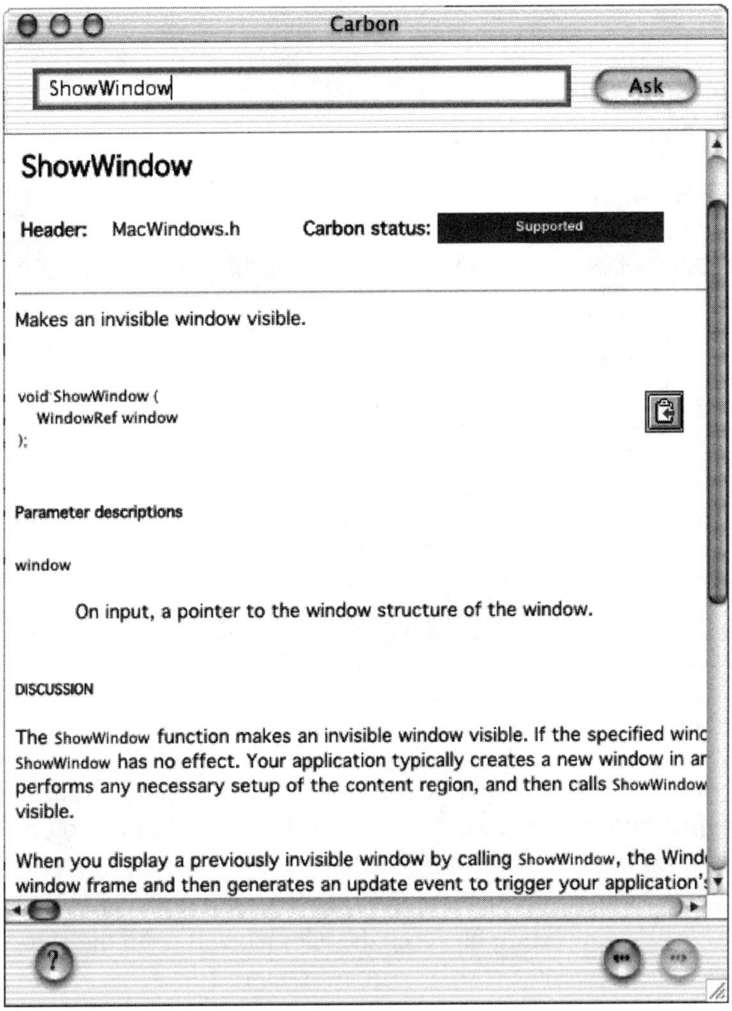

Figure 3-11. A Help Viewer page with a Clipboard button

2. Choose New Project from the File menu. A dialog opens with a list of template objects, as shown in Figure 3-12.

3. Select Carbon Application (Nib Based), then click Next. Nib refers to a project that uses Interface Builder to create user interface resources. You'll use Interface Builder later to modify the default interface you get with the project.

4. Type **Moon Travel Planner** as the project name (as shown in Figure 3-13) and click Set to choose a location to store the project. A sheet appears that lets you navigate to the location you want to store the project.

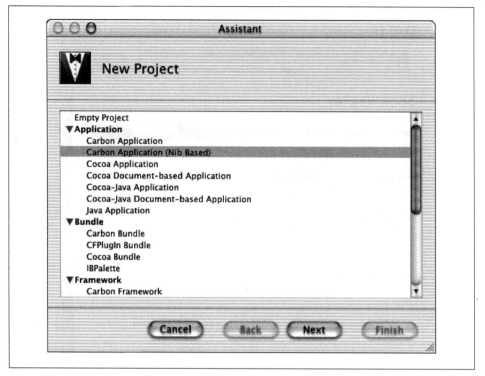

Figure 3-12. Choosing the type of project

5. Click Finish. The main window for Project Builder opens, with files for our new application in the Groups & Files list. Believe it or not, you now have a complete, although skeletal, application!

6. Take a look at the main function by clicking main.c in the Groups & Files list. If you can't see the main.c file, click the Files tab and open the Sources group. You should see the same code shown in Example 3-1.

Building and Running the Skeletal Application

The code should run without modification. Let's see if it does!

1. Click the Build button in the upper-left corner of the project window. The Build pane appears. When the build finishes, a message appears at the bottom of the project window. As long as you have not changed the source files, you should see the message "Build succeeded."

2. Click the Run button in the upper-left corner of the project window. Project Builder launches the application; the application displays an empty window.

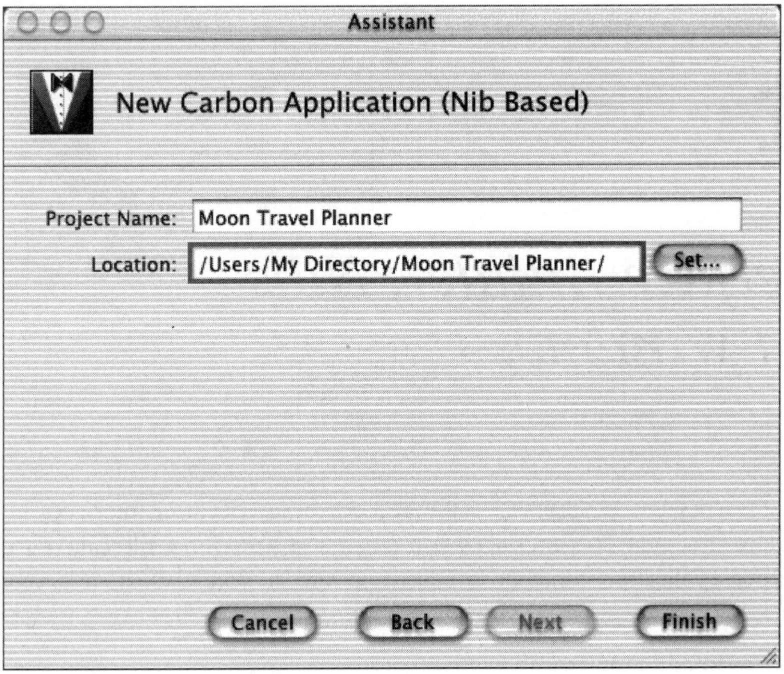

Figure 3-13. Specifying the project location

A shortcut is to press Shift-R to build and run the application. To avoid having Project Builder ask if you want files saved before building, set Project Builder's preferences to Always Save. To set this preference, choose Preferences from the Project Builder menu, click the Building icon, then choose Always Save from the Unsaved Files pop-up menu.

---

3. Press Command-Q to quit the sample application.

4. Choose Save from the File menu to save your project. You won't need to do this if you've set preferences to Always Save.

Recap

At this point, you've gotten familiar with Project Builder, and you've created a skeletal Carbon project, built it, and run the built application. In the next chapter, you'll be introduced to Interface Builder and use it to create some of the interface objects you'll need for the Moon Travel Planner application.

4

Interface Builder: Nibs and Windows

Interface Builder is a WYSIWYG tool that lets you lay out user interfaces in a simple, intuitive manner. The interfaces you create are stored in a file called a nib file, which your application can then access to create its windows, menus, and other elements. Interface Builder provides you with:

- Palettes to add interface elements
- Menus that help you align and lay out the interface
- Info windows to set up the behavior of interface elements

You can do so much with Interface Builder that it will take a couple of chapters to explore its features. In this chapter you'll:

- Look at the components of a nib file
- Check out what you can do with Info windows
- Take a look at the types of windows you can create in Interface Builder
- Use Interface Builder to modify a window

Then, you'll look at palettes and layout tools in Chapter 5, *Interface Builder: Tools and Controls*, where you'll add controls to a window. In Chapter 7, *Interface Builder: Menus*, you'll take a close look at the default menu bar provided by Interface Builder.

A Carbon Nib File

In the last chapter you saw that when Project Builder creates a Carbon (nib based) application, it provides a file named `main.nib` and puts it in the Resources group of the project. As you recall, the nib file contains the application's interface-based resources. It's an Interface Builder file (the "ib" in "nib" stands for Interface

Builder) that contains descriptions of the interface elements in your application. These descriptions use Extensible Markup Language (XML).

 In earlier versions of the Mac OS, developers created resources using either a resource compiler (such as Rez) or a utility program called a resource editor (such as Apple's ResEdit). The resources contained in a nib file are not the same as those contained in these old-style resources. In other words, you can't use Interface Builder to create old-style resources.

Example 4-1 shows what's needed to create a File menu using old-style resources that rely on text-based descriptions. Interface Builder automatically provides the File menu for you and lets you customize this and other menus it provides using WYSIWYG tools. You don't need to know anything about old-style resources to create a Carbon application; we've provided the listing just so you can see how this style of resource compares to Interface Builder.

Example 4-1: Defining a Menu Using Text-Based Resources

```
resource 'MENU' (kFileMenuID, "File menu")
    {
        kFileMenuID,                // Menu ID
        textMenuProc,               // Menu definition procedure
        0x7FFFFFFF,                 // Enable/disable flags for menu items
        enabled,                    // Enable/disable flag for menu
        kMenuTitleFile,             // Menu title
        {
            kItemNameClose, noIcon,             // Close command
                kItemKeyClose, noMark, plain,

            "-", noIcon, noKey, noMark, plain, // Separator

            kItemNameQuit, noIcon,              // Quit command
                kItemKeyQuit, noMark, plain
        }
    };
```

You can open the `main.nib` file from Project Builder by double-clicking its icon in the project window. This will launch Interface Builder and open the file.

The Default Items in a Nib File

When you open the default `main.nib` file you get from Project Builder, you should see the four windows shown in Figure 4-1:

- **Window.** This is the window that opens when your application runs.

- **Carbon Palette.** All the controls, menu items, and windows that you can drag into the interface are in the palette. You'll learn more about them in Chapter 5.

- **Main Menu.** This contains the items that appear in your application's menu bar. You'll take a closer look at what's included automatically in Chapter 7.

- **main.nib.** There are two panes in the main.nib: Instance and Images. The Instances pane displays icons of the interface objects in your nib file. The Images pane shows image resources available for you to use in the interface.

The default Instances pane contains icons that represent the menu bar and the main window. If you want to edit an item, double-click its icon. In Figure 4-1, the main menu and main window are already open. As you add other windows to your application, their icons appear in the Instances pane.

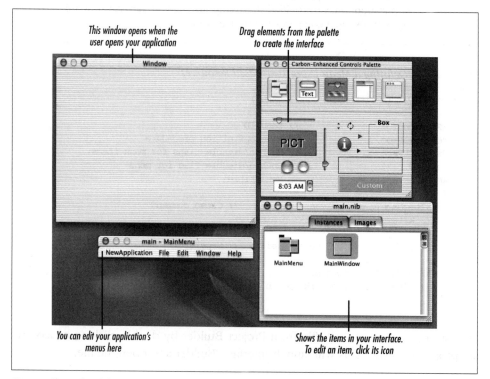

Figure 4-1. The default items in a nib file

Any image in the Images pane is available for use in the interface. The Images pane in Figure 4-2 shows three default images: caution, note, and stop. It also contains one image added to the application's Project Builder project. When you add a PICT resource to Project Builder, Interface Builder is informed automatically by Project Builder and the image appears in the Images pane.

You can use the default images in the appropriate dialogs along with your application's icon. (You'll read more about application icons in Chapter 13, *Desktop Icons.*) This will help users identify the severity of the message in the dialog and make sure they associate the message with your application.

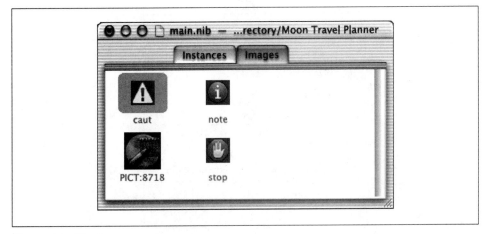

Figure 4-2. The Images pane

Info Windows

Info windows are likely to be the Interface Builder tool you'll use the most. An Info window provides information about an interface object (such as a window or menu) and lets you set attributes and other information that controls how the object behaves and appears to the user. You can even use an Info window to create a help tag for an object. (You'll do that in Chapter 12, *Providing Help.*)

The Info window and other Interface Builder tools are accessible from the Tools menu, shown in Figure 4-3. (You'll explore the Palettes and Alignment tools in the next chapter.) To display an Info window, click the interface object (window, menu, control, image, and so forth) whose attributes you want to inspect or modify, then choose Show Info from the Tools menu.

Tools	Window	Help
Show Info	⇧⌘I	
Palettes	▶	
Alignment	⇧⌘A	
Show Colors	⇧⌘C	

Figure 4-3. The Tools menu

After you choose Show Info, an Info window opens for that object. If an Info window is already open for another object, the Info window contents change to reflect the object you selected. Figure 4-4 shows an Info window for a window.

Figure 4-4. The Info window for a window

The Info window has a pop-up menu for accessing other information about the object. The menu items are Attributes (shown in the figure), Control, Size, and Help. Control information is available only for controls; that is, items that can issue commands or from which settings can be read by your application. You'll read more about these in Chapter 5. You can set a window's size in the Size pane and define a help tag for the window in the Help pane.

The Window Info Attributes pane is the one you'll use the most for setting up windows. The Title attribute specifies the text that shows in the title bar when the window is open (see Figure 4-6). In the next few sections we'll go over settings for Window Class, Theme Brush, Controls, Attributes, and Receives.

Window Classes

When you create a window in Interface Builder, you'll need to choose its class. The *Window Class* is an important attribute for any window, because it defines:

- How a window looks, such as whether it will have controls at the top and a title bar, and the font size of the title

- Whether the window is movable

- How the window behaves with respect to other windows (floats, takes over control of the screen, and so forth)

Table 4-1 provides a list of the window classes you can set in Interface Builder, along with guidelines for using them. The classes represent both windows and dialogs. *Dialogs* are windows that elicit a response from a user. Some dialogs are modeless; others are modal. You can find in-depth information about the use of windows and dialogs in *Inside Mac OS X: Aqua Human Interface Guidelines* (listed in Appendix A, *Additional Resources*).

A *modeless* dialog accepts user input and does not inhibit user activity. That is, the user is not required to make a response before doing anything else in a document or the application. A modeless dialog looks like a document window, but it can't be resized, zoomed, or scrolled. The user can make the dialog inactive and active, move it, and minimize it or close it like any document window. You can create a modeless dialog that doesn't close if you are displaying the status of an ongoing process. The title is generally the same as the name of the menu item that activates the dialog.

A *modal* dialog requires a response from the user. It can be application-modal or document-modal. An application-modal dialog prevents the user from doing anything else within a particular application until the user provides a response. However, the user can switch to other applications. A document-modal dialog prevents the user from doing anything else within a particular document until the user provides a response. The user can switch to other documents within the application, or to another application.

Table 4-1. Window Classes

Window Class	What It Is and What It's Used For
Alert	A system-modal dialog that displays problems and their remedies to users. Used to communicate warnings and error conditions. These are not recommended for use on Mac OS X. You should use a movable alert dialog instead.
Movable Alert	An application-modal dialog that displays problems and their remedies to users. Used to communicate warnings and error conditions.

Table 4-1. Window Classes (continued)

Window Class	What It Is and What It's Used For
Modal	A system-modal dialog that forces the user to provide necessary information before carrying out the current operation. These are not recommended on Mac OS X. You should use a movable modal dialog instead.
Movable modal	An application-modal dialog that forces the user to provide necessary information before carrying out the current operation.
Floating	A document window that floats above all document windows in an application. Used in tools-based applications for things like palettes.
Document	A document window. Used to present a view into file-based data that people create and store; can also be used to display controls.
Utility	A system-wide floating window (floats above all other windows). Used to provide tools or controls that users can work with on a system-wide level.
Help	A document window without a frame. Used for help tags.
Sheet	A document-modal dialog. Sheets roll down from the top of a window (similar to a window shade) and make it clear to the user to which window the sheet is attached. Used for document-specific dialogs, such as save and print.
Toolbar	A document window that floats above documents in an application, but below floating windows. Used to provide tools or controls that users work with while documents are open.

Theme Brush

The Theme Brush setting lets you coordinate the colors and patterns used in a window with the current theme. A *theme* is a user-editable combination of a given appearance with a system font, desktop picture or pattern, and highlight color.

A theme brush can be an RGB color or a pixel pattern, depending on the theme. When you use a Theme Brush setting, the operating system automatically applies the correct color or pattern for the interface object in the current theme. Interface Builder lets you choose from the list shown in Figure 4-5. The Black and White options provide a black or white background, respectively. All other options except Default result in a striped background, similar to the gray striped background you see in the window shown in Figure 4-5. The spacing between the stripes is determined by the option you choose (Dialog, Alert, and so forth). Default automatically picks the theme brush that's appropriate for the window class. Unless you have a reason to override the default, that's what you should normally choose.

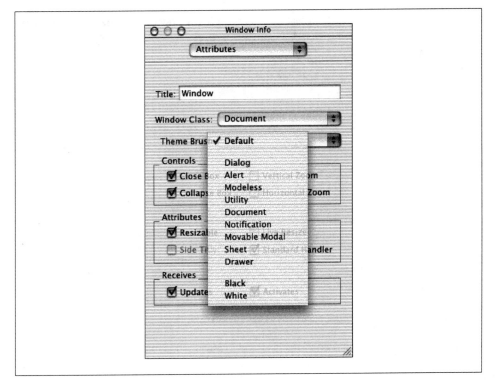

Figure 4-5. Theme Brush options

Controls

The Controls section in the Window Info Attributes pane lets you define which window buttons are available to the user. They're dependent on the window class, so some options in the Controls box are dimmed for some window classes.

Mac OS X provides three button controls for windows—close, minimize, and zoom. These are shown in Figure 4-6. When the user clicks the Close button the window closes. Clicking the Minimize button puts the window in the Dock. The Zoom button toggles the window size between the current size and the best size. (You can set the best size programmatically using the Window Manager.) The default "best size" is the full screen.

To set up window controls in Interface Builder do the following:

- If you want your window to have a Close button, set the Close Box option.

- To provide a window with the ability to minimize and go into the Dock, set the Collapse Box option.

- To provide the user with a Zoom button, click either the Horizontal Zoom or Vertical Zoom options, or click both options.

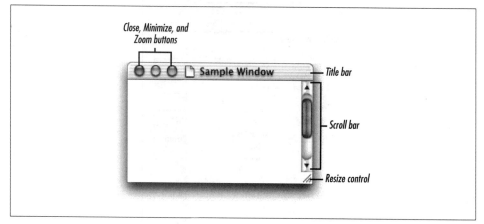

Figure 4-6. Standard window controls

Attributes

Window Attributes affect how the window moves and other window behavior. You can set four window Attributes options (see Figure 4-7):

- **Resizable.** Users can drag the resize control (shown in Figure 4-6) to change the size of the window.

- **Side Title.** The window title displays on the side of the window instead of the top. This is available only for the floating window class.

- **Live Resize.** If you set this, the window and its contents are redrawn as the user resizes the window. If it's not set, an outline of the window is drawn when the user resizes the window. Then the content is drawn when the user is done resizing the window.

- **Standard Handler.** The operating system handles the window's behavior in the standard manner if you select this option; your application doesn't need any code to process closing, minimizing, zooming, and resizing a window.

Receives

Use the Receives options for a window (shown in Figure 4-8) to set whether you want the window to receive update and activate events. An *activate event* indicates that a window is becoming active or inactive. Each activate event specifies the window to be changed and the direction of the change (i.e., whether it's becoming active or becoming inactive). An *update event* indicates that the contents of a window need updating. You'll usually want a window to receive these events.

Figure 4-7. Window Attributes options

Figure 4-8. Window Receives options

We'll use the tools we've discussed in this chapter to continue building our Moon Travel Planner application.

Moon Travel Planner: Modifying the Default Window

The main window for the Moon Travel Planner application you created in Chapter 3, *Project Builder Projects* is rather boring at this point. It shows nothing and is named Window. It will take a few chapters to whip this window into shape so it looks like the sketch in Chapter 2, *Specifying a Carbon Application: Moon Travel Planner.* In this section we'll get started by doing the following:

1. Open Interface Builder.

2. Revise the window title so it says something other than "Window."

3. Set Window Class, Controls, and Attributes.

4. Set the window's size.

5. Build and run the application to make sure it still works after our modifications.

Open Interface Builder

The Interface Builder application is located in the /Developer/Applications folder. Although you can double-click the Interface Builder icon to open it, we'll open Interface Builder from within Project Builder. Most of the time you'll have both open and move between them as you modify the interface and add code.

To open Interface Builder from within Project Builder:

1. Open the Moon Travel Planner project if it is not already open.

2. Double-click the `main.nib` file, located in the Resources group.

Revise the Window Title

The window's title is the text shown in the title bar (see Figure 4-6). You should change the title from Window to Moon Travel Planner:

1. Double-click the MainWindow icon in the Instances pane.

2. Choose Show Info from the Tools menu.

3. Type **Moon Travel Planner** in the Title text field, as shown in Figure 4-9, and press Return.

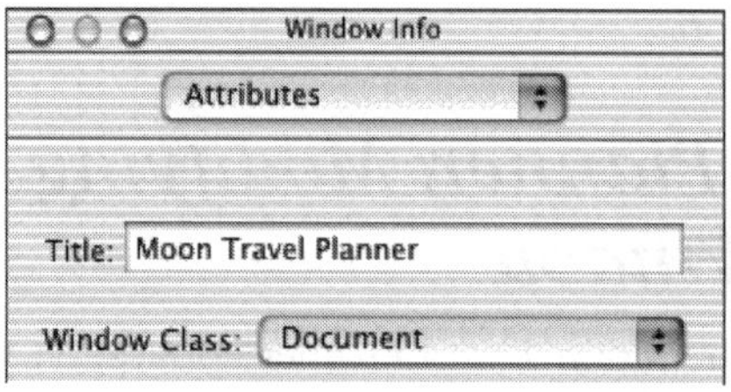

Figure 4-9. The title bar attribute for a window

Set the Window Class, Controls, and Attributes

A window's class, controls, and attributes taken together define the window's behavior:

1. Use the Window Class pop-up menu to set the main window's class to Document. See Table 4-1 for guidelines on when to use each window class. In the Window Info window, choose Document from the Window Class pop-up menu.

2. Use the Theme Brush pop-up menu to set to a gray striped background. In combination with the Document window class, Dialog causes a gray striped background to be displayed in the window. This is the type of background you should use for a document window that contains controls rather than the contents of a text file. Choose Dialog from the Theme Brush pop-up menu.

3. Specify a Collapse button as a control for our main window. The Moon Travel Planner window is our application's main window. It should stay open until the user quits the application, so the window doesn't need a Close button. Content can't be added to or deleted from the window, so there's no need for

a Zoom button. The window does, however, need a Collapse button to allow the user to minimize the window. In the Controls group, make sure Collapse Box is the only control checked.

4. Specify the Standard Handler attribute for our main window. The user should not be allowed to resize the window, so the Resizable and Live Resize options don't apply. In the Attributes group, make sure Standard Handler is the only option selected. This assures that any window activity (for example, moving the window) for which you do not write a handler gets taken care of by the operating system.

5. Look at the Receives options. You don't need to change the Receives options; use the defaults, which cause your window to receive update and activation events.

Set the Window's Size

The default window size is a bit different from what you'll need for the Moon Travel Planner application. Let's resize it so it's 300 pixels wide and 400 pixels high:

1. Choose Size from the pop-up menu at the top of the Window Info window.

2. Choose Width/Height from the pop-up menu on the right side.

3. Type **300** pixels for the width, and **400** for the height, then press Return.

Build, Run, and Check the Application

Although you haven't made a lot of alterations to the interface, it's a good idea to check to see if the application behaves according to what you've done so far:

1. Choose Save from Interface Builder's File menu.

2. Make Project Builder active by clicking its icon in the Dock.

3. Click the Build button in the upper-left corner of the project window.

4. Click the Run button in the upper-left corner of the project window.

5. Check the title shown in the window's title bar. The title bar should display Moon Travel Planner and should look similar to what's shown in Figure 4-10.

6. Make sure the window collapses into and expands from the Dock. Click the Minimize button. The window should collapse into the Dock. You should be able to expand the minimized window by clicking its icon in the Dock.

7. Choose Quit Moon Travel Planner from the Moon Travel Planner menu. Notice that the Moon Travel Planner menu and the Quit menu item were automatically added to your application.

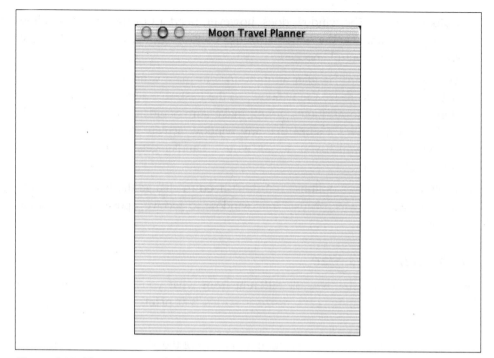

Figure 4-10. The Moon Travel Planner window when the application is running

Recap

You learned a little bit about Interface Builder nib files and Mac OS X windows, and were introduced to Info windows. You had an opportunity to use the Info window to revise a window's title and set its class, size, controls, and other attributes. Now you'll move on to Interface Builder's palettes and other tools that you can use to add controls (buttons, text fields, and so forth) to a window.

5

Interface Builder: Tools and Controls

Interface Builder provides palettes rich with controls and other items—such as push buttons, radio buttons, text labels, graphics, data browsers, and menus—you can add to your application's interface. Because Interface Builder uses graphical tools, it's fairly easy to create and lay out items in a window. The tricky part is to associate code with the controls so that when the user manipulates a control, the application responds.

You'll use Interface Builder in this chapter to:

- Take a close look at the objects you can add to an interface using Interface Builder palettes

- Check out the tools you can use to align interface objects in a window

- Add controls and other objects to the main window of the Moon Travel Planner application

Then, in Chapter 6, *Carbon Events*, you'll see how to write code that makes the controls spring to life.

Palettes and Layout Tools

To create an interface, you simply select the objects you want in the interface from one of Interface Builder's palettes, drag them to the appropriate location (a window, a menu, the desktop), and make sure the objects are arranged aesthetically, using *Inside Mac OS X: Aqua Human Interface Guidelines* as a guide. The guidelines are in Carbon Help (available in the Project Builder Help menu). For static objects, the job of adding them to the interface is done. For dynamic objects, you'll need to do a few more things.

Static objects include such things as a separator line in a menu, a text label, and a graphic. *Dynamic objects* include anything that changes, either because of a user's action or your application's. Some examples of dynamic objects include a window in which the user can edit text, a button the user can click, and a text field in which your application displays a computational result. Any interface you create will likely be a combination of both types of objects.

When you add a dynamic object to the interface, you'll need to assign it a control ID or a command signature. You'll assign these in Interface Builder, then you'll use these same values in your code to get and set control states, to identify a command issued from a menu, and to display information in a control or a window.

A *command signature* is a four-character sequence that uniquely identifies a command to the Finder and your application. Signatures for commands defined by Apple (such as redo, undo, copy) contain all lowercase characters. To avoid any possible conflicts with any Apple commands, you should use at least one uppercase character in the command signatures you define.

A *control ID* consists of a signature (a four-character sequence) and an ID (a 32-bit integer) that you assign to a control so that you can identify and address the control when your application runs. To avoid confusion with a control ID from another application or plug-in, a control ID should be unique. The best way to assure it is unique is to use the *application's signature* as the control ID's four-character sequence.

An application signature, or *creator code*, is a unique four-character sequence the Mac OS uses to identify your application. Apple Developer Technical Support maintains a database of creator codes to ensure that there are no duplications. You'll learn more about creator codes and how to obtain one in Chapter 13, *Desktop Icons*.

The operating system uses a data structure called a ControlID to store the signature and ID value assigned to a control. In this chapter, you'll assign a signature and ID for some of the controls you create in Interface Builder. For the signature, it's always best to use the application's creator code (also referred to as the application signature)—one that has been registered with Apple. (See Chapter 13 for more information on creator codes.) This assures the control ID will not conflict with a control ID for a control in another application. The creator code for the Moon Travel Planner application—MTPP—is already registered with Apple.

The Carbon Palettes Window

The Carbon Palettes window in Interface Builder provides you with five palettes: Menus, Controls, Enhanced Controls, Data Views, and Windows. You open the Carbon palettes window by choosing Palettes from Interface Builder's Tools menu. Clicking a button in the window's toolbar changes from one palette to another.

 When you hover the pointer over a button in the toolbar, a label appears.

Let's go through each of the palettes to see what interface objects are available and what you can do with each object.

Menus palette

Menus present lists of items—commands, attributes, or states—from which the user can choose. Menus are based on the interface principle of see-and-point: people don't have to remember command names because they can view all the available options at any time.

Interface Builder provides a default menu bar that contains standard menu items that most applications use. We'll cover these in detail in Chapter 7, *Interface Builder: Menus*. The Menus palette provides objects you can use to modify the default menu bar. Figure 5-1 shows the Menus palette.

The Menus palette contains the following items:

- The Application, File, Edit, and Window elements are fully loaded menus that you can drop into your application. Note that these menus were added automatically when you created the Moon Travel Planner application.

- The Submenu element can be either a top-level menu that you add to your menu bar or a hierarchical menu that you add to another menu. You can use it to create application-specific menus.

- The Item element is a single menu item that you can add to any menu.

- The blank element is a separator that you can add to any menu.

- You can add a contextual menu to your application using the menu object (on the right side). (You'll read more about contextual menus in Chapter 7.)

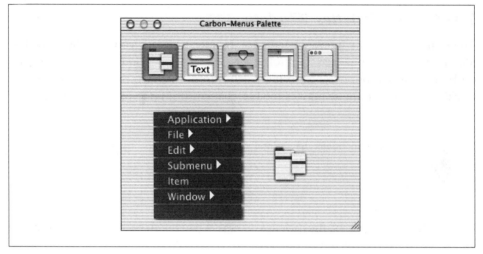

Figure 5-1. The Menus palette

Controls palette

Controls are onscreen objects the user can manipulate with the pointer to take an immediate action or to modify settings that effect a future action. Figure 5-2 shows the Controls palette provided by Interface Builder.

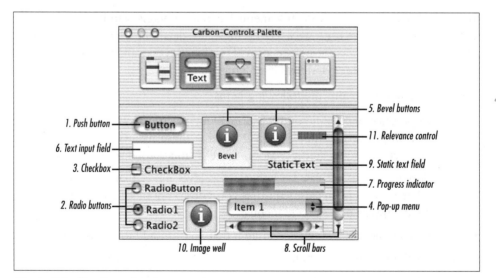

Figure 5-2. The Controls palette

The Controls palette contains those items most commonly used in the interface:

- **Push button.** A rounded rectangle with a text label that performs an instantaneous action.

- **Radio buttons.** Used for mutually exclusive, but related, choices.

- **Checkbox.** Provides options that can be either on or off.

- **Pop-up menu.** Presents mutually exclusive choices in a dialog or window.

- **Bevel button.** A rectangular button with a beveled edge that displays an icon or picture; it behaves similarly to a push button.

- **Text input field.** Allows users to type or modify text.

- **Progress indicator.** Informs the user of the status of a lengthy operation.

- **Scroll bars.** Allow users to view areas of a document or window that can't fit in the window.

- **Static text field.** Used for a dialog or other text the user can't edit.

- **Image well.** Displays an icon or picture; used as a target into which users can drag an item.

- **Relevance control.** Indicates how closely a search result matches search criteria.

Enhanced controls palette

Enhanced controls include controls, indicators, and grouping items that are more specialized than those found in the Controls palette. Some of these must be used together with another type of object. For example, a group box is always used to group two or more interface objects, such as checkboxes. Figure 5-3 shows the Enhanced Controls palette.

Enhanced controls include:

- **Sliders.** Enable users to choose from a continuous range of values.

- **PICT box.** Used as a container for a graphic you want to add to the interface.

- **Disclosure triangles.** Allow the display of information that elaborates on the primary information in a window.

- **Group box.** Associates related items.

- **User pane.** Lets you group items that appear on a pane in a tabbed dialog or draw a custom object that acts like a control.

- **Icon controller.** Used to create a control that displays the application icon.

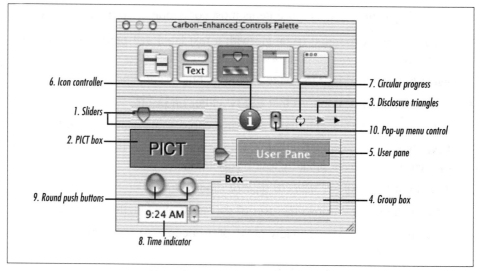

Figure 5-3. The Enhanced Controls palette

- **Circular progress.** Provides feedback to the user for operations that may take a long time.

- **Time indicator.** Used for setting a time (such as for an alarm) or for displaying current time.

- **Round push buttons.** Can be used as an alternative to rectangular push buttons.

- **Pop-up menu control.** Used to open a pop-up menu.

Data views palette

Data Views are interface objects (shown in Figure 5-4) that let you organize information you display to the user in a list or column view.

Interface Builder provides three data views:

- **Table viewer.** A type of data browser used to display multi-columned lists of information. You can set up the browser so the data in the columns are sortable.

- **Browser.** A type of data browser used to display scrolling lists.

- **Tab control.** Provides a way to present information in a multi-pane format by allowing users to switch from one user pane to another. You must use this in conjunction with user panes.

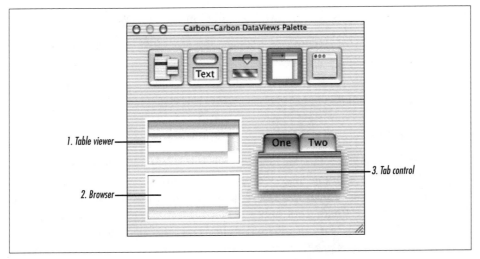

Figure 5-4. The Data Views palette

Windows palette

Windows provide a way for users to view and interact with data. Along with menus, they are the basic building blocks for any interface. A window is what you'll need to hold objects from the Controls, Enhanced Controls, and Data Views palettes. Figure 5-5 shows the Windows palette.

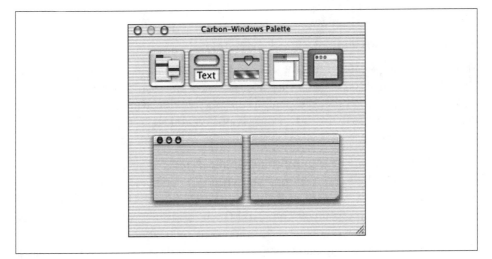

Figure 5-5. The Windows palette

You can select two types of windows from the Windows palette:

- **Windows.** Used for documents, dialogs, and any other windows that the user can close or minimize.

- **Panels.** Used for status or other windows that must remain open while an application is running.

Layout Tools

Aligning the objects in an interface can be a time-consuming and painstaking process. In Mac OS X, aligning interface objects is complicated by the fact that the objects have shadows, which most user interface metrics don't take into account. Fortunately, Interface Builder not only has layout tools you can use to make alignment precise and fairly easy, it also has built-in measurement guides that comply with *Inside Mac OS X: Aqua Human Interface Guidelines.*

You can choose from several options when you align objects. No doubt you'll take more than one approach. You can:

- Drag objects with the pointer

- Specify origin points in the Size pane of an Info window

- Use the Alignment menu or palette

- Use layout rectangles

- Follow Aqua-savvy guides

- Set up your own guides

You can use the pointer to drag objects into rough alignment. This won't be good enough for the final interface, but it's a start. If you know an object must be a certain size, you can open the Size pane in the object's Info window. Then, you can drag the object until it is placed in the proper coordinates. It's even faster if you just type the coordinate or size you want directly in the Size pane.

The Alignment submenu and the Alignment palette let you align objects. They each do the same thing, but with one you choose a command, and with the other you use a pop-up menu and click buttons. To align several objects, you select them, then choose an alignment command (such as Make Centered Column). Figure 5-6 shows the Layout menu and the alignment commands from which you can choose. The alignment commands use one of the interface objects you select as a reference and bring the other objects in alignment with the reference.

When you turn on layout rectangles, you'll see a rectangle around each object. The rectangles take Mac OS X shadows into account. So, as long as you align the rectangles rather than the objects themselves, you'll end up with a well-aligned interface. You can activate the rectangles by choosing Show Layout Rectangles from the Layout menu.

Layout	Tools	Window	Help	
Alignment ▶	Align Left Edges
	Align Right Edges
Bring to Front	Align Top Edges
Send to Back	Align Bottom Edges
Same Size	Align Vertical Centers
Size to Fit	Align Horizontal Centers
Transpose	Align Baselines
Group In ▶	Make Centered Column
Ungroup ⇧⌘G	Make Centered Row
Guides ▶	
Show Layout Rectangles ⌘L	

Figure 5-6. The Layout menu and the Alignment submenu

Perhaps one of the most useful layout commands is Aqua Guidelines in the Guides submenu, which is on by default. The Aqua Guidelines command turns on *Aqua guides*—lines that show up as you move interface objects in a window. If you drag an object to one of the guides, the object will be in compliance with the spacing outlined in *Inside Mac OS X: Aqua Human Interface Guidelines.*

You can press and hold the Command key to temporarily override the Aqua Guidelines setting. If Aqua Guidelines are on, holding the Command key toggles them off. If Aqua Guidelines are off, holding the Command key toggles them on.

There are a number of other assorted layout commands you'll find useful, including Bring to Front, Send to Back, Same Size, Size to Fit, Transpose, and Group In:

- Bring to Front and Send to Back rearrange the order of controls in the interface. For example, if you use a Group Box and a pop-up menu together, you might want to bring the pop-up to the front. Otherwise the Group Box may display a line over the pop-up menu.

- Same Size assures two objects have exactly the same dimensions; it is far easier to use than typing sizes, and certainly preferable to "eyeballing."

- Size to Fit is useful when you have an object that has a text label, such as a button. This makes the object large enough to fit the text and assures that the spacing around the text complies with *Inside Mac OS X: Aqua Human Interface Guidelines.*

- Transpose changes rows to columns and columns to rows. You can use this on a radio button group.

- Group In lets you put two or more objects in a container. This is handy when you've already created a number of objects, then decide you want to put some of them in a container, such as a Group Box.

Moon Travel Planner: Adding Objects to the Main Window

In the last chapter, you set up the main window for the Moon Travel Planner application. Now, you'll add objects to the main window so the window looks like the one we specified in Chapter 2, *Specifying a Carbon Application: Moon Travel Planner.* You'll need to do the following:

1. Open the nib file.
2. Add an item from the Enhanced Controls palette.
3. Add items from the Controls palette.
4. Add a PICT resource to the project.
5. Align objects.
6. Check the interface.

Open the Nib File

As you did in the last chapter, you'll open the nib file from the Moon Travel Planner project window:

1. If it is not already open, open the Moon Travel Planner project.
2. Double-click `main.nib` in the Resources group in the project window.
3. In Interface Builder, double-click the MainWindow icon in the Instances pane.

Add an Item from the Enhanced Controls Palette

As you recall, our sketch of the main window in Chapter 2 shows a graphic image at the top of the window, so let's start with that. To accomplish this, you'll add one object from the Enhanced Controls palette—a PICT control. A PICT control is really just a container for an image; you use it to lay out the interface. Later, you'll drag the image you want to appear in the interface on top of the PICT control.

1. Choose Palettes from the Palettes submenu in the Tools menu.

2. Click the Enhanced Controls button in the palette toolbar.

3. Add a PICT control to the top center of the interface. This is a container for the image of the moon. Drag a PICT box from the Enhanced Controls palette to the top center of the Moon Travel Planner window. Just use the "eyeball" method to place the PICT in the middle, but make sure it is no higher than what the blue Aqua guide (shown in Figure 5-7) suggests. We'll explain how to lay out the interface later, in the section "Align Objects with the Layout Tools."

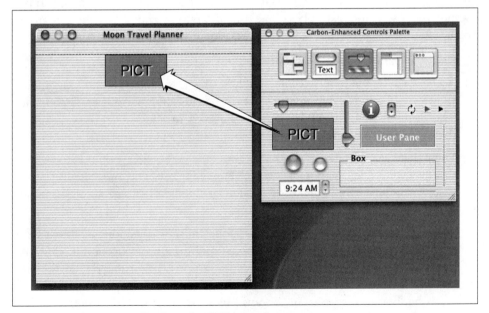

Figure 5-7. An Aqua guide above the PICT control

4. Resize the PICT control so it has the dimensions of the image you want to add. The moon image supplied with the tutorial materials is 100 by 100 pixels. (See the Preface for information on where to download the tutorial materials.) With the PICT control selected, choose Show Info from the Tools menu, choose Size from the pop-up menu, and type **100** in the height and width

fields, as shown in Figure 5-8. Then press Return. If the PICT pops out of place, just drag it so its top aligns with the Aqua guide.

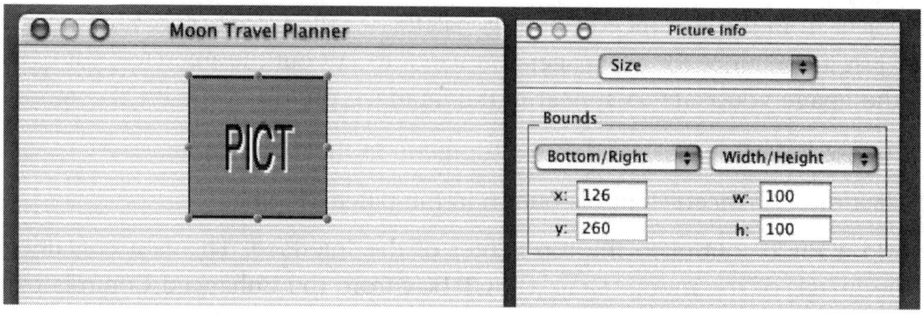

Figure 5-8. The Size pane for the PICT control

Add Items from the Controls Palette

The Controls palette has most of what you need to complete the Moon Travel Planner window: static text objects, a text field, buttons, and a radio button group. You'll start adding these at the top and work down:

1. Click the Basic Controls button in the Carbon toolbar.

2. Add a static text field just below the PICT. This is the label for the radio button group you'll add later. From the Controls palette, drag the object named Static Text to just below the PICT control, as shown in Figure 5-9. Once again, let the guide show you how close to place the static text to the PICT.

3. Enter **Mode of Transportation** as the static text field's value. Double-click the static text field, type **Mode of Transportation**, and press Return. If the field is too small for the text, click one of the "knobs" surrounding the text field and drag it until the text just fits.

4. Add a radio button group below the Mode of Transportation static text field. The user will select a mode of transportation from this group of radio buttons. From the Controls palette, drag the radio button labeled Radio 1 to the area just below the Mode of Transportation text field. The Radio 1 and Radio 2 radio buttons move as a unit because they belong to a radio button group. Use the Aqua guides as shown in Figure 5-10 to space the radio button group in relation to the Mode of Transportation text label. Don't worry too much about centering them, because you'll do this later.

   A radio button group is a great control to use when you want users to select one, and only one, option from among many. A radio button group automatically tracks a user's selection. Your application does not need to track, select, and deselect options; you only need to read the setting. You'll do that in Chapter 6 when you write the code associated with the radio button group.

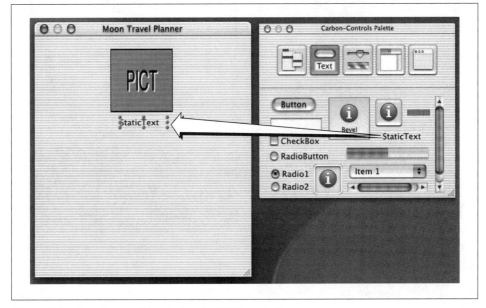

Figure 5-9. A static text object below the PICT control

5. Increase the number of radio buttons in the radio button group to 4. With the radio button group selected, choose Show Info from the Tools menu. Choose Attributes from the pop-up menu. As shown in Figure 5-11, you can use the Size box to change the number of rows and columns of a radio group. In the Rows field, type **4**, and press Return.

6. Resize the radio button group by dragging its corner so you can see all four radio buttons.

7. Label the radio buttons: Foot, Car, Commercial Jet, and Apollo Spacecraft. Double-click Radio 1 so the text becomes editable, type **Foot** and press Return. Use this procedure to label the other three radio buttons.

8. Enter **MTPP** as the radio button group's signature and **130** as its ID. You should use the application signature (otherwise known as creator code) for the signature. In the section "Palettes and Layout Tools" we mentioned the official, registered creator code for the Moon Travel Planner application is MTPP. You'll use this as the signature for any control that needs a control ID in the Moon Travel Planner application. In the Radio Group Info window, choose Control from the pop-up menu. In the Control ID box, type **MTPP** in the Signature field and **130** in the ID field. You'll need these values later when your program reads the radio button group setting.

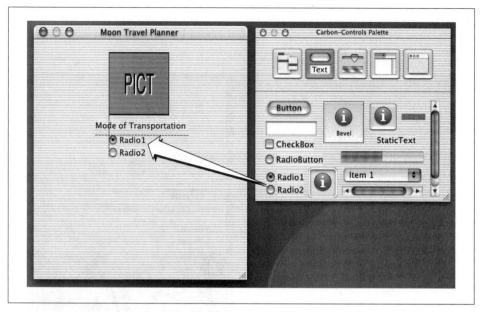

Figure 5-10. Aqua guides for the radio button group

9. Add the Compute Travel Time button. The Compute Travel Time button issues a command that calculates the travel time to the moon in days, based on the selected mode of transportation. Drag the Push button from the palette to the area below the radio button group, as shown in Figure 5-12.

10. Enter **Compute Travel Time** as the button's text. Double-click the button, type **Compute Travel Time**, and press Return. If the text isn't visible, select the button and choose Size to Fit from the Layout menu.

11. Enter **tRav** as the button's command. Choose Control from the pop-up menu in the Button Info window, type **tRav** in the Command text field, and press Return. When the user presses this button, it sends a tRav command to the Carbon Event Manager, which in turn calls your handler for the tRav command. You'll define the handler in the next chapter.

12. Make the Compute Travel Time button the default button. A default button pulses and is the button that's selected when the user presses Return. Choose Attributes from the pop-up menu in the Button Info window and select Default as the Button Type, as shown in Figure 5-13.

13. Add a static text field to the area below the radio button group. This labels the field that displays the computed travel time to the moon. From the palette, drag the object named Static Text to the area below the Compute Travel Time button.

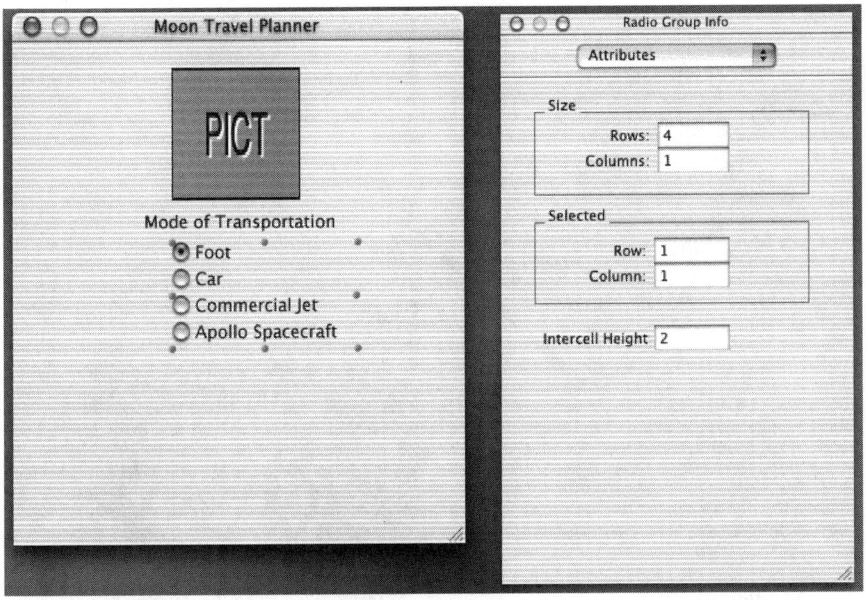

Figure 5-11. Radio group and info window

14. Enter **Travel Time in Days** as the static text field's value. Double-click the field, type **Travel Time in Days**, and press Return. If the field is too small for the text, make the field larger by dragging on of the "knobs" surrounding it.

15. Add a text field to the right of the Travel Time in Days label. This is the field in which the computed travel time is displayed. Drag the white box under the push button labeled Button from the Controls palette to the area next to "Travel Time in Days," as shown in Figure 5-14.

16. Enter **MTPP** as the text field's signature and **129** as the text field's ID. With the text field selected, choose Show Info from the Tools menu. Choose Control from the pop-up menu in the Edit Text Info window. In the Control ID section, type **MTPP** in the Signature field and **129** in the ID field, as shown in Figure 5-15. You'll need these values later when your program writes the computed travel time to the text field.

17. Add a Quit button. Drag a push button from the palette to the lower-right side of the main window. You should use the Aqua guides to place the button in the lower-right corner of the window, as shown in Figure 5-16.

18. Enter **Quit** as the button's text. Double-click the button, type **Quit**, and press Return.

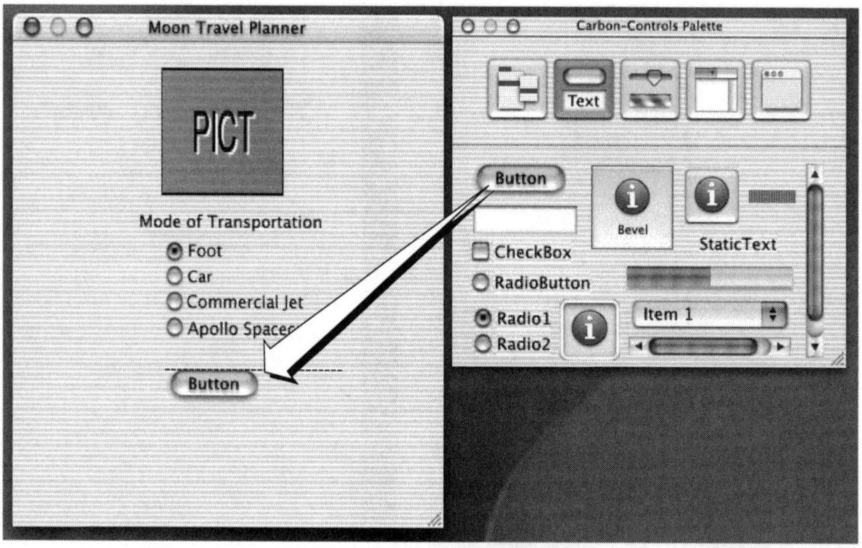

Figure 5-12. Push button added to the Moon Travel Planner window

19. Select quit as the button's command. Choose Control from the pop-up menu in the Button Info window, then choose Quit from the Command pop-up menu, as shown in Figure 5-17. When the user presses this button, the button sends a quit command to the Carbon Event Manager, which in turn calls a built-in handler that quits the application. As you can see, there are a number of other commands from which you can choose when you want to create a control that handles a standard task.

20. Choose Save from the File menu.

Add a PICT Resource

Your interface almost looks like the sketch in Chapter 2, except there is a PICT control instead of an image of the moon. Now it's time to add the moon image.

The image must be a PICT resource. You can create a PICT resource file with a graphics application, such as Adobe Photoshop. Make sure you save the file as a PICT resource file (not simply a PICT file) with the extension .rsrc. Once you have a PICT resource, you must add it to your Project Builder project. Then Project Builder adds it automatically to your Interface Builder nib file.

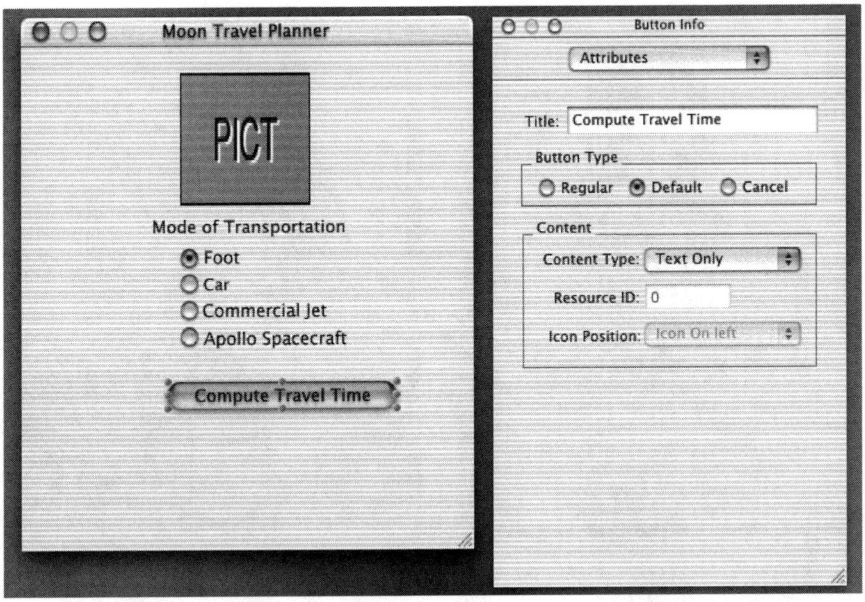

Figure 5-13. Compute Travel Time button set as a default button type

For the Moon Travel Planner application, use the moon.rsrc file provided with the tutorial materials (see the Preface for information on how to download the materials):

1. Copy the moon.rsrc file to the Moon Travel Planner folder. You must do this in the Finder. Drag the moon.rsrc file to the Moon Travel Planner folder.

2. Add the moon.rsrc file to the Moon Travel Planner project. Make the Moon Travel Planner project active by clicking the Project Builder icon in the Dock. Then choose Add Files from the Project menu, select the moon.rsrc file, and click Open. A sheet dialog appears, as shown in Figure 5-18. Select "Copy items into destination group's folder (if needed)," then click Add. Project Builder adds the file to the Resource group based on the file's extension. You should see the moon.rsrc file in the Resources group of the Groups & Files list. If you see the file, but it's not in the Resources group, just drag it to the Resources group.

3. Make Interface Builder active; click main.nib in the Project Builder file list.

4. Click the Images tab in the main.nib window. Notice that the Images pane in Figure 5-19 appears to have a duplicate image of the graphic you added. A duplicate image is usually a preview image created by the application you used to make the PICT resource. You can ignore it, or use an application such as ResEdit to open the PICT resource file and delete the preview image.

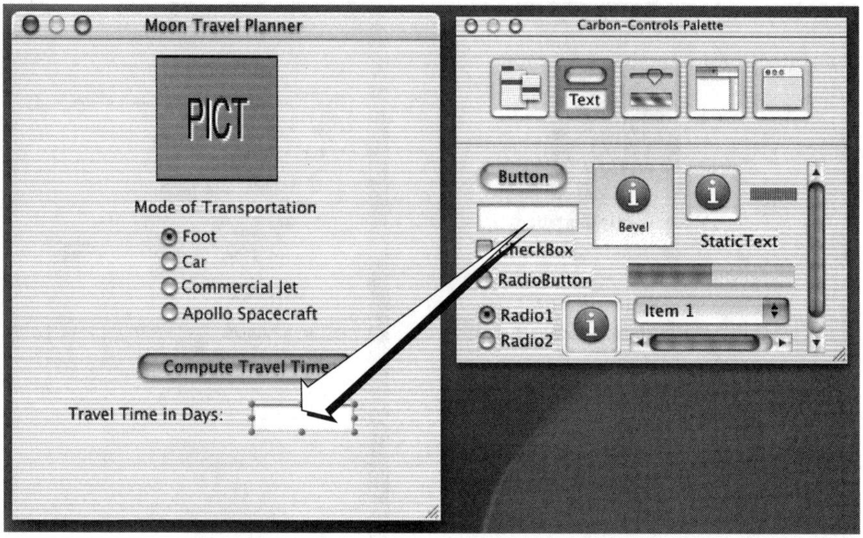

Figure 5-14. Text field to display travel time

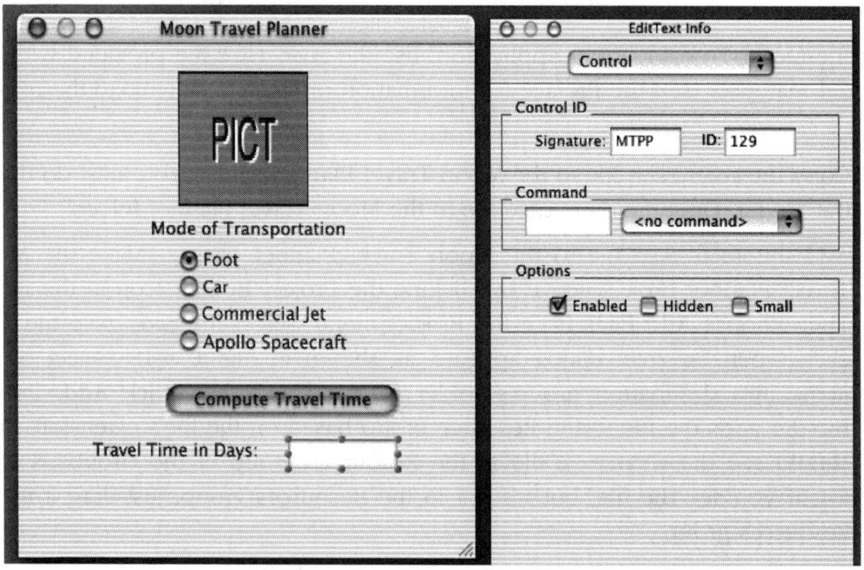

Figure 5-15. A control ID for a text field

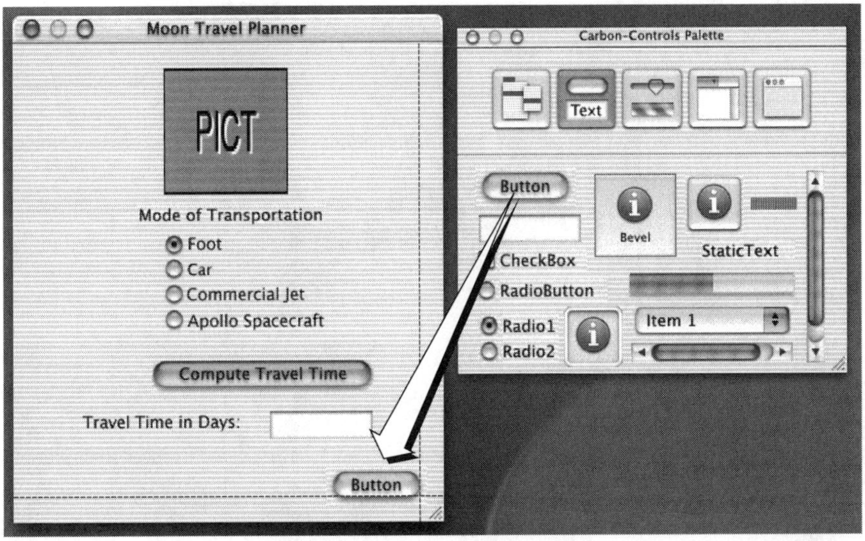

Figure 5-16. Quit button and Aqua guides

5. Drag the icon that looks like the moon and is named PICT to the PICT box, as shown in Figure 5-19. When you release the pointer, the moon image takes on the dimensions of the PICT control. Your window should look similar to Figure 5-21.

 An image always takes on the dimensions of the PICT control. If the dimensions of the PICT box don't have the same aspect ratio as the image you're adding, the image will be distorted.

Align Objects with the Layout Tools

If you've been using the Aqua guides as you've added interface objects, you only need to do a few more things to finish laying out the interface. You'll use layout rectangles and the Alignment menu along with the Aqua guides to complete the layout:

1. Choose Show Layout Rectangles from the Layout menu. Rectangles appear around each interface object, as shown in Figure 5-20.

2. Make sure the top of each object is spaced correctly from the bottom of the adjacent object. Move an object until you see an Aqua guide, then align the edge of the layout rectangle to the guide.

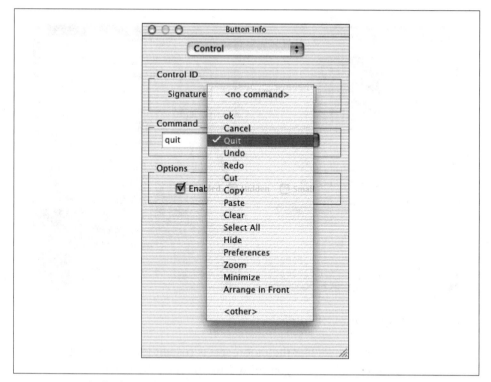

Figure 5-17. The built-in quit command from the Command pop-up menu

3. Use the Make Centered Column command to center the image, the Mode of Transportation text label, the radio button group, and the Compute Travel Time button. Select the items by clicking each as you press the Shift key or by clicking and dragging a selection rectangle around the items. Then choose Make Centered Column from the Alignment submenu in the Layout menu.

4. Use the Aqua baselines to align the Travel Time in Days text field with the Travel Time in Days label. Select the Travel Time in Days text field and move it so the baseline shown by the Aqua guides aligns with the baseline of the Travel Time in Days label.

5. Center the Travel Time in Days text field and the Travel Time in Days label. Use the Size pane in the Info window to make sure the Bottom Left x value of the Travel Time in Days label is equal to the Bottom Right x value of the Travel Time in Days text field.

6. Make sure the Quit button is aligned properly. Move the Quit button. As you approach the corner, you should see the Aqua guides appear, as shown in Figure 5-20. Make sure the top of the Quit button isn't too close to the Travel Time in Days label and text field. If it is, you may need to adjust the window height and move the Quit button lower.

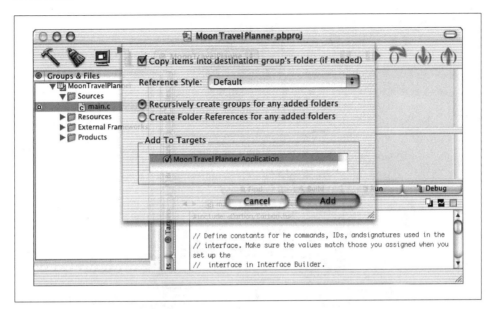

Figure 5-18. Add Files dialog in Project Builder

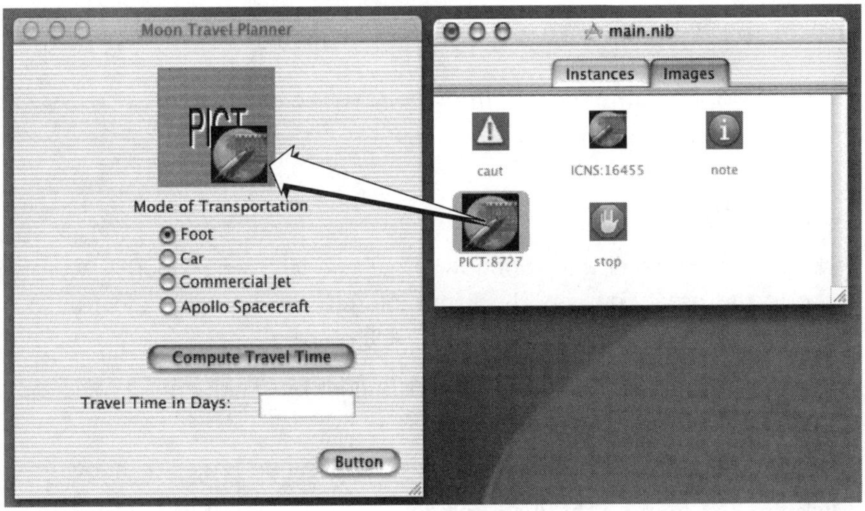

Figure 5-19. Dragging a PICT resource to a PICT control

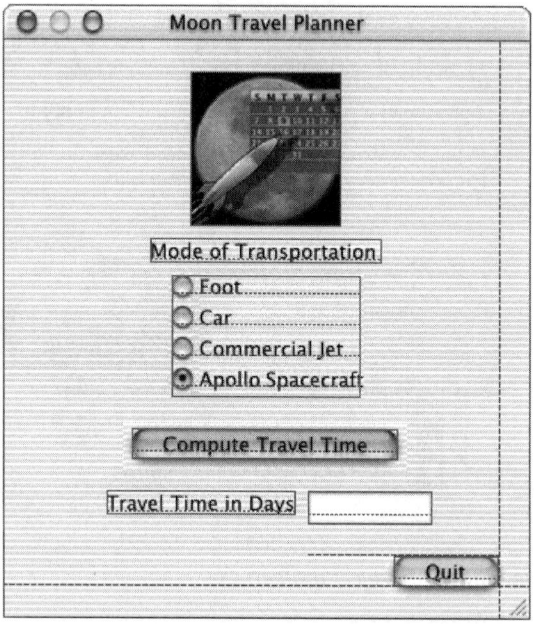

Figure 5-20. Layout rectangles around all controls, and Aqua guides for the Quit button

7. Choose Hide Layout Rectangles from the Layout menu.

8. Choose Save from the File menu.

Check the Interface

By now, the Moon Travel Time window should be laid out properly. What will it look like to the user? You can check the interface by building and running the application in Project Builder. That's what you'll do next:

1. Switch from Interface Builder to Project Builder by clicking the Project Builder icon in the Dock.

2. Click the Build button in the Moon Travel Application project window.

3. Click the Run button. The main window for the Moon Travel Planner should open and look something like the window shown in Figure 5-21.

4. Click Quit.

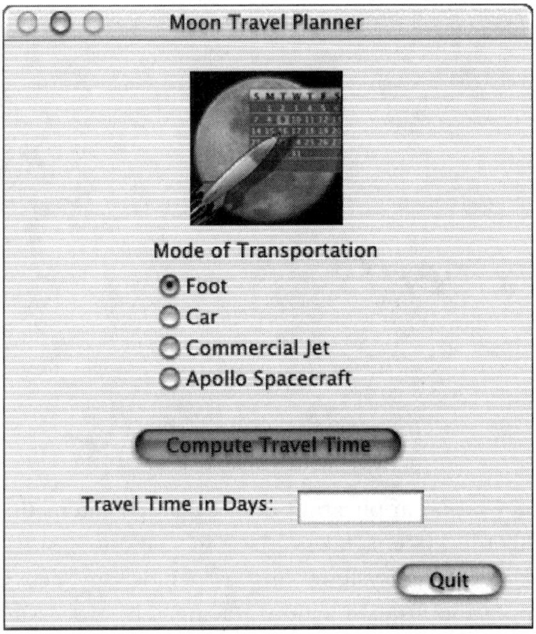

Figure 5-21. The main window for the Moon Travel Planner when the application runs

Recap

We've taken a look at the interface objects—controls, windows, menus, data views—available on Interface Builder's palettes. We've seen how Aqua guides and other layout tools can be used to align an interface fairly quickly while staying within the guidelines specified by the *Aqua Human Interface Guidelines*. You've also had an opportunity to use the palettes and layout tools to finish the main window for the Moon Travel Planner application. You should have a great-looking interface and an application that doesn't do much. Next you'll write some code to make the Moon Travel Planner main window interface spring to life.

6

Carbon Events

Everything a typical Carbon application does, whether interacting with the user or communicating with the system, takes place in response to an event sent to the application by the operating system. *Events* include any activity that requires a response by the application—user actions, changes in processing status, hardware activity, and other occurrences. The core task of any Carbon application is to respond to events.

Carbon supports two event-handling models, although only one is recommended. The first is the legacy Mac OS Event Manager model, referred to as the classic Event Manager. The second is the Carbon Event Manager model. It's the one we'll cover in this chapter, and the event model your Carbon application should use. An application that uses this model tells the Carbon Event Manager what events are of interest. Then the application doesn't do anything until the Carbon Event Manager detects one of the events the application wants to handle. So, when someone using your application is asleep at the keyboard, your application is simply waiting. No processing cycles are wasted; it's a very efficient model.

Another big advantage to using the Carbon Event Manager is that it greatly reduces the amount of code needed to write a basic application. It provides standard handlers for most types of user interaction, so you can concentrate on writing code that's unique to your application.

In this chapter, you'll look at Carbon events and how to handle them. In particular, you'll:

- Get an overview of how events are handled with the Carbon Event Manager

- Learn the essential terminology—event targets, types, and references

- See what default handlers can do for you

- Write a Carbon event handler

Carbon Event Handling

Let's follow a typical user event—a mouse click-through the system. The user clicks a button in the interface. The action of the user pressing a mouse button sets off a low-level event from the device driver that controls the mouse. The I/O Kit, which forms the foundation of all device drivers on Mac OS X, creates the event, puts it in the window server's event queue, and notifies the window server. (The window server is a core service that manages windows. All user actions occur in a window or in a menu associated with a window.) The window server takes the event off the queue, consults a database of open windows, then sends the event to the process that owns the window in which the event occurred. The Carbon Event Manager gets the event from the window server, packages it in an appropriate form, and passes it to the event-handler mechanism specific to the application. This mechanism ensures that the event is handled by the function associated with the control the user clicked. Figure 6-1 depicts the subsystems that generate, repackage, and forward an event to its destination.

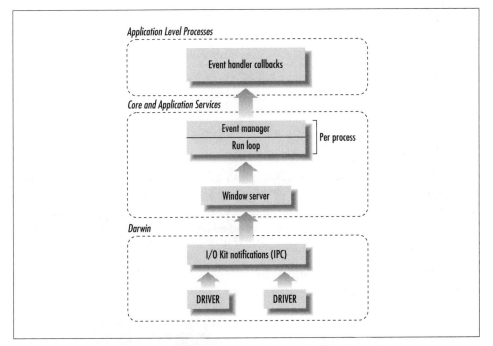

Figure 6-1. A mouse click handled by Mac OS X and the Carbon Event Manager

Carbon uses a callback mechanism to handle events. You define your application's response to various types of events by writing event handler functions and registering them with the Carbon Event Manager. Then, each time an event occurs, the Carbon Event Manager calls back the handler function you installed for that type of event.

Implementing handler-based event management in your application is fairly straightforward. It involves these steps:

1. Identify the events your application must handle.

2. Write handlers (functions) to respond to the events.

3. Install the handlers. This informs the Carbon Event Manager of the events your application handles and which handlers respond to those events.

4. Call the function RunApplicationEventLoop. The Carbon Event Manager does the rest. When the Carbon Event Manager detects an event that your application handles, the manager calls your handler.

The tricky part is to figure out, in Carbon Event Manager lingo, to what events your application responds. This involves learning some new terms and then looking up some predefined constants in the Carbon Event Manager documentation. Basically, you must:

- Identify where events of interest to your application occur (the *event target*)

- Specify what events are of interest (*event type*) to your application

Once you've defined what you're looking for, your application must be prepared to dig out event information from an *event reference* it gets from the Carbon Event Manager.

Event Targets

Carbon events happen, at a general level, in a window or in a menu. On a more specific level, events occur in a user pane, a control, a radio button, and so forth. The interface object (window, control, etc.) in which an event occurs is called the *event target*. When you install an event handler you must specify an event target.

An event target can have any number of events associated with it. For example, an event handler for an application's main window (the event target) could process command events, window events, and mouse events.

Event Types

An *event type* is a pair of values—an event class and an event kind—that define an event. As you identify the events your application handles, you need to find the pair of constants (event class and event kind) associated with each event.

Most Carbon events fall into one of nine *event classes*: application, command, control, keyboard, menu, mouse, tablet, text input, and window.

- **Application.** Associated with application-wide events, such as quitting and launching.

- **Command.** Issued from such objects as menu items and buttons in the interface.

- **Control.** Associated with controls in the interface, such as radio buttons, checkboxes, and sliders.

- **Keyboard, mouse, and tablet.** Issued by the device of the same name.

- **Menu and window.** Actions that happen in menus and windows, such as opening a menu or closing a window.

- **Text input.** Specialized text events, such as mapping a character index to a screen position.

Table 6-1 lists the major event classes and the Carbon Event Manager constants you need to use when you refer to an event class in your application.

Table 6-1. Carbon Event Classes

Event Class	Event Class Constant
Application	kEventClassApplication
Command	kEventClassCommand
Control	kEventClassControl
Keyboard	kEventClassKeyboard
Menu	kEventClassMenu
Mouse	kEventClassMouse
Tablet	kEventClassTablet
Text Input	kEventClassTextInput
Window	kEventClassWindow

An *event kind* indicates a specific event within an event class. Some event classes have only a few event kinds (such as the command class); others (such as the window class) have many event kinds. To define an event type, in addition to the event class, you'll need to look up the constant associated with the event kind. You can find the event kind constants for each of the event classes listed in Appendix B, *Carbon Event Classes and Kinds*.

When you specify an event in your application, you use a structure of type Event-TypeSpec. Let's say your application is supposed to do something every time the user clicks a button in the interface. The event you want to handle is classified as a command (a command class event). The specific action you want to take is to process the command. You'd specify the event type as follows:

```
EventTypeSpec myEventSpecification = {kEventClassCommand,
    kEventCommandProcess};
```

Event References

When the Carbon Event Manager detects an event for your application, it returns an event reference to your application. The *event reference* is a pointer to an opaque structure that contains general information about the event's class, kind, and time of occurrence. An *opaque structure* is a data structure you can't "open up" to directly examine or manipulate its internal elements. You can, however, obtain information about the event's attributes by passing the event reference to various Carbon Event Manager accessor functions provided for this purpose. For instance, the functions Get EventClass and GetEventKind each accept an event reference as a parameter and return a 32-bit integer representing the event's class and kind, respectively:

```
EventRef theEvent;
UInt32    eventClass;
UInt32    eventKind;
eventClass = GetEventClass (theEvent);
eventKind  = GetEventKind (theEvent);
```

Similarly, the Carbon Event Manager function GetEventTime returns the time an event occurred, expressed as a double-length integer of type EventTime measured in seconds since the system was started up:

```
EventRef    theEvent;
EventTime   timeInSeconds;

timeInSeconds = GetEventTime (theEvent);
```

In addition to generic event attributes like class, kind, and time, an event can have additional *event parameters* whose number and nature vary depending on the event type. Each parameter has an *event parameter name* and an *event parameter type*, both of which are denoted by constants defined in the Carbon interface. For instance, a mouse-down event has these four event parameters:

- kEventParamMouseLocation. A point (parameter type typeQDPoint) giving the global screen coordinates at which the mouse button was pressed.

- kEventParamMouseButton. An integer code (parameter type typeMouseButton) identifying which button was pressed (allowing support for a one-, two-, or three-button mouse).

- kEventParamKeyModifiers. A set of flag bits (parameter type typeUInt32) telling which modifier keys, if any, were being held down at the time the button was pressed.

- kEventParamClickCount. An integer (parameter type typeUInt32) telling how many times the button was clicked in the same location (1 for a single click, 2 for a double click, and so on).

Other event types have different parameters associated with them; see Appendix C, *Parameter Names and Types for Common Event Kinds.* All such parameters are accessed with the same Carbon Event Manager function, GetEventParameter, which takes as arguments an event reference, the name and type of the requested parameter, the size of the expected value in bytes, and a pointer to a memory buffer of that size in which to return the value. (There is also a pair of arguments for returning the actual parameter type and size of the value returned; you can specify NULL for these arguments if you don't need this information or don't expect the actual type and size to differ from those requested.) Thus, for example, you might obtain the screen coordinates for a mouse-down event as follows:

```
EventRef    theEvent;
Point       mousePoint;

GetEventParameter (theEvent,
                   kEventParamMouseLocation,
                   typeQDPoint, NULL,
                   sizeof(mousePoint), NULL,
                   &mousePoint);
```

Default Event Handlers

Carbon provides a default event handler for each type of event target (window, menu, control, and application). The default handler defines a standard response to each type of event that a particular target may receive. The one for windows, for instance, implements all the standard behavior for manipulating a window with the mouse—dragging it by its title bar, closing it by clicking the Close button, resizing it by dragging the resize control, and so on. By installing the default handler when you create a window, you automatically inherit all of this standard behavior with no additional effort on your part. You can then proceed to install additional handlers of your own for those aspects of the window's behavior that are specific to your individual application, such as drawing the window contents or responding to the user's mouse actions inside it. Events of those specific types will be reported to your own installed handlers for processing; all others will instead be passed through to the default handler to deal with in the standard way. This frees you from having to provide your own handler for each of the hundred or so events that Carbon may throw at you. With the default event handler to back you up, you can focus your attention on those events whose behavior you need to modify or customize in some way and leave the rest to the default handler.

Sometimes the default event handler's response to a single event can trigger an elaborate cascade of other events. Consider, for example, what happens when the user presses the mouse button in a window's resize control. The mouse press generates an event of type kEventMouseDown, reporting such information as the time and location at which the button was pressed, what modifier keys were being held down at the time, and so forth. Responding to this event involves hit-testing the mouse location to determine that it lies in the window's resize control, tracking the mouse's movements for as long as the button is held down, providing appropriate visual feedback on the screen, and finally resizing the window when the button is released. Theoretically, you could provide a handler function for mouse-down events to do all this yourself, but it's generally more convenient to let the default event handler manage all these chores for you in the standard way. It does this by generating a sequence of further events representing various stages in the process of responding to the original mouse press:

1. A hit-test event (kEventWindowHitTest) to analyze the mouse location and determine what object on the screen received the mouse press.

2. A click-resize-region event (kEventWindowClickResizeRgn) indicating that the mouse button was pressed in the resize control of one of your windows.

3. A get-minimum-size (kEventWindowGetMinimumSize) and a get-maximum-size (kEventWindowGetMaximumSize) event requesting the smallest and largest dimensions to which the user should be allowed to resize the window.

4. The following cycle of events, repeated for as long as the mouse button is held down:

   • A mouse-dragged event (kEventMouseDragged) reporting the mouse's coordinates.

   • A window bounds-changing event (kEventWindowBoundsChanging) indicating that the window's size is about to change.

   • A get-grow-image-region event (kEventWindowGetGrowImageRegion) requesting the size and shape of the window outline to be drawn for visual feedback on the screen.

5. A mouse-up event (kEventMouseUp) when the mouse button is released.

6. A draw-frame event (kEventWindowDrawFrame) to redraw the window's structural elements (frame, title bar, and so forth) in the new size.

7. A window bounds-changed event (kEventWindowBoundsChanged) indicating that the window's size has changed.

8. A window update event (kEventWindowUpdate) indicating that the portion of the window's contents visible on the screen has changed and must be redrawn.

9. A draw-content event (kEventDrawContent) to redraw the window's interior contents.

This proliferation of events may seem daunting, but most of them are really intended to be processed by the default event handler itself, with no active intervention on your part. The only reason for sending all these events is to give you the flexibility to step in at various points in the process and take control yourself if you choose to do so. Maybe you want to reimplement the draw-frame event to change the standard rectangular window frame to an octagonal viewing port for your starship simulation, or intercept mouse-dragged events to play a cool sound effect while the user is dragging the mouse around. Most of the time, you'll just leave these events for the default handler to manage in its own way.

Defining an Event Handler

When you define your own event handler, it must conform to this prototype:

```
pascal OSStatus HandlerName (EventHandlerCallRef  nextHandler,
                             EventRef             theEvent
                             void*                userData);
```

where HandlerName is the name you assigned to the function.

The parameter theEvent is an event reference describing the event to be handled. Your handler can use this value to obtain information about the event by passing it to one of the Carbon accessor functions, such as GetEventClass, GetEventKind, and GetEventParameter, as discussed above.

The handler returns a status code of type OSStatus as its function result: noErr to show that it has successfully handled the specified event or eventNotHandledErr to indicate that it hasn't. In the latter case, the Carbon Event Manager will relay the event to the next handler after this one in the chain of handlers for the given type of event, continuing up the chain until it finds a handler willing to accept and process the event. You can also explicitly propagate an event up the handler chain yourself by calling the Carbon Event Manager function CallNextEventHandler, passing it the value you received for the nextHandler parameter. This value is an *event handler call reference*, an opaque structure denoting the next handler after this one in the chain. This technique of event propagation is useful for incorporating the standard response to an event into your own handler while adding any desired pre- or postprocessing of your own.

The event handler's third parameter, `userData`, is a pointer to an arbitrary data value that your program can use for any purpose of its own. You specify the value of this item when you install your event handler; the Carbon Event Manager will then pass this same value back to the handler function each time it's called.

Installing an Event Handler

The basic Carbon function for installing an event handler is called `Install-EventHandler`:

```
OSStatus InstallEventHandler (EventTargetRef       target,
                              EventHandlerUPP      handlerProc,
                              UInt32               numTypes,
                              const EventTypeSpec* typeList,
                              void*                userData,
                              EventHandlerRef*     handlerRef);
```

The second parameter, `handlerProc`, is a universal procedure pointer (UPP) to your handler function. The Carbon Event Manager function `NewEventHandlerUPP` returns a UPP of the required type; for instance:

```
EventHandlerUPP  handlerUPP;

handlerUPP = NewEventHandlerUPP(MyHandler);
```

where `MyHandler` is the name of your handler function.

A universal procedure pointer (UPP) is a generalized procedure pointer that lets code with different calling conventions call each other. Some Carbon functions require you to pass UPPs for callbacks because the calling routine doesn't know in advance if your code is Mach-O based or CFM-based.

The target parameter to `InstallEventHandler` identifies the event target on which the handler is to be installed. You can obtain a reference to the desired target by calling one of the Carbon functions `GetApplicationEventTarget`, `GetWindowEvent-Target`, `GetMenuEventTarget`, or `GetControlEventTarget`. For convenience, the Carbon Event Manager also defines a set of specialized macros, `InstallWindowEventHandler`, `InstallMenuEventHandler`, and `InstallControlEventHandler`, which accept the targeted object as a parameter, obtain the corresponding target reference for you, and pass it to `InstallEventHandler`. The remaining parameters to these macros are the same as for the function `InstallEventHandler`. For example, the macro call:

```
InstallWindowEventHandler (theWindow, handlerUPP,
                        numTypes, typeList,
                        userData, &handlerRef);
```

is equivalent to:

```
theTarget = GetWindowEventTarget(theWindow);
InstallEventHandler (theTarget, handlerUPP,
                    numTypes, typeList,
                    userData, &handlerRef);
```

A similar macro, `InstallApplicationEventHandler`, needs no parameter to identify the application itself as the target; the call:

```
InstallApplicationEventHandler (handlerUPP,
                        numTypes, typeList,
                        userData, &handlerRef);
```

is equivalent to:

```
theTarget = GetApplicationEventTarget();
InstallEventHandler (theTarget, handlerUPP,
                    numTypes, typeList,
                    userData, &handlerRef);
```

In all of these cases, the `typeList` parameter specifies the event types for which the handler is to be installed. This parameter is nominally declared as a pointer to an event type specifier giving the class and kind of a single event type; but since the C language considers pointers and arrays to be equivalent, it may actually designate an array of such specifiers for more than one type. The `numTypes` parameter tells how many event types are being specified. For example, the following code installs a single handler for both key-down and key-repeat events:

```
EventTypeSpec    eventTypes[2];
EventHandlerUPP  handlerUPP;
```

```
eventTypes[0].eventClass = kEventClassKeyboard;
eventTypes[0].eventKind  = kEventRawKeyDown;

eventTypes[1].eventClass = kEventClassKeyboard;
eventTypes[1].eventKind  = kEventRawKeyRepeat;

handlerUPP = NewEventHandlerUPP(KeyboardHandler);

InstallApplicationEventHandler (handlerUPP,
                                2, eventTypes,
                                NULL, NULL);
```

The userData parameter to InstallEventHandler is a pointer to an arbitrary data value. As we've already seen, any value you supply for this parameter will later be passed back to your handler function each time it's called. You can use this parameter for any purpose that makes sense to your program.

Finally, handlerRef is an output parameter that returns an *event handler reference*, an opaque structure representing the new event handler. The handler reference is needed as a parameter to such Carbon Event Manager functions as AddEventTypesToHandler and RemoveEventTypesFromHandler, for dynamically changing the event types to which a handler applies, and RemoveEventHandler, for deinstalling it. If you're not going to be using any of these operations, you can simply pass NULL for the handlerRef parameter, indicating that no handler reference should be returned. In particular, the handler will be disposed of automatically when you dispose of the target object it's associated with, so there's no need to call RemoveEventHandler explicitly unless for some reason you want to deinstall the handler while the underlying target object still exists.

MoonTravel Planner: Writing an Event Handler

Now that you know what an event handler is supposed to look like, we're ready to add one to the Moon Travel Planner application. Here's what you'll do:

1. Identify the events your handler processes.

2. Write the main window event handler and the compute travel time function called by the handler.

3. Install the main window event handler.

4. Call the application event loop function.

5. Make sure the code works.

Identify Events

As you recall from Chapter 2, *Specifying a Carbon Application: Moon Travel Planner*, a user can select a mode of transportation, then click a button to compute the travel time to the moon. When you created the interface, you assigned a command to the Compute Travel Time button. Your application needs to handle this command when it's issued—a command class event kEventClassCommand.

Everything else that happens in the window—moving it, minimizing it, clicking a radio button—can be handled by the default handler for the window. (Recall you selected Standard Handler in Chapter 4, *Interface Builder: Nibs and Windows*.)

Now that you've identified the event (a command class event) in which your application is interested, you need to declare an event type specifier to indicate to the Carbon Event Manager the event for which to call the handler.

Open the Moon Travel Planner project. In the main.c file file, copy the following to the main function, after the declaration OSStatus err:

```
EventTypeSpec     mainSpec = {kEventClassCommand,
                                 kEventCommandProcess};
```

Write the Main Window Event Handler

In this section, you'll write an event handler, MTPMainWindowEventHandler, for the main window and a function, MTPComputeCommandHandler, called by the main window event handler. Note that we'll preface the functions and constants for the Moon Travel Planner application with MTP to distinguish them from functions and constants supplied by the Carbon programming interface.

Functions and constants from the Carbon programming interface contain either a prefix or keyword that indicates to which manager or technology they belong. For example, functions that take care of controls in the interface have the word Control somewhere in the function name, such as GetControlID. Functions from Core Foundation are prefaced by CF, such as CFStringCreateWithFormat.

We'll point out the manager or technology associated with each function. If you want complete, technical documentation on a function or related functions, you can consult the Carbon API (application programming interface) documentation by choosing Carbon Help in the Project Builder Help menu.

The main window event handler

You need to declare the event handler and then write the actual handler. The function declaration for the handler must follow the prototype discussed in the section "Defining an Event Handler." Declare the handler by copying the following to the main.c file, at the top, just after the statement #include <Carbon/Carbon.h>:

```
// Function declarations for the window event handlers
pascal OSStatus MTPMainWindowEventHandler (EventHandlerCallRef myHandler,
                                           EventRef event,
                                           void *userData);
```

You need to declare the constants and global variables used in the MTPComputeCommandHandler. Note that many of these constants represent the commands, IDs, and signatures you assigned to objects when you created the interface. Some represent constants you'll use in a switch statement to determine which formula to use to calculate travel time. Others represent constants you'll use to calculate travel time.

Copy the declarations shown in Example 6-1 to the main.c file, at the top, just after the statement #include <Carbon/Carbon.h>:

Example 6-1: Main Window Event Handler and Compute Command Function Declarations

```
// Define constants for the commands, IDs, and signature used
// in the interface. Make sure the values match those you assigned when
// you set up the interface in Interface Builder.
#define kMTPApplicationSignature        'MTPP'
#define kMTPComputeCommand              'tRav'
#define kMTPTravelTimeFieldID                 129
#define kMTPModeOfTransportButtonGroupID      130


// Define constants to use in the moon travel time computation.
#define kMTPHoursPerDay 24
#define kMTPDistanceToMoon 384467  // kilometers


// Define constants to identify the mode of transportation.
#define kMTPFootMode              1
#define kMTPCarMode               2
#define kMTPCommercialJetMode     3
#define kMTPApolloSpacecraftMode  4


// Define a window reference to the main window
WindowRef         gMainWindow;
```

The main window event handler will handle the command issued by the user when the user clicks the Compute Travel Time button in the window. You'll need to use the function GetEventParameter to get the exact command. Once you know what the command is, you can call other functions in your application to carry out the command.

Next, copy the function in Example 6-2 into the main program (main.c), after the main function.

Example 6-2: The Main Window Event Handler

```
pascal OSStatus MTPMainWindowEventHandler (EventHandlerCallRef myHandler,
                        EventRef event, void *userData)
{
    OSStatus        result  = eventNotHandledErr;                   // 1
    HICommand       command;

    GetEventParameter (event, kEventParamDirectObject, typeHICommand, NULL,
                            sizeof (HICommand), NULL, &command);    // 2
    switch (command.commandID)

        {
        case kMTPComputeCommand:                                    // 3
            MTPComputeCommandHandler ((WindowRef) userData);        // 4
            result = noErr;
            break;
        }
    return result;
}
```

Here's what the function does:

1. Set the value of `result` to `eventNotHandledErr` to assure that if the event passed to the handler is not handled, the Carbon Event Manager gets passed back `eventNotHandledErr`. If your handler doesn't handle an event, the Carbon Event Manager will handle it if it can.

2. The Carbon Event Manager function `GetEventParameter` gets the command ID associated with the command. The command IDs are the four-character codes you assigned to the buttons and commands in the interface and declared as constants in the section "Identify Events."

3. The `k` denotes a constant. The preface `kMTP` denotes a constant defined in the Moon Travel Planner application. The constant's value `'tRav'` (defined in Example 6-1) corresponds to the command (`'tRav'`) you entered in the Info window in Chapter 5, *Interface Builder: Tools and Controls*, for the Compute Travel Time button.

4. `MTPComputeCommandHandler` computes travel time and displays the result. You'll write this function next.

The compute command handler

When the main window event handler gets the compute travel time command, it calls a function to compute travel time. In this section, you'll write a function that:

1. Reads the value of the radio button group.

2. Chooses a calculation based on the value of the radio button group.

3. Does the calculation.

4. Converts the numerical result to a string.

5. Writes the string to the travel time field. You'll need to declare the command
   handler. Copy the following to the `main.c` file, just after the declaration for the
   main window event handler:

```
// Function declarations for command handlers
pascal void MTPComputeCommandHandler (WindowRef window);
```

The function is shown in Example 6-3. Copy it into the main program, after the
function `MTPMainWindowEventHandler`.

Example 6-3: A Handler That Computes Travel Time Based on Mode of Transportation

```
pascal void MTPComputeCommandHandler (WindowRef window)
{
  ControlHandle    modeOfTransportButtonGroup,                          // 1
                   travelTimeField;
  ControlID  modeOfTransportControlID = {kMTPApplicationSignature,      // 2
                   kMTPModeOfTransportButtonGroupID};
  ControlID  travelTimeControlID = { kMTPApplicationSignature,
                   kMTPTravelTimeFieldID };
  CFStringRef      text;
  double           travelTime;
  SInt32           transportModeValue;
  OSErr          status;

  GetControlByID (window, &modeOfTransportControlID,                    // 3
                   &modeOfTransportButtonGroup);
  GetControlByID (window, &travelTimeControlID, &travelTimeField);
  transportModeValue = GetControl32BitValue (modeOfTransportButtonGroup); // 4
  switch (transportModeValue)                                          // 5
    {
      case kMTPFootMode:
        // Foot - good walking time is 4 miles per hour
        travelTime = (kMTPDistanceToMoon/(4.0/0.62))/kMTPHoursPerDay;
        break;
      case kMTPCarMode:
        // Car - 70 miles per hour on the highway, no speed limit in space!
        travelTime = (kMTPDistanceToMoon/(70/0.62))/kMTPHoursPerDay;
        break;
      case kMTPCommercialJetMode:
        // Commercial Jet - 600 miles per hour.
        travelTime = (kMTPDistanceToMoon/(600.0/0.62))/kMTPHoursPerDay;
        break;
      case kMTPApolloSpacecraftMode:
        // Apollo 11 took 4 days to get to the moon.
        travelTime = 4;
        break;
      default:
```

Example 6-3: A Handler That Computes Travel Time Based on Mode of Transportation (continued)

```
        travelTime = 0;
        break;
  }
  text = CFStringCreateWithFormat(NULL, NULL, CFSTR("%2.1f"),travelTime);  // 6
  status = SetControlData( travelTimeField, kControlEntireControl,
            kControlEditTextCFStringTag,sizeof (CFStringRef), &text);     // 7
  CFRelease (text);                                                        // 8
  DrawOneControl (travelTimeField);                                        // 9
}
```

Here's what the function does:

1. A `ControlHandle` is a reference to a structure that contains information about a control, such as its location in the interface, title, value, whether it's visible, and so forth. You need to pass this reference to a function that accesses the structure.

2. You need to pass a control's `ControlID` when you get or set information associated with the control. The `ControlID` is a structure that contains the application's creator code (signature) and ID associated with a control. In Chapter 5 you set signatures and IDs for controls. You use these values (or constants that represent these values) when you declare a `ControlID` in the `MTPComputeCommandHandler` function.

3. You call the Control Manager function `GetControlByID` twice: once to get the control handle associated with the Mode of Transportation radio button group and a second time to get the control handle associated with the Travel Time field. `GetControlByID` takes three parameters: a reference to the window in which the control resides; the `ControlID` for the control (whose value you set in item 2, above); and a control handle.

4. The Control Manager function `GetControl32BitValue` returns a value that indicates which radio button in the radio button group is selected. You must pass the control handle to the radio button group.

5. Calculations are based on the mode of transportation selected, but do not take into account the effects of gravity and inertia. Miles are converted to kilometers by dividing by 0.62.

6. The Core Foundation String Services function `CFStringCreateWithFormat` converts the floating point number to a `CFString`. The "printf-style" format string `%2.1f` indicates how the string should be formatted.

7. The Control Manager function `SetControlData` sets the Travel Time text field to the value of the string, but does not draw the field. It takes five parameters:

- A handle to the control whose data you want to set.

- The part code of the control part for which data is to be set. In this case our control (a text field) has no parts, so you need to pass kControlEntireControl. Control part constants are defined in the Control Manger reference documentation.

- A constant representing the control-specific data you wish to set. In this case you need to put CFString data into the field, so you use the constant kControlEditTextCFStringTag. Editable text control data tag constants are defined in the Control Manager reference documentation.

- The size (in bytes) of the data pointed to by the fifth parameter.

- A pointer to the buffer containing the data that you are sending to the control.

8. The Core Foundation Base Services function CFRelease releases the memory associated with the CFString.

9. The Control Manager function DrawOneControl redraws the Travel Time text field with the new string.

Install the Main Window Event Handler

The event target is a window, so you can use one of the macros discussed in the section "Installing an Event Handler" to install our handler InstallWindowEventHandler.

In the main function, after the line DisposeNibReference(nibRef), add the following code:

```
InstallWindowEventHandler (gMainWindow,
        NewEventHandlerUPP (MTPMainWindowEventHandler),
        1, &mainSpec, (void *) gMainWindow, NULL);
```

InstallWindowEventHandler tells the Carbon Event Manager to call the window's event handler whenever a specified event type happens in the window. These are the parameters to the function InstallWindowEventHandler:

- The target of the event handler—in this case, the window to which the handler should be registered, which is the main window.

- A pointer to the window event handler—the function NewEventHandlerUPP returns a pointer to the function you just wrote, MTPMainWindowEventHandler.

- The number of events for which the handler is registered—in this case, 1, a command.

- A pointer to the event types handled by the event handler—you defined these as `mainSpec`.

- A value that's passed to the window event handler when the Carbon Event Manager calls the handler—in this case, a pointer to the window to which the handler is registered, that is, the main window.

- An event handler reference—in this case, `NULL`.

Modify the main function

When you created a skeletal application in Chapter 3, *Project Builder Projects*, Project Builder provided several lines of code for you that you now need to modify. Notice in the main function the code to create and show the main window uses a variable called `window`. The Moon Travel Planner application will eventually have four windows, so you'll rename the generic `window` to `gMainWindow`. You declared this global (the g denotes global) variable in the previous section, the section "Write the Main Window Event Handler."

Modify these lines of code in the main function so they use `gMainWindow`:

```
err = CreateWindowFromNib(nibRef, CFSTR("MainWindow"), &window);
ShowWindow (window );
```

When you're done, they should look like this:

```
err = CreateWindowFromNib (nibRef, CFSTR ("MainWindow"), &gMainWindow);
ShowWindow (gMainWindow);
```

Finally, you can delete this line from the main function because the main window is now held in a global variable (gMainWindow):

```
WindowRef window;
```

Call the Application Event Loop Function

The function `RunApplicationEventLoop` is already in the main function. As you recall from Chapter 3, it's one of the lines of code provided "for free" by Project Builder. So let's build, run, and test the application to make sure the events are handled properly.

1. Choose Save from the File menu.

2. Click the Build button in the upper-left corner of the Moon Travel project window.

3. Click the Run button in the upper-left corner of the project window.

4. Select a mode of transportation and click the Compute Travel Time button. Does the value in the Travel Time field change? Is it the value you expect?

5. Click the Quit button. Does the application quit? If so, you are ready to move on!

Recap

We've discussed one of the most important Carbon technologies in this chapter—the Carbon Event Manager. You followed a typical event through the operating system and saw how it's handled. Then we discussed the key concepts you need to set up event handlers for Carbon events. You had an opportunity to see how Carbon's default handlers work, and then to actually write an event handler for the Moon Travel Planner application.

Now that the Moon Travel Planner application is more than just a pretty face and actually does something—compute travel time—you can move on. There is still a lot to do to create the application described in Chapter 2. Next you'll take care of menus.

7

Interface Builder: Menus

Every Carbon application must support menus—the standard ones supplied by Mac OS X and those your application provides. Menus allow users to view or choose from a list of choices any commands or attributes provided by your application. You can add application-specific menus and customize many of the standard menu items to suit your application's needs.

The easiest way to create, display, and set up the behavior of pull-down, hierarchical, and contextual menus is to use Interface Builder. It provides you with a menu bar that's already loaded with the standard menus and items. To set up the menus for your application, do the following steps:

1. Modify the default menu bar by:

   • Disabling the items your application doesn't need

   • Preparing the items your application needs

   • Adding application-specific menus and menu items

2. Add code to your project to:

   • Call Interface Builder Services to create the menu bar from the nib file

   • Process the menu commands

In this chapter, you'll:

• Look at a typical menu bar for an application running on Mac OS X

• Go through the menu bar provided by Interface Builder to see which items are set up for you and which ones you need to prepare

- Discuss hierarchical and contextual menus

- Modify the menu bar for the Moon Travel Planner application

The Menu Bar

The Mac OS has a menu bar with a number of standard menus and menu items that should appear in any application. Figure 7-1 shows the menu bar for the Finder on Mac OS X. The Apple menu on the left is always present. The menu to the right of the Apple menu is the Application menu; it takes the name of the application that's running. On Mac OS X, the Finder is an application, so the menu is named Finder. The Application menu, along with the menus called out to the right of it, make up an application's menus. Some are standard, such as File, Edit, Window, and Help, while others are specific to the application. The View and Go menus are specific to the Finder.

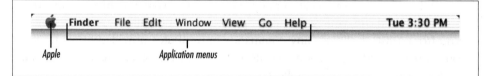

Figure 7-1. The menu bar for the Finder on Mac OS X

When the user opens a menu from the menu bar, they see a pull-down menu, as shown in Figure 7-2. Menus should have a one-word title that represents what's in the menu. The ellipsis character indicates the user must supply more information after choosing the item. In the case of the Go to Folder command, the user is presented a dialog and must choose or type a location. Menu items that aren't followed by an ellipsis character indicate the item will issue a command when it's chosen. Menu items should do something (such as save a file, show a movie) or change an attribute (such as change the font size).

A keyboard equivalent provides an alternative to choosing an item from the menu. Mac OS X reserves certain keyboard combinations as equivalents to menu commands; these shortcuts affect all applications. As long as a combination isn't reserved, you can assign it to a menu item. You can find a complete list of reserved keyboard equivalents in *Inside Mac OS X: Aqua Human Interface Guidelines* in Carbon Help (available in the Project Builder Help menu).

The menu bar provided with Interface Builder (shown in Figure 7-3) is a template you'll modify to suit the needs of your application. Interface Builder automatically includes standard menus—Application, File, Edit, Window, and Help. (If you open Interface Builder and the menu bar isn't open, double-click the MainMenu icon in the Instances pane.)

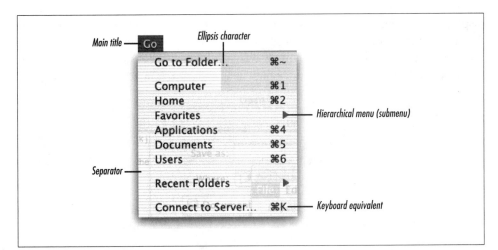

Figure 7-2. The standard parts of a pull-down menu

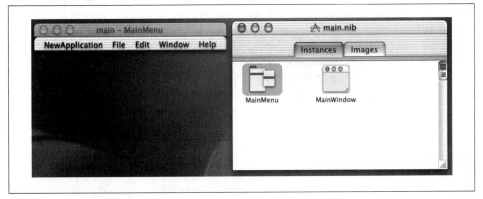

Figure 7-3. The menu bar provided with Interface Builder

In this section, we'll go through each menu in the menu bar to see what you get "free" with Interface Builder. As you go through each menu, you'll see that some items are already wired to do something, while others you'll need to assign a command to and then provide the code that gets invoked by the command. Once you see what's in the menu bar, we'll take a look at two other types of menus you can create: hierarchical and contextual menus.

Application Menu

The Application menu contains items that apply to your application as a whole, rather than to a specific document or window. Figure 7-4 shows the Application menu template as it looks in Interface Builder. The template contains the only item you can modify, About NewApplication. When a user chooses the About menu item, it should issue a command that opens your application's About window to display version and copyright information. You have to do a few things to make the menu item issue a command and open the About window: assign the item a command (which you'll do later in this chapter), write code to open the About window, and create the window (which you'll do later in Chapter 10, *Property Lists*).

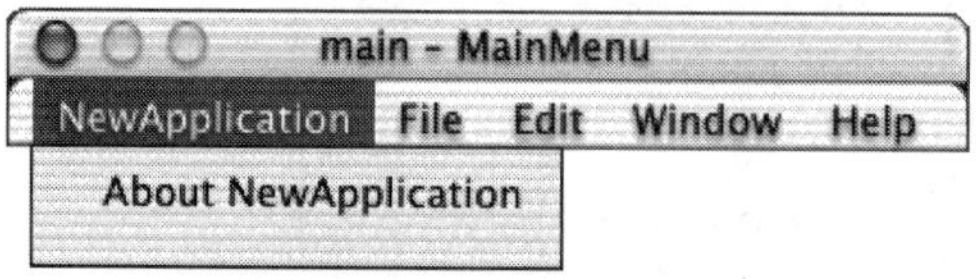

Figure 7-4. The Application menu template as it looks in Interface Builder

When your application actually runs, the Application menu will contain all the standard items (such as Quit) shown in Figure 7-5 in addition to the About item. The operating system automatically includes the other items for you.

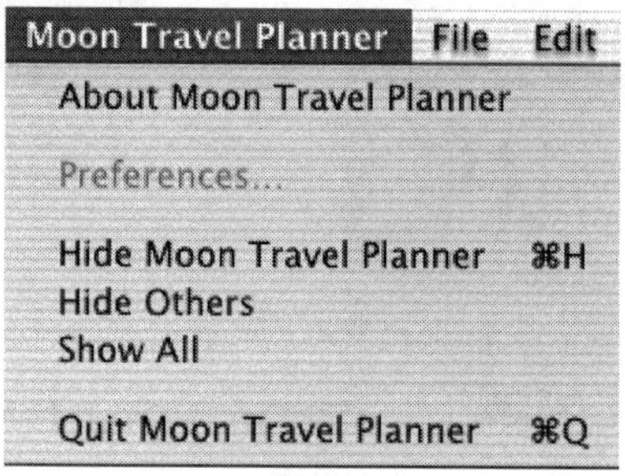

Figure 7-5. The Moon Travel Planner application menu

File Menu

The File menu contains commands that can be applied to a document. The standard File menu is shown in Figure 7-6. In most cases, each command should apply to a single file. The commands are necessary for any application that is document-centered. If you write an application that doesn't use documents and for which none of the File menu commands apply, you can disable the items in the File menu.

None of the File menu items are configured to do anything. For each item your application plans to provide to the user, you must assign a command and then implement the minimum expected behavior for that item by calling the appropriate functions from the Carbon programming interface. The commands must be programmed by you to do the following:

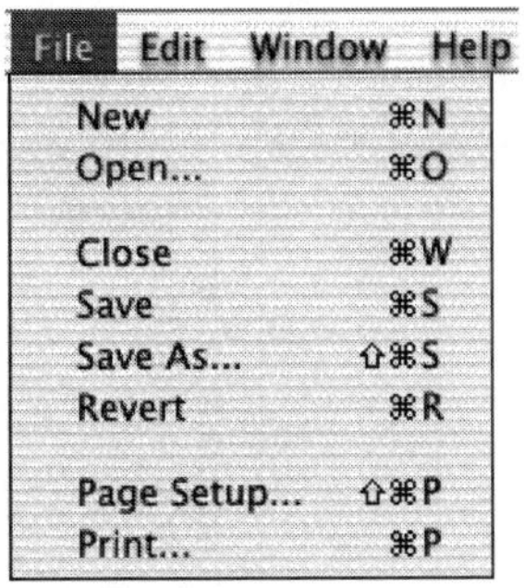

Figure 7-6. The standard File menu

- **New.** Opens a new document named untitled.

- **Open.** Displays the standard dialog so the user can open an existing document.

- **Close.** Closes the active window. If it's a window in which the user has made changes, you should provide an opportunity to save changes. In a single-window application, closing the window should not quit the application.

- **Save.** Saves the active document and leaves the document open.

- **Save As.** Opens a dialog to let the user enter a new filename for the active document, saves a copy of the active document with the new user-defined name, and leaves the original document open.

- **Revert.** Reverts to the last saved version of the document.

- **Page Setup.** Opens a dialog in which the user can specify printing parameters, such as size and orientation.

- **Print.** Opens a dialog for specifying printing options, such as printer, page range, and number of copies.

Later in this book, we'll show you how to write code to implement Open, Close, Save, Save As, Page Setup, and Print.

Edit Menu

Commands that allow users to change or edit the contents of a document or to move data between applications are in the Edit menu. The editing commands use a system utility—the *Clipboard*—for temporary storage of data that's cut or copied from a document. Data remains on the Clipboard until the user replaces the contents with a new cut or copy operation. Figure 7-7 shows the Edit menu you get with Interface Builder.

If you need to see what's on the Clipboard, go to the Finder and choose Show Clipboard from the Edit menu.

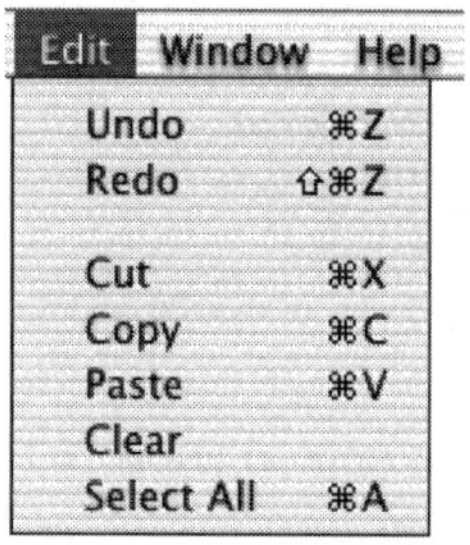

Edit	Window	Help
Undo		⌘Z
Redo		⇧⌘Z
Cut		⌘X
Copy		⌘C
Paste		⌘V
Clear		
Select All		⌘A

Figure 7-7. The Edit menu you get with Interface Builder

Unlike the File menu, every item in the Edit menu is already assigned a command. You need to implement the following standard behavior:

- **Undo.** Reverses the effect of the user's last operation.

- **Redo.** Reverses the effect of the user's just-completed Undo operation.

You don't need to implement the following items for a text field added using Interface Builder. The commands will behave as follows automatically. However, if you are developing an application that provides more sophisticated text handling, you will need to implement them. For example, if you are using the Multilingual Text Engine functions provided in Carbon, you will need to handle these commands:

- **Cut.** Removes selected data and stores it on the Clipboard.

- **Copy.** Copies the selected data and stores it on the Clipboard.

- **Paste.** Inserts whatever is on the Clipboard at the location of the insertion point.

- **Clear.** Removes selected data but does not store it on the Clipboard.

- **Select All.** Selects and highlights every object in a document.

Some Edit items might not always be appropriate. For example, if no action has been taken by the user, then Undo should not be enabled. It should appear dimmed to the user. Your application must implement code that enables and disables menu items appropriately.

Window Menu

The Window menu provides commands for managing multiple document windows. Figure 7-8 shows a Window menu with two items, Minimize and Arrange in Front. When an application runs, the menu also lists the application's open document windows and those windows that are minimized.

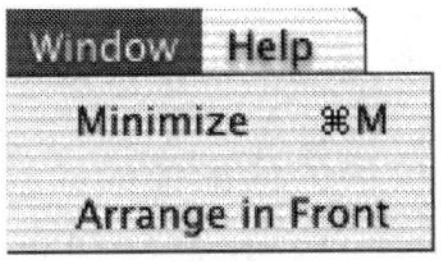

Figure 7-8. The Window menu

The Minimize and Arrange in Front items are already assigned commands and are set up to behave as follows:

- **Minimize.** Puts a window in the Dock.

- **Arrange in Front.** Brings all windows belonging to the application to the front, while maintaining the order of the windows.

Help Menu

If your application provides onscreen help (and it should), the Help menu is always the rightmost menu. The first item is the name of the application and the word "Help" (Moon Travel Planner Help, for example). If you plan to provide users with a standard Apple help book for your application, you won't need to use Interface Builder's Help menu. In fact, as you'll see later in this chapter, you'll need to delete the Help menu, as the Help menu and handling the Help menu item comes "for free" with the use of a standard Apple help book.

However, if you plan to provide help in a form other than a standard Apple help book, you'll need to use Interface Builder's Help menu. You'll also need to assign commands to Help menu items and implement code to open help for your application.

Figure 7-9. The Help menu in Interface Builder

Hierarchical Menus

You can use *hierarchical menus* to offer additional menu item choices without taking up more space in the menu bar. When the user points to a menu item that has a submenu indicator, a submenu appears. Submenus have all the features of menus, including keyboard equivalents, status markers (such as checkmarks), icons, and so on. Figure 7-10 shows a hierarchical menu.

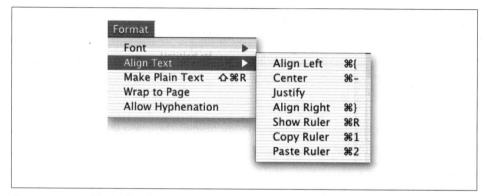

Figure 7-10. A hierarchical menu

The default menus provided by Interface Builder do not include any hierarchical menus. You can easily add one by dragging a submenu object from the Menus palette. See Chapter 5, *Interface Builder: Tools and Controls*, for more information on the Menus palette.

Contextual Menus

A *contextual menu* is one that appears next to an item when the user presses the Control key while clicking the item. The contextual menu provides convenient access to often-used commands associated with the item. Figure 7-11 shows the Finder's contextual menu for the Clock utility.

If you use a contextual menu in your application, include a small subset of the most commonly used commands in the appropriate context. You can add a contextual menu using the menu object provided in Interface Builder's Menu palette.

Moon Travel Planner: Modifying the Menu Bar

The procedures for modifying the menu bar in Interface Builder are similar to those you used to modify the main window in Chapter 4, *Interface Builder: Nibs and Windows*.

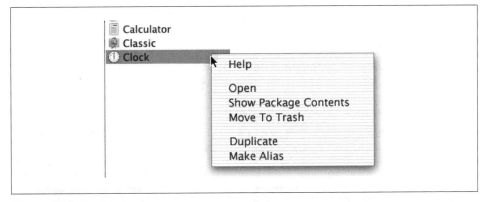

Figure 7-11. A contextual menu

- Drag an object from the Menus palette to the menu bar to create new menus and menu items.

- Use the Info window to change menu item attributes and controls.

- Double-click an item and type to change its name.

In this section, you'll modify the menu bar so it's customized for the Moon Travel Planner application. You'll do the following:

1. Disable the items you won't need.

2. Set up the items the application needs.

3. Add an application-specific menu to the menu bar.

4. Add code to your project to create the menu bar.

5. Test the menus.

Disable the Items You Won't Need

Let's take a look at the default menu bar and disable any items you won't need for the Moon Travel Planner application. The application won't provide the ability for users to create new files, so you can disable the New menu item in the File menu. Users will be able to choose Open, Close, and Save As commands from the File menu. But you'll disable Revert and Save. The Moon Travel Planner won't provide any editing capabilities, so you'll disable the items in the Edit menu.

Open the menu bar by clicking main.nib in the Resources group of the Moon Travel Planner project, then double-click the MainMenu icon in the Instances pane.

Disable each unneeded item by following these steps:

1. Click a menu (such as File) to open it.

2. Click the item in the menu you want to disable.

3. Choose Show Info from the Tools menu.

4. Choose Attributes from the pop-up menu.

5. Make sure Enabled is not selected, as shown in Figure 7-12. When an item is not enabled, it appears dimmed to the user.

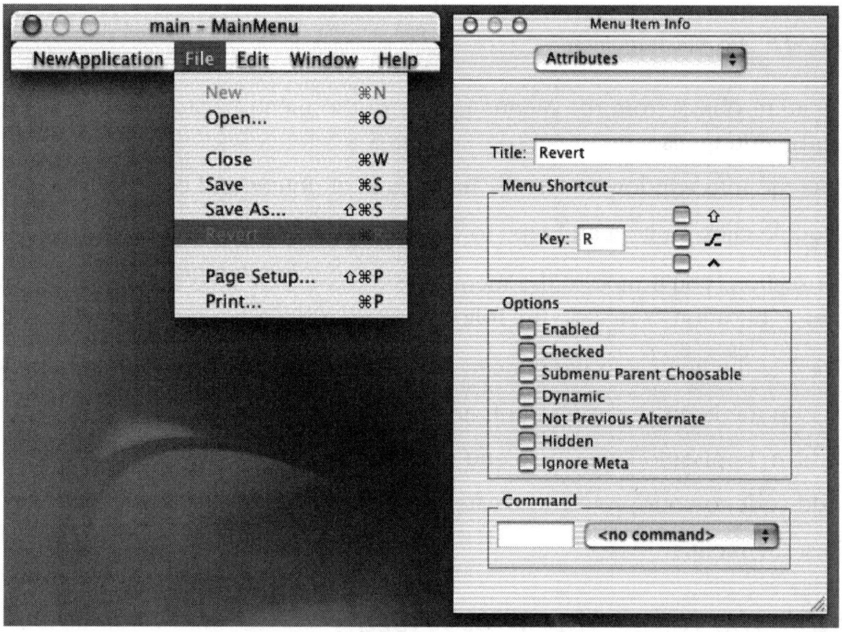

Figure 7-12. Enabled is not selected for unneeded menu items

Set Up the Items You Know You'll Need

You must assign a command to every menu item your application makes available to the user. A command must:

- Consist of four characters

- Have at least one uppercase character (Apple reserves the use of commands that are all lowercase characters.)

- Be unique within your application

When a user chooses a menu item from a menu, the Menu Manager issues the command you assigned to it. The Carbon Event Manager passes the command to your application to handle. Then, your application calls the function that handles it.

It takes two steps to get a menu item working for your application: assigning the command and writing the code to handle it. In this section you'll add commands for each menu item you'll use in the Moon Travel Planner. You'll write the code to process commands in other parts of this book.

 As you assign a command to a menu item, make a note of it. You'll need to refer to a command when you write the code to handle it.

Add an About command

The About command will open a window that displays version and copyright information for the application.

1. Click the NewApplication menu, then double-click the About NewApplication menu item.

2. Type **About Moon Travel Planner**.

3. Choose Show Info from the Tools menu.

4. Choose Attributes from the pop-up menu.

5. Assign **aBtb** as the command. In the Command section, type **aBtb** in the text field (as shown in Figure 7-13) and press Return.

Add an Open Itinerary command

The Open command will allow users to open a file that contains a suggested itinerary for a trip to the moon. Because the user will only be able to open files that have a special itinerary type, you should first change the name of the Open menu item to Open Itinerary, then add a command.

1. Click the File menu, then double-click the Open menu item.

2. Type **Open Itinerary...** and press Return. The ellipsis indicates to the user that more information is required to carry out the command. In this case, the ellipsis indicates a dialog will appear.

3. Assign **oPit** as the command. From the pop-up menu at the top of the Menu Item Info window, choose Attributes. In the Command section, type **oPit** in the text field, and press Return.

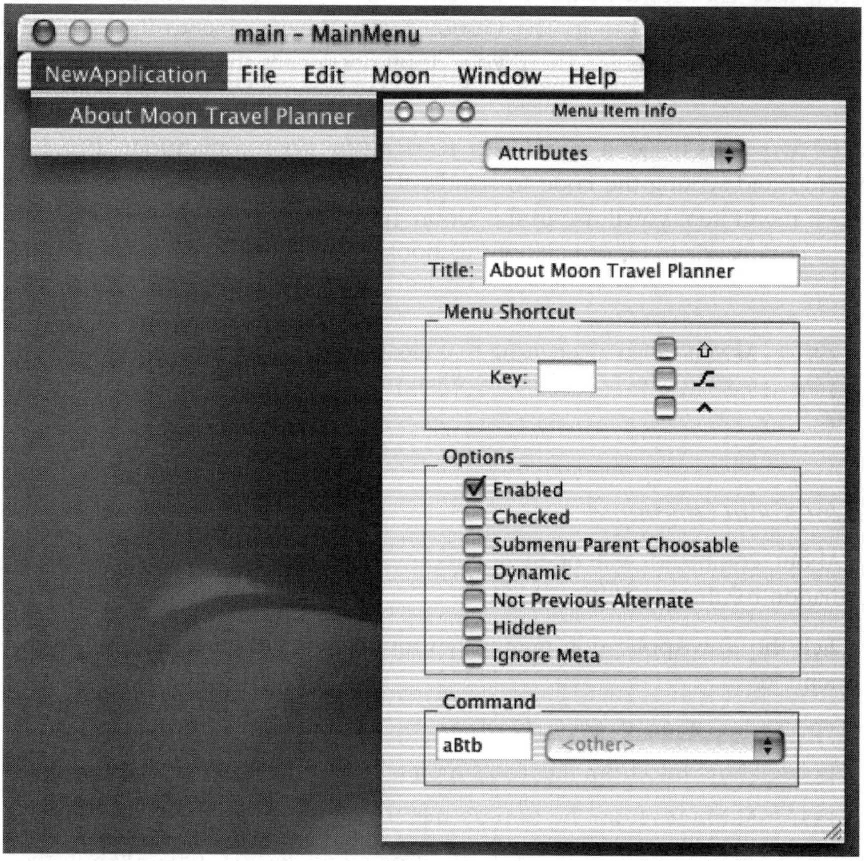

Figure 7-13. A command for the About menu item

Add Commands for Close and Save As

Users should be able to close and open an itinerary, or save an itinerary under a different file name. Add these commands to the Close and Save As menu items:

- Enter **cLse** as the Close menu item's command.

- Enter **sAit** as the Save As menu item's command.

Add Commands for Page Setup and Print

In Chapter 8, *Text and Localization*, you'll create a window (Facts for the Traveler) that displays facts for those considering travel to the moon. You should add page setup and print commands to allow users to print the facts. Add these commands to the Page Setup and Print menu items:

- Enter **pGsu** as the Page Setup menu item's command.

- Enter **pRnt** as the Print menu item's command.

Delete the Help Menu

In Chapter 12, *Providing Help*, you'll add a help book to the Moon Travel Planner application, write code that registers the help book, and set properties that specify the help book name and folder. Mac OS X automatically sets up a Help menu and names the Help menu item based on the properties you set. In our case, the Help menu item will be named Moon Travel Planner Help. The operating system also handles the command issued when the user chooses Moon Travel Planner Help from the Help menu. So there is no need for us to use the Help menu provided by Interface Builder. You must delete it, otherwise your application will have two Help menus:

1. Click the Help menu.
2. Press Delete.

Add an Application-Specific Menu to the Menu Bar

Not everything an application needs is in the default menu bar; you usually need to add at least one application-specific menu. You can find help for designing an application-specific menu in *Inside Mac OS X: Aqua Human Interface Guidelines*.

You already know from the Moon Travel Planner specification (see Chapter 2, *Specifying a Carbon Application: Moon Travel Planner*) that you need to add an application-specific menu called Moon. The Moon menu should have two menu items—Compute Travel Time and Show Facts. The Compute Travel Time menu item will issue the same command issued by the Compute Travel Time button in the main window. The Show Facts menu item will issue a command that opens a window to display enticing facts about the moon as a tourist destination.

You'll use the Menus palette to add a new menu to the default menu bar:

1. In Interface Builder, choose Palettes from the Tools menu, then click the Menus icon (the circled icon in Figure 7-14) in the palette's toolbar.

2. Drag a Submenu object from the Menu palette to the space between the Edit and Window menus, as shown in Figure 7-15.

3. Name the menu **Moon**. Double-click the word Submenu, type **Moon**, and press Return.

4. Name the Item **Compute Travel Time**. Double-click the Item menu item, type **Compute Travel Time**, and press Return.

Figure 7-14. The Menus palette

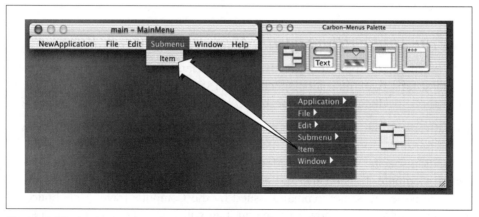

Figure 7-15. A submenu item inserted in the menu bar

5. Assign Command-K as the Compute Travel Time menu item's keyboard equivalent. Click the menu item and choose Show Info from the Tools menu, then type **K** in the Key text field of the Menu Shortcut box as shown in Figure 7-16.

6. Enter **tRav** as the menu item's command. Type **tRav** in the Command text field of the Menu Item Info window and press Return. When the user chooses Compute Travel Time, the Carbon Event Manager sends the tRav command to your application. In Chapter 6, *Carbon Events*, you wrote the handler that takes care of the tRav command issued by the Compute Travel Time button in the main window. Note the menu item uses the same command. As long as the main window is active when the user chooses the Compute Travel Time item from the Moon menu, the handler takes care of the command. It doesn't matter whether the menu or the button issues the command.

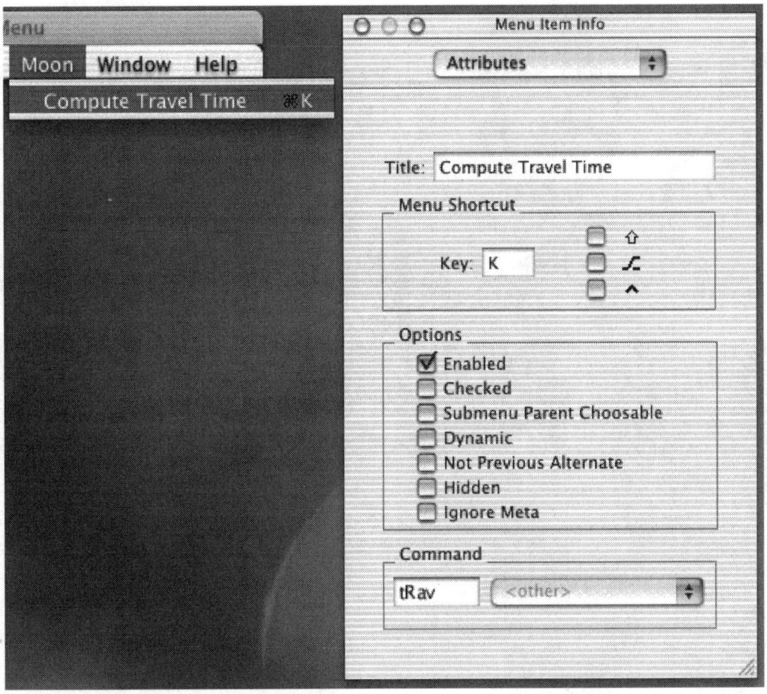

Figure 7-16. The Compute Travel Time menu item and Info window

7. Add a new item to the Moon menu. Drag an Item object from the Menu palette to the space below the Compute Travel Time menu item, as shown in Figure 7-17. When the Item is over a "legal" spot, the pointer changes to show a small + sign and a line appears at the location where the Item is placed.

8. Name the menu item **Show Facts**. Double-click the Item menu item, type **Show Facts**, and press Return. In most cases, a menu item should be written as an action so it's clear to the user what happens when the item is chosen. Although the window's title is Facts for the Traveler, we've named the menu item Show Facts.

9. Assign Shift-Command-F as the Show Facts menu item's keyboard equivalent. Click the Show Facts menu item, then type Shift-Command-F in the Key text field of the Menu Shortcut box.

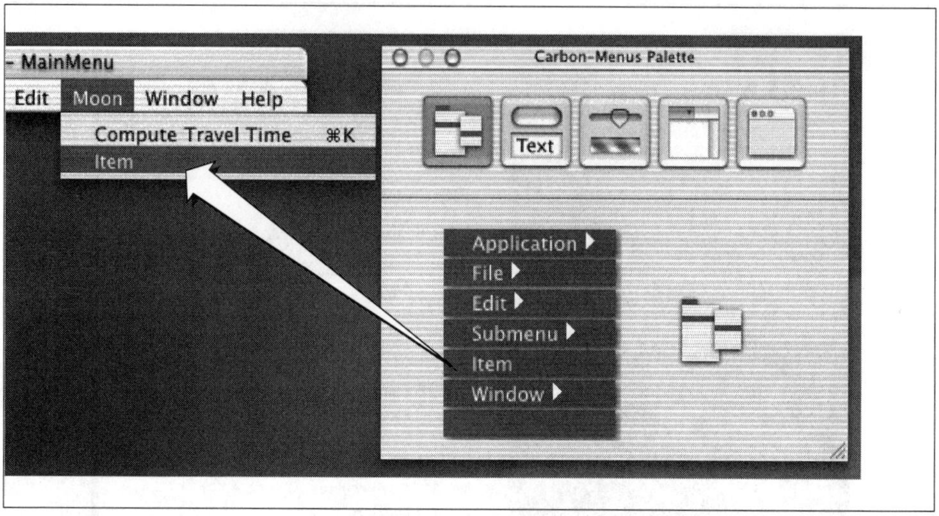

Figure 7-17. Adding a new menu item to a menu

> You should assign Shift-Command-F rather than Command-F, because in some applications, Command-F is used for the Find command. Although you could use this equivalent here because the Moon Travel Planner application doesn't have a Find command, it's not recommended. Using common keyboard equivalents in an uncommon way could make your application less intuitive for users accustomed to the commonly used combinations.

10. Enter **fAct** as the menu item's command. Type **fAct** in the Command text field of the Menu Item Info window and press Return.

11. Save the nib file. Make sure your changes are saved before you add code to the Moon Travel Planner project.

Add Code to Your Project

You need to add code to the main function of the Moon Travel Planner project to create the menu bar from the nib file you modified and to handle the commands issued by menu items.

Create the menu bar

Project Builder already provides code that creates the menu bar from the nib file when your application launches. Let's take a look at that code:

1. Make Project Builder active by clicking its icon in the Dock.

2. Click `main.c` in the Groups & Files list.

3. Look at the two lines of code in the `main` function in the `main.c` file, just after the `CreateNibReference` statement. The Interface Builder Services function `SetMenuBarFromNib` takes two parameters, a nib reference and a `CFString` object. You pass the nib reference returned from the function `CreateNibReference` (see Chapter 3, *Project Builder Projects*). You use the function `CFSTR` to convert the string "MainMenu" to a `CFString` object. The string you provide must match exactly the name of the menu object in the Instances pane of Interface Builder. `SetMenuBarFromNib` reads the menu bar definition from the nib file, allocates memory for it, creates it, and sets it as the current menu bar. The function `require_noerr` exits the application if there is an error that prevents the menu bar from being created from the nib file.

Handle menu commands

Although there are a number of commands that need to be handled by your application, you won't write the code for them in this chapter. You'll do that throughout the book, as follows:

- About Moon Travel Planner (`aBtb`). See Chapter 10.

- Open Itinerary (`oPit`). See Chapter 11, *Files*.

- Close (`cLse`). You'll write code to close the itinerary window in Chapter 11, the Facts for the Traveler window in Chapter 8, and the About window in Chapter 10.

- Save Itinerary As (`sAit`). See Chapter 11.

- Page Setup (`pGsu`). You already set up handling this command in Chapter 6 but in Chapter 9, *Printing* you'll write the functions that do page setup.

- Print (`pRnt`). You already set up handling this command in Chapter 6 but in Chapter 9 you'll write the functions that do the printing.

- Compute Travel Time (`tRav`). You already set this up in Chapter 6.

- Show Facts (`fAct`). See Chapter 8.

In the meantime, you can build and run the application, but the commands that aren't yet handled won't do anything.

Test the Menus

Let's build and run the application to make sure the Moon menu looks okay and the Compute Travel Time menu item works:

1. Click the Build button in the upper-left corner of the Moon Travel Planner project window.

2. Click the Run button in the upper-left corner of the project window.

3. Click a mode of transportation.

4. Choose Compute Travel Time from the Moon menu. Does the value in the Travel Time field change? If so, you are ready to move on!

5. Choose Quit Moon Travel Planner from the Moon Travel Planner menu.

Recap

You've taken a look at the default menu bar provided by Interface Builder and at the items in each of the menu bar's menus. You've seen that some items, such as edit items, come "prewired" with commands, while other items you need to set up for your application. If an application needs menus or menu items other than the default ones, you can create new ones using the Menu palette. It's also possible to disable menu items your application doesn't need.

You created a new menu and menu items and adjusted the default menu items for the Moon Travel Planner application. You also saw that a command issued by a button in the interface can also be issued from a menu item (Compute Travel Time). Next you'll take a look at localization and, in particular, how to set up an application so it's easy to make available in multiple languages or for multiple locations.

8

Text and Localization

Few applications exist that don't display text either in the interface (dialogs, buttons, window title bars, and so forth) or in a window (text from a file). If you plan to distribute your application in more than one language, you'll need a strategy for *internationalizing* it, that is, *localizing* the application as appropriate for a particular language or region of the world.

Resources simplify the process of internationalizing an application. An application bundle (explained in Chapter 3, *Project Builder Projects*) can contain multiple sets of resources, grouped by language and locale. By combining all these resources in one package, you can create one version of your application that is localized for multiple languages. Translations of the application's text strings are among the resources stored with the executable in the application's bundle.

Project Builder supports localization by organizing resources into language-specific, or .lproj folders. We won't cover all localization issues in this chapter. Instead, we'll focus on how to use language-specific folders to store strings. To that end, you'll:

- Review language-specific (.lproj) folders
- Provide an overview of what you can put in them
- Look at a localizable strings file and how to retrieve a string from it
- Create a window and a localizable strings file that contains text to display in the window

Language-Specific Folders

When you create a project in Project Builder, it checks to see under which development region you're running the operating system. Then it creates the appropriate .lproj folder in which you can place all resources that are localized, or at least appropriate for localization. For an English development region, a project has an English.lproj folder. For a Spanish development region, a project has a Spanish.lproj folder, and so forth.

To localize an English application for French, you must create a French.lproj folder. Then you put all the resources localized for French into that folder. You create other folders for each language or locale you plan to localize.

At the very least, a language-specific folder should contain:

- An InfoPlist.strings file for localized versions of information properties associated with the application that a user will see, such as name and version
- A Help folder that contains help files for your application
- One or more nib files for the resources created using Interface Builder
- A Localizable.strings file for the text strings used in the application

Figure 8-1 shows a set of language-specific folders for the Moon Travel Planner application. The folders have a parallel structure. Note the names of the items in each folder are not localized, but the resources in the each item have been translated appropriately. In the next sections, you'll take a look at what's in each resource.

InfoPlist.strings File

An information property list is a file containing key-value pairs that describe properties of the application, such as the version and copyright information. Some properties, such as the application signature, are never seen by the user. Other properties, such as the application name and version, are displayed in the interface in such places as an About window or the Finder's Info window.

In Chapter 10, *Property Lists*, you'll learn how to modify information properties from within Project Builder. However, all that does is to create a property list for the language of the primary development region, stored in a file called Info.plist. You must put the properties the user will see into an InfoPlist.strings file, create localized versions of that file, and store each localized InfoPlist.strings file in the appropriate language-specific directory (a typical InfoPlist.strings file is shown in Figure 8-2). This convention assures that your application gets the appropriate string for the language environment in which the application launches.

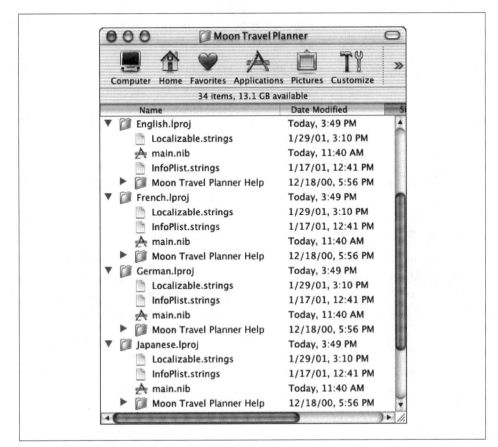

Figure 8-1. Typical localized resources for an application

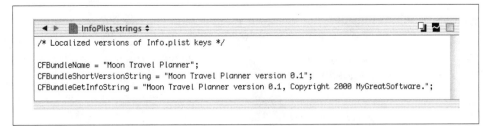

Figure 8-2. A typical InfoPlist.strings file as viewed from a Project Builder project

Help Folder

The help folder contains HTML files that display in the Apple Help Viewer. You need to make sure the files conform to the guidelines for Apple Help. You can find the guidelines along with a tutorial for creating a help folder in the Apple Help Software Development Kit (SDK), available from the Apple Developer web site. Information on adding a help folder to an application and registering a help book with the Help Center is covered in Chapter 12, *Providing Help*.

You need to localize help content and any special index terms and keywords you include in the files. As long as you place the appropriate localized help folder in each language-specific directory, your application should launch the version of help that matches the language or locale of the user's operating system.

Nib Files

Any nib-based Carbon application will have at least one nib file that contains the resources for the main menu and a main window. Any interface object that displays text needs to be localized. Menus, window titles, and labels for controls are some of the items that usually contain text.

When you create a nib-based Carbon project, Project Builder automatically puts a nib file called `main.nib` in the language-specific folder (such as `English.lproj`) for the development region of the operating system. You need to put localized versions of your project's nib files into the appropriate language-specific folders.

Localizable Strings Files

There are many cases when an application needs to display text, such as for a login screen. It makes sense to store these strings so they can be localized, rather than hard-coding them in the application.

Strings that need to be localized should be defined in a separate file named `Localizable.strings`. After you've translated the strings, you'd put the localized version of the file into the appropriate language-specific folder.

You can put any number of strings in a `Localizable.strings` file. To distinguish one string from another, you need a key. You'll use the key to retrieve the text when you need to display it in your application. Figure 8-3 shows a sample file that contains one string with the key "LoginScreen."

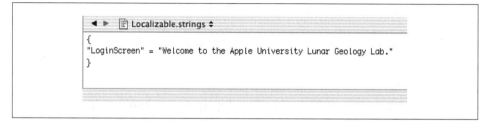

Figure 8-3. A sample Localizable.strings file as viewed from a Project Builder project

You create a `Localizable.strings` file in Project Builder by choosing New File from the File menu. Create an empty file named `Localizable.strings` and then add it to the Resources group in your project.

The contents of the file must follow this syntax:

- It must begin and end with braces.

- Each string must be defined as a key-value pair. The text key must be followed by an equal sign and that must be followed by the string value. Both the key and the string must be enclosed by straight quotation marks.

- Key-value pairs must be separated by a semi-colon.

Do not translate the text keys, just the strings. You use the key to retrieve the string; the user doesn't see the key. You use the Core Foundation Bundle Services function `CFCopyLocalizedString` to get the string associated with the key. This function takes two parameters:

- **Key.** A `CFStringRef` data type; the string you used as a key for the text.

- **Comment.** A `CFStringRef` data type; a string you can use to specify a comment about the key.

`CFCopyLocalizedString` returns the text associated with the key as a `CFStringRef` data type.

 A `CFStringRef` is a reference to a `CFString` object. `CFString` objects are opaque data structures used by Mac OS X to efficiently store string data.

Example 8-1 shows you'd retrieve the text shown in Figure 8-3. The function `CFSTR` converts a string (such as "LoginScreen") to a `CFStringRef` data type.

Example 8-1: Retrieving a String from a Localizable.strings File

```
CFString text

text = CFCopyLocalizedString (CFSTR("LoginScreen"),CFSTR("The
                    greeting shown to the user in the login window"));
```

Moon Travel Planner: Displaying Localized Text

According to our specification (see Chapter 2, *Specifying a Carbon Application: Moon Travel Planner*), the Moon Travel Planner application needs a window, Facts for the Traveller, that displays facts about the moon to entice travelers to visit. The list of facts is a perfect candidate for a Localizable.strings file.

You'll need to do the following to create the window:

1. Create a new window to display the facts.

2. Add a text field.

3. Create a Localizable.strings file and add content for the window.

4. Write a function to display the text.

5. Modify the main window event handler so it handles the command that opens the facts window.

6. Write a handler for the moon facts window. You need this handler to close the window. Later, you'll need the handler to take care of print commands. (Recall that the specification calls for this window to be printable. You'll write the printing code in Chapter 9, *Printing*.)

7. Make sure text displays properly in the window.

Create a New Window

There are two ways you can use Interface Builder to create a new window: add a window to the existing main.nib file or create a new nib file for the window. In this section you'll add a window to the existing nib file. Later, in Chapter 11, *Files*, you'll learn how to create a new nib file for a window.

1. Double-click the main.nib file in the Moon Travel Planner project.

2. Create a new window. Click the Windows button in the Palette toolbar. Then drag the window icon from the left side of the palette to the desktop, as shown in Figure 8-4.

3. Name the window object **MoonFacts**. This is the name by which you'll refer to the window in your code. In the Instances pane of the main.nib window, double-click the word "Window" that's under the icon of the window you just created, type **MoonFacts**, and press Return. The icon's name should be the same as that shown in Figure 8-5.

4. Enter **Facts for the Traveler** as the window's title. The title is the text users see in the title bar at the top of the window. With the window active,

choose Show Info from the Tools menu, choose Attributes from the pop-up menu at the top of the Info window, type **Facts for the Traveler** in the Title text field, and press Return.

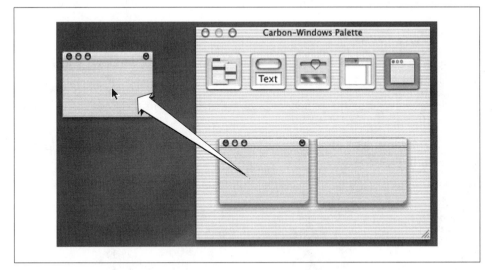

Figure 8-4. A new window dragged from the Windows palette

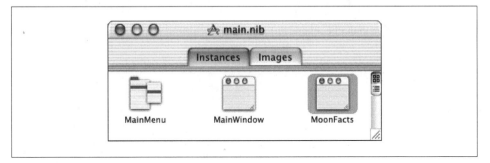

Figure 8-5. The MoonFacts icon in the Instances pane

5. Set the window's class. Choose Document from the Window Class pop-up menu.

6. Set a Theme Brush for the window. You need to give the window a gray-striped background. Choose Dialog from the Theme Brush pop-up menu.

7. Set the window's controls. In the Controls group, make sure Close Box and Collapse Box are the only options selected.

8. Set the window's attributes. In the Attributes group, make sure Standard Handler is the only option selected. You can let the operating system handle most of the standard behavior for the window.

9. Resize the window to 400 by 300 pixels. Choose Size from the pop-up menu at the top of the Show Info window, choose Width/Height from the right Content Rect pop-up menu, and type **400** for width and **300** for height. Then press Return.

Add a Text Field

Although it is possible to display information directly in a window, you'll add a text field to make the text appear as if it's framed (see Figure 8-6):

1. Add a text field to the window. Drag a text field from the Controls palette to the window.

2. Resize the text field. Drag the text field so it just fits within the Aqua guides, as shown in Figure 8-6.

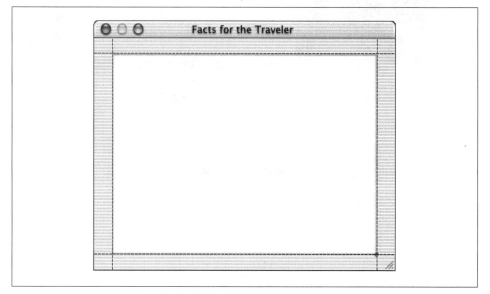

Figure 8-6. Aqua guides showing where to place a text field

3. Set the signature to MTPP and the text field's ID to 131. In the Edit Text Info window, choose Control from the pop-up menu. In the Control ID box, type the Moon Travel Planner creator code—**MTPP**—in the Signature field and **130** in the ID field. Make a note of the ID. When you write code to display text in the text field, you'll need the text field ID and the signature so the application knows where to draw the text.

4. Position the window where you'd like it to appear when the user opens it. You should make sure that when the Facts for the Traveler window is open the user can also see the main window, similar to what's shown in Figure 8-7.

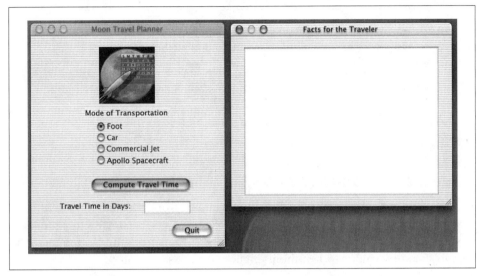

Figure 8-7. Windows positioned as they will appear when the application runs

5. Choose Save from the File menu.

Create Content for the Window

You'll store the text for the window in a Localizable.strings file in the Moon Travel Planner project. As you localize the application for other languages or regions, all you need to do is translate the strings (but not the keys) in the Localizable.strings file.

You need to create a new file and name it Localizable.strings:

1. Make the Moon Travel Planner project window active. Click the Project Builder icon in the Dock.

2. Add a Localizable.strings file to your project. Choose New File from the File menu and double-click Empty File. In the dialog that appears, name it Localizable.strings and add the file to the English.lproj folder. The file should automatically appear in the Resources group in your project.

3. Open the Localizable.strings file. Click Localizable.strings in the Groups & Files list. The empty file opens in the right side of the Project Builder window.

4. Add a text key and text to the file. Type the following (or make up your own text) into the `Localizable.strings` file:

```
{ "Facts" = "Atmosphere: None. Outdoor temperatures
range from -173 C to +126 C, so forget the sun block and be sure
to pack a pressurized suit. Indoor dress is casual. Raingear optional.
\r\rRecreation: Golf (miniature and traditional), hiking. No swimming
or scuba diving; the Sea of Tranquility doesn't actually contain
any water. \r\rDon't Miss: Apollo 11 landing site. Luna 5 crash
landing site. The monolith. \r\rWhat to Avoid: I, Clavius, a musical
revue history of the moon, showing hourly on the outdoor stage."
}
```

Note the string contains formatting information (`\r`) to indicate returns.

5. Save the Moon Travel Planner project.

Write a Function to Display the Window

You need to write code that creates the window from the nib file (`main.nib`). When a window is created, it is hidden by default. So you also need to write code to show the window when the user chooses Show Facts from the Moon menu and then to hide the window when the user clicks the Close button.

Adding function and global declarations

First, you need to declare the `MTPShowMoonFactsWindow` function. Copy the following declaration to the `main.c` file, just after the function declaration for the Compute Travel Time command handler:

```
pascal void MTPShowMoonFactsWindow (WindowRef window);
```

You need to declare some global constants to represent the Show Facts menu command and the ID you assigned to the moon facts text box. You'll also declare a constant to represent the text key—"Facts"—associated with the string in our `Localizable.strings` file. You assigned the menu command when you created the Moon menu in Chapter 7, *Interface Builder: Menus*.

Put these constant declarations in the main file:

```
#define   kMTPShowMoonFactsCommand     'fAct'
#define   kMTPMoonFactsFieldID         131
#define   kMTPMoonFactsTextKey         "Facts"
```

You need to declare a window reference for the moon facts window. Modify the declaration for the main window—`gMainWindow`—so it includes the moon facts window:

```
WindowRef       gMainWindow,
                gMoonFactsWindow;
```

Creating the window

You need to add code to the `main` function so it constructs the interface from the `main.nib` file you modified in Interface Builder. Copy the following statement to the `main` function in the `main.c` file, after the statements that create the main window:

```
// Create the Facts for the Traveler window
err = CreateWindowFromNib (nibRef, CFSTR("MoonFacts"),
                                    &gMoonFactsWindow);
require_noerr (err, CantCreateWindow);
```

Writing the show moon facts window function

The function `MTPShowMoonFactsWindow` does the following:

* Shows the Moon Facts window if it is not visible

* Expands the window if the window is in the Dock

* Retrieves a string from the `Localizable.strings` file and writes it to the window

Copy the function in Example 8-2 to the main program, after the function `MTPComputeCommandHandler`.

Example 8-2: Show Moon Facts Window Function

```
pascal void MTPShowMoonFactsWindow (WindowRef window)
{
    CFStringRef      text;
    ControlHandle    moonFactsBox;
    ControlID        moonFactsControlID = {kMTPApplicationSignature,
                                          kMTPMoonFactsFieldID };

    GetControlByID (window, &moonFactsControlID, &moonFactsBox);        //1
    ShowWindow (window);                                                //2
    SelectWindow (window);
    text = CFCopyLocalizedString (CFSTR(kMTPMoonFactsTextKey),
                                  NULL);                                //3
    SetControlData (moonFactsBox, 0, kControlEditTextCFStringTag,
                                  sizeof (CFStringRef),
                                  &text);                               //4
    CFRelease (text);                                                   //5
    DrawOneControl (moonFactsBox);                                     //6
}
```

Here's what the function does:

1. The Control Manager function GetControlByID gets the control handle associated with the text field in which the facts about the moon are displayed.

2. The Window Manager function ShowWindow makes the window visible. If the window is in the Dock the function expands the window to its normal size.

3. The Window Manager function SelectWindow makes the window active and frontmost.

4. The Core Foundation Bundle Services function CFCopyLocalizedString returns the string associated with the kMTPMoonFactsTextKey ("Facts") from the Localizable.strings file. It returns the result as a reference to a CFString.

5. The Control Manager function SetControlData sets the moon facts text field to the value of the string, but does not draw the string.

6. The Core Foundation Base Services function CFRelease releases the memory associated with the CFString object.

7. The Control Manager function DrawOneControl redraws the moon facts text field with the new string.

Modify the Main Window Event Handler

When a user chooses the Show Facts command from the Moon menu, your application must handle the command by calling the function MTPShowMoonFactsWindow. The main window event handler must take care of the Show Facts command.

You need to add a case to the switch statement to the main window event handler you wrote in Chapter 6, *Carbon Events*, that takes care of the Show Facts command.

Add this code to the switch statement in (MTPMainWindowEventHandler):

```
case kMTPShowMoonFactsCommand:
     MTPShowMoonFactsWindow (gMoonFactsWindow);
     result = noErr;
     break;
```

Write a Handler for the Moon Facts Window

You've taken all the steps to create a window that shows localized content, and you've modified your code so the user can choose a command from the Moon menu to open the window. Now you need to handle the window once it's open. Recall from Chapter 2 that the user should be able to print the Facts for the Traveller window and set up the page before printing it. So you'll need to handle those commands. You'll also need to handle closing the window.

Why not use the standard handler to close the window? When you set up the window attributes for the window, you selected Standard Handler as one of the window's attributes. The standard handler for the close event disposes of a window when the user clicks the Close button. But because the Moon Travel application creates the Facts for the Traveler window once (when the application opens) and disposes of the window once (when the application quits), the standard close event isn't appropriate. The Moon Travel Planner application must open and close the Facts for the Traveler window by showing and hiding the window instead of creating and disposing of it. So you'll need to set up the handler to take care of the window event (kEventClassWindow) that is of the event kind kEventWindowClose.

If your application has windows that require a lot of memory, it's preferable to dispose of the window when it's closed and create it again when it needs to be opened.

Now that you know what your handler needs to do, you can go through the same steps you went through to write the main window event handler:

1. Identify the events the handler takes care of.

2. Write the code for the handler.

3. Install the handler.

Identify events

The three events we identified fall into two type of events: command events (setting up and printing the page) and window events (closing the window).

Command events are in the command event class (kEventClassCommand). The specific kind of event in which your application is interested is a process command (kEventProcessCommand). In particular, your handler must take care of the Print and Page Setup commands you added in Chapter 7.

A window close event is in the window event class (kEventClassWindow). The specific kind of event you need to handle is a close event (kEventWindowClose).

You need to declare an event type specification for the two events. As you recall from Chapter 6, an event type is made up of an event class and event kind. You can declare the event type specification by copying the following to the main function, after the EventTypeSpec declaration for mainSpec:

```
EventTypeSpec  moonSpec[] = {{kEventClassCommand, kEventCommandProcess},
                            {kEventClassWindow, kEventWindowClose}};
```

Write the code for the handler

The handler for the moon facts window must first check to see which kind of event (window close or process command) it has been given by the Carbon Event Manager. If the kind is a process command event, the handler then needs to check the specific command to see whether it's Print (pRnt), Page Setup (pGsu), or neither one. If it's neither, the event gets passed back to the Carbon Event Manager. If it's Print or Page Setup, the application must call the appropriate function. You'll write functions that implement setup and printing in Chapter 9.

Before you write the handler, declare it by copying the following to the main.c file, just after the function declaration for the main window event handler:

```
pascal OSStatus MTPMoonFactsWindowEventHandler (
                        EventHandlerCallRef myHandler,
                        EventRef event, void *userData);
```

Notice it conforms to the prototype specified in Chapter 6.

You need to declare global constants for the commands you set up in Interface Builder. These are the commands you assigned to the Close, Print, and Page Setup menu commands. Copy the following into the main.c file, just after the constants you've already defined for the command IDs:

```
#define kMTPCloseCommand        'cLse'
#define kMTPPrintCommand        'pRnt'
#define kMTPPageSetupCommand    'pGsu'
```

Now you can add the handler. Copy the function in Example 8-3 into the main program, after the function MainWindowEventHandler. Make sure you comment out the functions MTPDoPrint and MTPDoPageSetup. You haven't written those yet, so to build, run, and test the code, you'll need to have them commented out. You can uncomment them once you've added those functions in the next chapter.

Example 8-3: The Moon Facts Window Event Handler

```
pascal OSStatus MTPMoonFactsWindowEventHandler (
                        EventHandlerCallRef myHandler,
                        EventRef event, void *userData)
{
    OSStatus        result = eventNotHandledErr;
    UInt32          eventKind;
    HICommand       command;
    eventKind = GetEventKind (event);                           // 1
    switch (eventKind)
    {
        case kEventWindowClose:                                 // 2
            HideWindow ( (WindowRef) userData);                 // 3
```

Example 8-3: The Moon Facts Window Event Handler (continued)

```
            result = noErr;
            break;
        case kEventCommandProcess:                              // 4
            GetEventParameter (event, kEventParamDirectObject,
                    typeHICommand, NULL, sizeof (HICommand), NULL,
                    &command);                                  // 5
            switch (command.commandID)
            {
                case kMTPCloseCommand:                          // 6
                    HideWindow ( (WindowRef) userData);
                    result = noErr;
                    break;
                case kMTPPrintCommand:
//                  MTPDoPrint (gMoonFactsWindow);              // 7
                    result = noErr;
                    break;
                case kMTPPageSetupCommand:
//                  MTPDoPageSetup (gMoonFactsWindow);          // 8
                    result = noErr;
                    break;
            }
        }
    return result;
}
```

Here's what the function does:

1. The Carbon Event Manager function `GetEventKind` returns the kind of the event.

2. If the event is a window close event, then it handles it, otherwise it returns the result code `eventNotHandledErr` to indicate the Carbon Event Manger should handle the event.

3. The Window Manager function `HideWindow` hides the Facts for the Traveler window.

4. If the event is a command process event, you need to figure out exactly which command needs to be handled.

5. The Carbon Event Manager `GetEventParameter` gets the command.

6. If the user chooses Close from the File menu, you'll call the same functions you would call if the user clicked the Close box.

7. If the command is a Print command, call `MTPDoPrint`. This function doesn't yet exist, so you should comment out the line.

8. If the command is a Page Setup command, call `MTPDoPageSetup`. This function doesn't yet exist, so you should comment out the line.

Install the moon facts window event handler

Just as you did for the main window event handler in Chapter 6, you use the Carbon Event Manager function `InstallWindowEventHandler` to register the moon facts window event handler. Add the following code to the main function, after the line in which you installed the main window event handler:

```
InstallWindowEventHandler (gMoonFactsWindow,
        NewEventHandlerUPP (MTPMoonFactsWindowEventHandler),
        2, moonSpec, (void *) gMoonFactsWindow, NULL);
```

These are the parameters to the function `InstallWindowEventHandler`:

- The target of the event handler—in this case, the window to which the handler should be registered, which is the Facts for the Traveler window.

- A pointer to the window event handler—the function `NewEventHandlerUPP` returns a pointer to the function you just wrote, `MTPMoonFactsWindowEventHandler`.

- The number of events for which the handler is registered, in this case two.

- A pointer to the event types handled by the event handler—you defined these in the array `moonSpec`.

- A value that's passed to the window event handler when the Carbon Event Manager calls the handler—in this case, a pointer to the window to which the handler is registered, that is, the Facts for the Traveler window.

- An event handler reference—in this case, `NULL`.

Make Sure the Text Displays Properly

The function `RunApplicationEventLoop` is already in your code, in the `main` function. As long as you've commented out the Print and Page Setup functions, you can build and run the application to make sure the window opens and displays the text:

1. Click the Build button in the upper-left corner of the Moon Travel Planner project window.

2. Click the Run button in the upper-left corner of the project window.

3. When the application opens, choose Show Facts from the Moon menu. You should see a window that looks like Figure 8-8.

4. Click the Minimize button in the moon facts window. You should see the Facts for the Traveler window shrink and move into the Dock. The standard handler takes care of this.

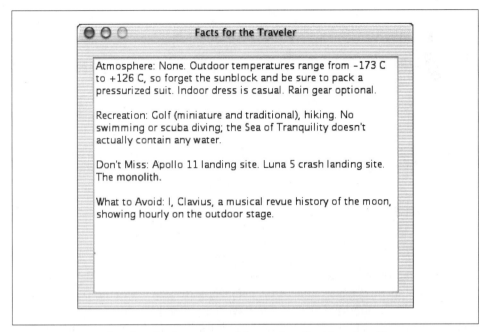

Figure 8-8. A window that displays text read from a Localizable.strings file

5. Click the Facts for the Traveler window icon in the Dock to expand it. The window should expand out of the Dock, to its full size.

6. Click the Close button in the moon facts window. Your handler takes care of this by hiding the window.

7. Click Quit in the Moon Travel Planner window.

If the window behaves properly, you're ready to move on!

Recap

You saw how using language-specific folders for user-readable application properties, help content, interface resources, and strings can facilitate localizing your application. In particular, you looked at using a strings file to store text that will be displayed in a window. You ended the chapter by creating a new window for the Moon Travel Planner application to display facts about the moon, and then reading those facts from the `localizable.strings` file. In the next chapter you'll tackle printing.

9

Printing

Printing is one of the basic functions provided by most applications. When printing a document, a user may first wish to specify settings such as the page size and orientation, the scaling percentage, the page range, and the number of copies. A user may also wish to specify a printer from a list of available printers and choose settings specific to that printer, such as paper tray, duplex printing, or print quality. The application itself may supply additional printing options, such as whether to print odd or even numbered pages or registration marks. If the user doesn't specifically choose any setting, the application should supply reasonable default values if possible.

Because printing involves many variables, your application may have a lot of work to do to deliver robust printing support. However, Mac OS X provides features to help your application gather and work with printing information. These features involve interaction that takes place between the user, the application, the operating system, and the printer:

- Your application can call on Mac OS X to display the Page Setup dialog, shown in Figure 9-1. The Page Setup dialog lets the user choose page format settings, such as paper size, orientation, and scale, before printing. You can save these settings with a document and use them again when the document is reopened.

- When a user chooses to print a document, your application calls on Mac OS X to display the Print dialog, shown in Figure 9-2. The Print dialog lets the user choose print settings, such as the printer, page range, and number of copies. Applications can extend both the Page Setup and Print dialogs to add application-specific options, and printer manufacturers can also extend the Print dialog with printer-specific options.

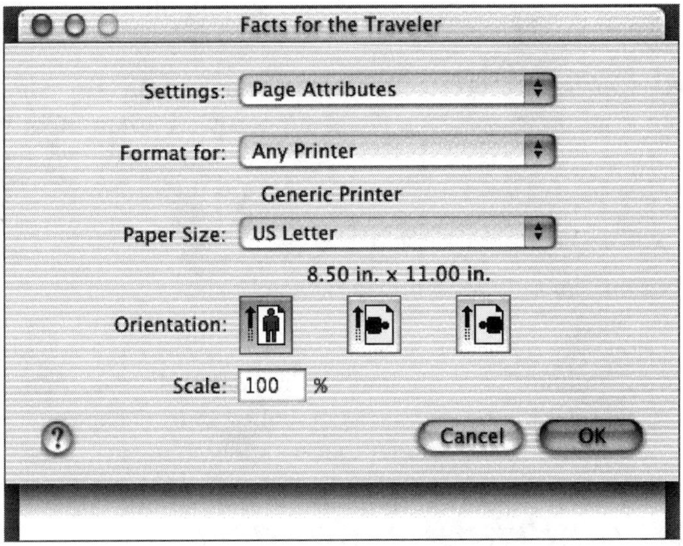

Figure 9-1. The Page Setup dialog, showing default values

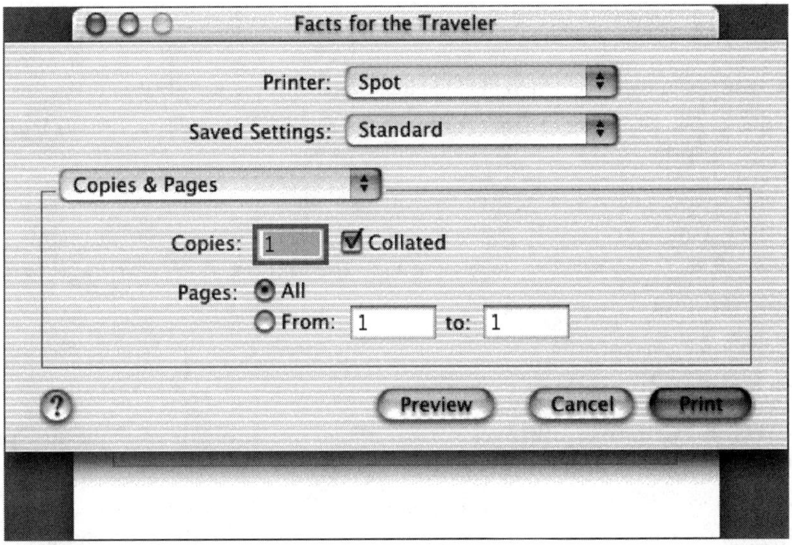

Figure 9-2. The Print dialog, showing default values

- Mac OS X provides printing data types to keep track of user selections in the Page Setup and Print dialogs. Your application uses instances of these data types in calls to printing functions. You can extend some of these types with your own data, save them with documents, and use them when the document is opened and printed.

In this chapter you'll learn about the Carbon Printing Manager, which can help your application supply powerful printing support with a consistent user experience. You'll learn key concepts for printing with the Carbon Printing Manager, including:

- How to organize a printing session
- How to set up a print loop to print a range of pages
- How to handle printing errors

You'll also write printing code for the Moon Travel Planner application. Once you're familiar with the printing concepts described in this chapter, you should be able to adapt them for printing in other Carbon applications you write.

The Carbon Printing Manager

Mac OS X includes a flexible new printing system based on a modular client/server architecture. The printing system:

- Uses PDF-based rendering, providing PDF capability for all printers, including inexpensive raster printers
- Allows applications to draw in "virtual pages" and map those pages to "physical pages" at print time, breaking the connection between the drawing page and the printing page
- Provides applications and printer drivers with control over individual user interface elements in the system's printing dialog boxes, so applications and drivers don't need to completely replace the standard Print or Page Setup dialog boxes with custom versions
- Includes robust support for Carbon applications through the Carbon Printing Manager

In Mac OS X, Carbon applications can initiate multiple, simultaneous printing tasks. Each printing task is referred to as a *printing session,* and each printing session is independent of other printing sessions. Printing sessions can run in separate threads, or you can create multiple sessions within a single-threaded application. You'll read more about threads in Chapter 14, *Beyond Moon Travel: Advanced Topics.*

The *Carbon Printing Manager* was designed to let Carbon applications take advantage of new features in Mac OS X, while still working correctly in previous versions of the Mac OS. For example, the Carbon Printing manager supports printing sessions on Mac OS 8 and 9, although each application can have only one printing session running in a single thread, due to limitations of the underlying Classic printing architecture.

This book doesn't cover how to create a Carbon application that can run on versions of the Mac OS earlier than Mac OS X, although the printing code in this chapter should compile and run on either platform. If you want to write an application that can run and print on both platforms, see the *Carbon Porting Guide* in Carbon Help (available in the Project Builder Help menu).

Carbon Printing Manager functions can conceptually be divided into three groups:

- **Session functions.** These can create and manage printing sessions.

- **Nonsession functions.** These don't support sessions. They operate identically on all Carbon platforms, but inherit some of the limitations of the Classic Printing Manager.

- **Universal functions.** These are available with both session and nonsession printing functions.

The rest of this chapter will deal only with the universal and session functions, which are strongly recommended for all Carbon applications.

A Sample Printing Session

For any printing session, an application will need to:

- Instantiate a Carbon Printing Manager printing session object for the session

- Instantiate a Carbon Printing Manager page format object to store information from the Page Setup dialog, such as paper size and orientation

- Instantiate a Carbon Printing Manager print settings object to store information from the Print dialog, such as page range and number of copies

- Instantiate an application-defined data type (call it the `AppPrintInfo` structure) to store printing information, including references to the three previous objects, plus additional information such as pointers to application printing data and functions

- Provide certain printing functions, such as a function to draw one page of a document

The data types for printing session, page setup, and print settings objects are described in detail in the section "Data Types for Working with Printing Sessions" and Carbon Printing Manager functions are described in more detail in the section "Functions for Working with Printing Sessions."

 The main Carbon Printing Manager data types you'll use are PMPrintSession, PMPageFormat, and PMPrintSettings. The Carbon Printing Manager provides functions to extend these opaque data types to contain data you supply, but you won't do that here. Although instances of these types are sometimes referred to as objects, that doesn't mean you'll have to write any object-oriented code. The Carbon Printing Manager hides the underlying implementation and provides procedural functions to access the internal data of these structures. But of course you can freely call these functions from object-oriented code.

As you work through this sample printing session, you'll see a number of data objects and functions. Functions that start with PM are Carbon Printing Manager functions; those that start with App must be defined by your application. Later sections will provide additional information about the Carbon Printing Manager functions and data types mentioned here. To see a full implementation of a printing session for a working application, see the section "Moon Travel Planner: Adding Printing to the Moon Facts Window."

Suppose a user opens a text document in the application. Your application would perform steps similar to the following:

- Create a window to display the document information.

- Create an instance of the AppPrintInfo structure and store it with the window. If your application stores page format information with the document, extract it, call PMUnflattenPageFormat to create a page format object, and store a reference to the object in the AppPrintInfo structure; otherwise, store an empty reference for now. Store empty references for a printing session object and for a print settings object in the AppPrintInfo structure. Your application will create the objects when needed for printing. Store references to various application functions that will be called during printing, such as the AppDraw-Page function, in the AppPrintInfo structure.

- If the user chooses Page Setup from the File menu, call PMCreateSession to create a printing session object. Also call PMCreatePageFormat to create a page format object, if one hasn't already been created, and call PMSessionDefault-PageFormat to set it to default values for this session. If the page format object already exists, call PMSessionValidatePageFormat to ensure that the object is valid within the context of the printing session. Call PMSessionUseSheets to indicate the Page Setup dialog should use sheets (a Mac OS X feature in which a printing dialog is attached to the window of the document being printed). Call PMSessionPageSetupDialog to display the Page Setup dialog. Preserve page setup information in the page format object. When the Page Setup dialog is dismissed, call PMRelease to release the session object.

- If the user chooses Print from the File menu, create a session object and set up a page format object (creating it if necessary) as in the previous step. Call PMCreatePrintSettings to create a print settings object and call PMSessionDe-faultPrintSettings to set it to default values for this session. Call PMSessionUseSheets to indicate the Print dialog should use sheets. Call the Carbon Printing Manager function PMSessionPrintDialog to display the Print dialog.

- If the user accepts the Print dialog, call a print loop function, passing the App-PrintInfo structure to provide the data needed for printing. Call PMGetFirst-Page and PMGetLastPage to get the user-specified page range, and call AppPa-gesInDoc to verify the legal page range. Call PMSessionBeginDocument to begin the print job. Loop over the user-specified page range, calling PMSessionBegin-Page and calling your application's AppDrawPage function to print each page and PMSessionEndPage on completion. After printing, or after the user cancels the print job, call PMSessionEndDocument to end the print job and PMRelease to release the print settings and printing session objects.

- When the user saves the document, most applications save the page format data (choices made by the user on the Page Setup dialog) with the document. Your application can use the PMSetPageFormatExtendedData function to store application-specific information with the page format data.

The next section takes a more detailed look at the print loop function and the Carbon Printing Manager functions it typically calls.

A look at the print loop

The print loop is simply the piece of code that calls all the necessary functions to print a selected page range of a document. By the time the print loop function is called, your application has performed some preparation for printing, as described in the previous section: your application has created and initialized its own print information structure; it has created Carbon Printing Manager objects for the printing session, page format, and print settings; and your application's print information structure has references to these objects.

The user may have used the Page Setup dialog to change page format options. Finally, the user has displayed the Print dialog and decided to print all or a range of pages. Your application calls the print loop function, passing a pointer to the print information structure. The following pseudocode shows the calls a typical print loop might make, with the calls divided among Carbon Printing Manager functions, other Carbon functions, and application-defined functions. Not all error handling is shown, but the print loop should check for errors after each call that may return one:

```
AppPagesInDoc (application function to verify legal page range)
PMGetFirstPage (get the selected page range, first to last)
PMGetLastPage (adjust if selected range outside legal range)
(now know how many pages to print in the print loop)
PMSetFirstPage (set page range that will show up in progress dialog)
PMSetLastPage
PMSessionBeginDocument (begin a new print job)
    (for each page to be printed)
    PMSessionError (check for an error before starting a new page;
                    if error, break out of loop)
    PMSessionBeginPage (prepare to print the current page)
        PMSessionGetGraphicsContext (get printing port)
        SetPort (Carbon function to set current drawing port
                    to printing port)
        AppDrawPage (application function to draw one page)
        SetPort (Carbon function to restore saved port)
    PMSessionEndPage (finish printing current page)
PMSessionEndDocument (end the print job)
AppPostPrintingErrors (application function to display any error to user)
PMRelease (release print settings and printing session objects)
```

This print loop adheres to requirements described in the section "Sequence and Scope for Printing Functions," as well as to the error handling described in the section "Error handling." You'll notice that very few of the functions called in the print loop are application-defined functions—most are Carbon Printing Manager functions or other Carbon functions. Your application supplies functions only to determine the maximum number of pages in its document, to print one page, and to display errors (if any).

For a full-scale print loop from a working application, see the `MTPDoPrintLoop` function in the section "Moon Travel Planner: Adding Printing to the Moon Facts Window."

Error handling

Your application should always check for error conditions while printing. As usual, you should check for an error from every function that can return one. Within a print loop that uses Carbon Printing Manager session functions, as described in this chapter, you should also check for errors by calling PMSessionError before beginning each new page. If PMSessionError returns a value other than noErr, you should quit printing and close the page and document (depending on the location of the error). If the error value is anything other than kPMCancel (which indicates the user canceled printing), you should also display an error alert to the user.

For a simplified implementation of this type of error handling, see the descriptions for the MTPDoPrintLoop and MTPPostPrintingErrors functions in the section "Moon Travel Planner: Adding Printing to the Moon Facts Window."

Sequence and Scope for Printing Functions

The application code that prints a range of pages is called a print loop because it loops to print each page in the range. The Carbon Printing Manager enforces a sequence of steps in a print loop and defines a valid scope for each printing function. This means that your application must call certain functions before calling others. Functions used out of sequence generate an error value of kPMOutOfScope. The rules for calling sequence and scope are different for session and nonsession printing functions. This section provides a brief overview of the requirements for session printing. For additional details, see the Carbon Printing Manager documentation in Carbon Help (available in the Project Builder Help menu).

The following list of functions shows the calling sequence and scope requirements for some of the most commonly used session functions:

```
PMCreateSession
    PMSessionDefaultPageFormat
    PMSessionValidatePageFormat
    PMSessionDefaultPrintSettings
    PMSessionValidatePrintSettings
    PMSessionUseSheets
    PMSessionPageSetupDialog
    PMSessionPrintDialog
    PMSessionBeginDocument
        PMSessionBeginPage
            PMSessionGetGraphicsContext
        PMSessionEndPage
    PMSessionEndDocument
PMRelease
```

In general, functions may be called in any order with respect to other functions at the same or lower scope level (represented in the list by indentation). For example, you can call PMSessionGetGraphicsContext only within the scope of a call to

PMSessionBeginPage, which in turn must be within the scope of a call to PMSessionBeginDocument. But within the scope of a call to PMCreateSession, you can call PMSessionDefaultPageFormat and PMSessionDefaultPrintSettings in any order.

> The series of steps between the function calls to PMSessionPrintDialog and PMSessionEndDocument (that is, from the display of the Print dialog until the last page is printed in the print loop) is commonly refered to as a print job.

Naturally "begin" functions (such as PMSessionBeginPage) must be called before their corresponding "end" functions (PMSessionEndPage). And some calls make sense only in a certain order within a given scope. For example, if you are using sheets, as the code in this chapter does, you must call PMSessionUseSheets before calling the PMSessionPageSetupDialog or PMSessionPrintDialog function to display a dialog as a sheet.

The following list shows some of the universal printing functions, which can be called at any time:

```
PMCreatePageFormat
PMCreatePrintSettings
PMFlattenPageFormat
PMUnflattenPageFormat
PMGetPageFormatExtendedData
PMSetPageFormatExtendedData
PMGetAdjustedPaperRect
PMGetAdjustedPageRect
PMGetOrientation
PMSetOrientation
PMFlattenPrintSettings
PMUnflattenPrintSettings
PMGetPageRange
PMSetPageRange
```

Although these functions are designed to be called at any time, it is currently required that you call PMSessionValidatePageFormat before calling PMGetAdjustedPaperRect or PMGetAdjustedPageRect.

Many of these functions are used in the sample code in this chapter. Two functions that are not used, but that may be of interest, are PMFlattenPageFormat and PMUnflattenPageFormat. You can use these functions to save and restore information from the opaque PMPageFormat data structure, which stores information displayed in the Page Setup dialog (shown in Figure 9-1). You use PMFlattenPageFormat, for example, to flatten a page format object before writing it to a handle, document, or other location, and PMUnflattenPageFormat to recreate a PMPageFormat object after reading flattened data.

Because you can use the PMSetPageFormatExtendedData function to store application-tion data with a page format object and the PMGetPageFormatExtendedData function to retrieve the data, the PMFlattenPageFormat and PMUnflattenPageFormat functions provide a convenient way to save and restore additional application-specific data along with the standard page format data.

The functions PMFlattenPrintSettings and PMUnflattenPrintSettings perform a similar duty for saving and restoring information from the opaque **PMPrintSettings** data structure, which stores information displayed in the Print dialog (shown in Figure 9-2). However, most applications will not need to save settings information. An application can extend a print settings object with the PMSetPrintSettingsExtendedData and PMGetPrintSettingsExtendedData functions.

An application can extend an instance of the PMPrintSession data type with the PMSessionSetDataInSession and PMSessionGetDataFromSession functions, but the Carbon Printing Manager does not supply functions to flatten and unflatten an instance of this type. Therefore, you can use the extended data structure only within the lifetime of the printing session object (before releasing it).

Data Types for Working with Printing Sessions

Don't look for direct access to global data structures in the Carbon Printing Manager—that's so 20th century. Instead, the Carbon Printing Manager relies primarily on the opaque data structures shown in Table 9-1. The table also shows the functions you use to create these data types and, for those that can be extended to store application-specific data, the functions for extending them. Each of the creation functions returns a reference to an instance of the specified data type.

Table 9-1. Printing Session Data Types

Data type	Create with/extend with	Description
PMPrintSession	PMCreateSession / PMSessionSetDataInSession PMSessionGetDataFromSession	Represents a single printing session.
PMPageFormat	PMCreatePageFormat / PMSetPageFormatExtendedData PMGetPageFormatExtendedData	Stores information about how pages of a document should be printed, such as paper size and orientation.
PMPrintSettings	PMCreatePrintSettings / PMSetPrintSettingsExtendedData PMGetPrintSettingsExtendedData	Stores such information as the print quality and the range of pages to print for a particular print job.

Table 9-1. Printing Session Data Types (continued)

Data type	Create with/extend with	Description
PMPrinter	PMSessionGetCurrentPrinter	Represents a printer. May contain such data as resolution, driver creator, and language information for the printer. Many applications won't need to use this data type.

Previous sections provided examples of how to use these data types. The next section provides information on functions that work with these types.

Functions for Working with Printing Sessions

Because the primary printing data types for printing sessions are opaque, you cannot directly access any of their internal data. Instead, the Carbon Printing Manager defines accessor functions for manipulating the data in these structures. Table 9-2 shows some of the accessors and other functions available to work with an instance of the opaque data type PMPrintSession.

The Carbon Printing Manager doesn't supply functions for saving an instance of a printing session because it's not recommended that you save one. An application typically creates an instance of a printing session as needed (such as before displaying the Page Setup or Print dialog) and releases it when it is no longer needed (as when the print loop has completed).

Table 9-2. Functions for Working with the PMPrintSession Data Type

Function	Description
PMCreateSession	Initializes a PMPrintSession object and creates a context for printing operations for a single printing session.
PMRelease	Decrements the reference count for a printing object (such as an instance of a session, page setup, or print settings data type). When an object's reference count reaches 0, the object is deallocated.
PMSessionBeginDocument	Establishes a new print job.
PMSessionEndDocument	Closes the print job started with PMSessionBeginDocument.
PMSessionBeginPage	Informs the printing system that the drawing that follows is part of a new page.

Table 9-2. Functions for Working with the PMPrintSession Data Type (continued)

Function	Description
PMSessionEndPage	Finishes printing the current page.
PMSessionGetCurrentPrinter	Obtains a reference to the **PMPrinter** object for the current printer.
PMSessionGetDataFromSession PMSessionSetDataInSession	Obtains (or sets) the data the application previously stored in a printing session object.
PMSessionGetGraphicsContext	Obtains the graphics context associated with the current page.
PMSessionPageSetupDialog	Displays the Page Setup dialog and records the user's selections in a **PMPageFormat** object.
PMSessionPrintDialog	Displays the Print dialog and records the user's selections in a **PMPrintSettings** object.
PMSessionUseSheets	Specifies that a printing dialog be displayed as a sheet (that is, attached to the window of the document being printed).

Table 9-3 shows some of the accessors and other functions available to work with an instance of the opaque data type **PMPageFormat**, which is used to store information displayed in the Page Setup dialog. Applications typically store page format information with documents and also maintain it between printing sessions, because users expect changes made in the Page Setup dialog to persist with the document. The table describes functions for creating an instance of this data type, setting it to default values, validating it for the current printing session, extracting information from it, and so on.

Table 9-3. Functions for Working with the PMPageFormat Data Type

Function	Description
PMCreatePageFormat	Creates a new **PMPageFormat** object.
PMSessionDefaultPageFormat	Assigns default parameter values for the specified printing session to an existing **PMPageFormat** object.
PMSessionValidatePageFormat	Ensures that a **PMPageFormat** object is valid within the context of the specified printing session.
PMFlattenPageFormat	Flattens a **PMPageFormat** object for storage in a user document or other location.
PMUnflattenPageFormat	Creates a **PMPageFormat** object from a flattened representation produced previously by PMFlattenPageFormat.
PMGetPageFormatExtendedData PMSetPageFormatExtendedData	Obtains (or sets) extended page format data for the application.

Table 9-3. Functions for Working with the PMPageFormat Data Type (continued)

Function	Description
PMGetAdjustedPageRect PMSetAdjustedPageRect	Obtains (or sets) the page size, taking into account orientation, application drawing resolution, and scaling settings.
PMGetAdjustedPaperRect PMSetAdjustedPaperRect	Obtains (or sets) the paper size, taking into account orientation, application drawing resolution, and scaling settings.
PMGetScale, PMSetScale	Obtains (or sets) the scaling factor currently applied to the page and paper rectangles.

Table 9-4 shows some of the accessors available to work with an instance of the opaque data type PMPrintSettings, which is used to store information displayed in the Print dialog. Applications don't typically store print settings information, because users expect the Print dialog to show current default values. The table describes functions for creating an instance of this data type, setting it to default values, validating it for the current printing session, extracting information from it, and so on.

 The Print dialog contains a Saved Settings pop-up menu that lets users select from various saved settings, so most applications shouldn't need to worry about saving settings themselves.

Table 9-4. Functions for Working with the PMPrintSettings Data Type

Function	Description
PMCreatePrintSettings	Creates a new PMPrintSettings object.
PMSessionDefaultPrintSettings	Assigns default parameter values for the specified printing session to an existing PMPrintSettings object.
PMSessionValidatePrintSettings	Ensures that a PMPrintSettings object is valid within the context of the specified printing session.
PMFlattenPrintSettings	Flattens a PMPrintSettings object for storage in a user document or other location.
PMUnflattenPrintSettings	Creates a PMPrintSettings object from a flattened representation produced previously by PMFlattenPrintSettings.
PMGetPrintSettingsExtendedData PMSetPrintSettingsExtendedData	Obtains (or sets) extended print settings data for the application.

Table 9-4. Functions for Working with the PMPrintSettings Data Type (continued)

Function	Description
PMGetCopies, PMSetCopies	Obtains (or sets) the number of copies that the user has requested to be printed.
PMGetFirstPage, PMSetFirstPage	Obtains (or sets) the number of the first page to be printed.
PMGetLastPage, PMSetLastPage	Obtains (or sets) the number of the last page to be printed.
PMGetPageRange, PMSetPageRange	Obtains (or sets) the valid range of pages that can be printed.

Where to Go from Here

This section should have provided a good description of the basic concepts you'll use to print with the Carbon Printing Manager. If you're working on an application with complex printing needs, see the following:

- For more information on the Mac OS X printing architecture, see *Inside Mac OS X: System Overview*, available in Carbon Help (available in the Project Builder Help menu).

- For additional information on printing, see the Carbon Printing Manager documentation in Carbon Help.

Moon Travel Planner: Adding Printing to the Moon Facts Window

In Chapter 8, *Text and Localization*, you created the Facts for the Traveler (or moon facts) window to display various information about the moon. To add printing support to the moon facts window, you perform these steps:

1. Define constants for working with printing.

2. Define data types for working with printing.

3. Define prototypes for printing functions.

4. Write printing functions.

5. Add a print error format string to the `Localizable.strings` file.

6. Add print setup code to the `main` function.

7. Adjust code in the moon facts window event handler.

8. Test the Page Setup and Print commands to prove it all works.

These steps are described in the sections that follow.

Define Constants for Working with Printing

In this section, you'll define additional constants you'll need to hook up printing for the moon facts window.

In Chapter 6, *Carbon Events*, you defined the constant kMTPApplicationSignature for the Moon Travel Planner application. In Chapter 8, you defined the constants kMTPPageSetupCommand and kMTPPrintCommand for the Page Setup and Print commands, as well as kMTPMoonFactsTextKey to identify the moon facts window text. You'll use all these constants in your printing code.

Now you'll need to define constants to use when you store and retrieve printing information for the moon facts window and when you display printing errors. Copy the following definitions to the main.c file, below the definition for kMTP-PrintCommand:

```
#define kMTPPrintInfoProperty 'Piwp'
#define KMTPPrintFormatStrKey   "Error format"
```

The constant kMTPPrintInfoProperty includes the word "Property" because you'll use it to store and retrieve print information as a property of the moon facts window. (The print information structure is described in the section "Define Data Types for Working with Printing.") You'll use the constant KMTPPrintFormatStrKey to obtain a localized format string to use when displaying printing errors.

Define Data Types for Working with Printing

In this section, you'll define a structure for storing print information, as well as pointer and function data types you'll need for printing.

To print the contents of the moon facts window, you need a convenient way to pass information among your printing functions and in calls to Carbon Printing Manager functions. One such piece of information is a structure to keep track of printing information. You'll define that structure below, but the C programming language allows you to define a pointer to a structure before defining the structure itself. You'll do that, because you'll need the structure pointer for another type defined below. Copy the following type definition to the main.c file, right after the last constant definition:

```
typedef struct MTPDocumentPrintInfo * MTPDocumentPrintInfoPtr;
```

You'll also need a pointer to the function that draws one page of the moon facts window. One of the parameters for the drawing function is a pointer to our print information data structure. That's why you defined the pointer before the structure. To be able to pass a pointer to a drawing function, copy the following type declaration to the `main.c` file, right after the previous type definition:

```
typedef OSStatus (*MTPDrawDocPageProc)
    (MTPDocumentPrintInfoPtr documentPrintInfoPtr,UInt32 pageNumber);
```

You'll see how this pointer type is used in the section "Add Printing Code to the Main Function," the section "MTPCreatePrintInfoForWindow," and the section "MTPDoPrintLoop."

To keep track of printing information, the Moon Travel Planner defines the **MTPDocumentPrintInfo** structure. Copy the following lines to the `main.c` file, after the **MTPDrawDocPageProc** definition:

```
struct MTPDocumentPrintInfo
{
    PMPrintSession printSession;                          // 1

    PMPageFormat pageFormat;                              // 2
    PMPrintSettings printSettings;                        // 3

    PMSheetDoneUPP pageSetupDoneUPP;                      // 4
    PMSheetDoneUPP printDialogDoneUPP;                    // 5

    MTPDrawDocPageProc drawDocPageProc;                   // 6
};
typedef struct MTPDocumentPrintInfo MTPDocumentPrintInfo; // 7
```

This structure provides the following fields:

1. A printing session to use for all moon facts printing. **PMPrintSession** is an opaque data structure defined by the Carbon Printing Manager.

2. A page format object to track format information, such as paper size and orientation. **PMPageFormat** is an opaque data structure defined by the Carbon Printing Manager.

3. A print settings object to track settings information, such as page range and number of copies. **PMPrintSettings** is an opaque data structure defined by the Carbon Printing Manager.

4. A pointer to a function the Carbon Printing Manager calls when the user closes the Page Setup dialog.

5. A pointer to a function the Carbon Printing Manager calls when the user closes the Print dialog.

6. A pointer to a function that draws one page of the moon facts window. The definition for the pointer type (**MTPDrawDocPageProc**) is shown above.

7. The last item is not a field of the structure, but merely a type definition for the structure itself.

You'll learn how to initialize this data structure in the `MTPCreatePrintInfoForWindow` function.

Define Prototypes for Printing Functions

In this section you'll define function prototypes for the Moon Travel Planner's printing functions. Copy the following lines to the `main.c` file, right after the function prototypes for window event and command handler functions:

```
OSStatus MTPCreatePrintInfoForWindow (
                WindowRef theWindow,
                MTPDrawDocPageProc drawDocPageProc,
                PMSheetDoneUPP pageSetupDoneProc,
                PMSheetDoneUPP printDialogDoneProc);
OSStatus MTPSetupPageFormatForPrinting(
                MTPDocumentPrintInfoPtr documentPrintInfoPtr);
pascal void MTPPageSetupDoneProc (
                PMPrintSession printSession,
                WindowRef documentWindow,
                Boolean accepted);
void MTPDoPageSetup (WindowRef parentWindow);
pascal void MTPPrintDialogDoneProc (
                PMPrintSession printSession,
                WindowRef documentWindow,
                Boolean accepted);
void MTPDoPrint ( WindowRef parentWindow );
OSStatus MTPDrawMoonFactsPage (
                MTPDocumentPrintInfoPtr documentPrintInfoPtr,
                UInt32 pageNumber);
UInt32   MTPPagesInDoc (MTPDocumentPrintInfoPtr documentPrintInfoPtr);
void MTPPostPrintingError (OSStatus status);
void MTPDoPrintLoop (MTPDocumentPrintInfoPtr documentPrintInfoPtr);
```

These functions are described in the following section.

Write Printing Functions

It's time to write printing code for the Moon Travel Planner application. It may seem like you need a lot of functions to print some simple text, but the printing code in this chapter provides several benefits:

- It demonstrates a variety of printing concepts, including how to display the Page Setup and Print dialogs and how to set up a print loop to print each page in a document.

- It supports the really cool Mac OS X feature of sheets—the Page Setup and Print dialogs appear as sheets that pop out of the title bar of the moon facts window. A sheet is part of the window it appears on, providing a convenient way to associate a dialog with a window.

- It provides a reusable template that you can easily adapt to print other, more complicated documents.

To print the text from the moon facts window, you'll need to create the following functions:

1. MTPCreatePrintInfoForWindow. Initializes a print data structure and stores it with the window to print.

2. MTPSetupPageFormatForPrinting. Prepares a valid page format object for use with page setup or printing and creates a print session object.

3. MTPPageSetupDoneProc. Called by the Carbon Printing Manager when the user dismisses the Page Setup dialog, regardless of whether the user accepted the dialog or canceled it.

4. MTPDoPageSetup. Displays the Page Setup dialog (shown in Figure 9-1).

5. MTPPrintDialogDoneProc. Called by the Carbon Printing Manager when the user dismisses the Print dialog, regardless of whether the user accepted the dialog or canceled it.

6. MTPDoPrint. Displays the Print dialog (shown in Figure 9-2).

7. MTPDrawMoonFactsPage. Draws the specified page in the location specified by the page format object.

8. MTPPagesInDoc. Returns the maximum number of pages to print in the document.

9. MTPPostPrintingErrors. Displays an alert to notify the user that a printing error has occurred.

10. MTPDoPrintLoop. Loops over the specified page range, calling the draw page routine for each page.

The next sections describe the code for these functions.

MTPCreatePrintInfoForWindow

The MTPCreatePrintInfoForWindow function initializes a print data structure and stores it with the window to print (in this case, the moon facts window). Copy the code shown in Example 9-1 to the main.c file, below the MTPAbout-WindowCommandHandler function.

Example 9-1: A Function to Create Print Information for a Window

```
OSStatus MTPCreatePrintInfoForWindow (
                    WindowRef theWindow,
                    MTPDrawDocPageProc drawDocPageProc,
                    PMSheetDoneUPP pageSetupDoneProc,
                    PMSheetDoneUPP printDialogDoneProc)
{
    MTPDocumentPrintInfoPtr documentPrintInfoPtr = NULL;
    OSStatus status = noErr;

    documentPrintInfoPtr =
        (MTPDocumentPrintInfoPtr) NewPtr(sizeof(MTPDocumentPrintInfo));// 1

    if (documentPrintInfoPtr)                                          // 2
    {
        documentPrintInfoPtr->printSession = NULL;                     // 3
        documentPrintInfoPtr->pageSetupDoneUPP = pageSetupDoneProc;    // 4
        documentPrintInfoPtr->printDialogDoneUPP = printDialogDoneProc;// 5
        documentPrintInfoPtr->drawDocPageProc = drawDocPageProc;       // 6
        documentPrintInfoPtr->pageFormat = kPMNoPageFormat;            // 7
        documentPrintInfoPtr->printSettings = kPMNoPrintSettings;      // 8

        status = SetWindowProperty(theWindow, kMTPApplicationSignature,// 9
                    kMTPPrintInfoProperty,
                    sizeof(MTPDocumentPrintInfoPtr),
                    &documentPrintInfoPtr);
    }
    else
        status = MemError();                                           // 10

    if ((status != noErr) && (documentPrintInfoPtr != NULL))          // 11
        DisposePtr( (Ptr) documentPrintInfoPtr);

    return status;                                                     // 12
}
```

Here's how the `MTPCreatePrintInfoForWindow` function works:

1. It calls the Memory Manager function `NewPtr` to allocate memory for a print information structure. If the call is successful, the pointer `documentPrintInfoPtr` points to the allocated memory.

2. If the previous step was successful, it sets values for the print information structure.

3. It sets the printing session reference to `NULL`, indicating the object hasn't been created yet. This object won't be created until it is needed—when the user opens the Page Setup or Print dialog.

4. It stores a reference to a function the Carbon Printing Manager calls when the user dismisses the Page Setup dialog. The reference comes from the `pageSetupDoneProc` parameter.

5. It stores a reference to a function the Carbon Printing Manager calls when the user dismisses the Print dialog. The reference comes from the `printDialogDoneProc` parameter.

6. It stores a reference to a function the Moon Travel Planner's `MTPDoPrintLoop` function calls to print a single page. The reference comes from the `drawDocPageProc` parameter.

7. It sets the page format reference to a value that indicates the page format object hasn't been created yet. This object won't be created until it is needed—when the user opens the Page Setup or Print dialog.

8. It sets the print settings reference to a value that indicates the print settings object hasn't been created yet. This object won't be created until it is needed—when the user opens the Print dialog.

9. It calls the Window Manager function `SetWindowProperty` to store a pointer to the print information structure as a property of the window. The constants `kMTPApplicationSignature` and `kMTPPrintInfoProperty` identify the property, which other printing functions can access by calling the Window Manager function `GetWindowProperty`. These constants are described in the section "Define Constants for Working with Printing."

10. If it couldn't create the print information structure by calling `NewPtr`, it calls the function `MemError`, which yields the result code produced by the last Memory Manager function the application called directly (`NewPtr`).

11. If there was an error after allocating the print information structure, `MTPDoPageSetup` calls the Memory Manager function `DisposePtr` to dispose of the allocated memory.

12. It returns a value indicating whether the function successfully created and initialized a print information structure for the window. A return value of `noErr` indicates success.

MTPSetupPageFormatForPrinting

The `MTPSetupPageFormatForPrinting` function prepares a valid page format object for use with the Page Setup or Print dialog. Both of those dialogs require a printing session object, so the function also creates a printing session object, though it is possible to create a page format object without a printing session. If any error occurs before the function completes, it frees any objects it created.

Copy the code shown in Example 9-2 to the `main.c` file, below the `MTPCreatePrintInfoForWindow` function.

Example 9-2: A Function to Set Up a Page Format Object for Printing

```
OSStatus MTPSetupPageFormatForPrinting(
            MTPDocumentPrintInfoPtr documentPrintInfoPtr)
{
    OSStatus status = noErr;
    PMPrintSession printSession = NULL;
    PMPageFormat pageFormat = kPMNoPageFormat;

    status = PMCreateSession(&printSession);                       // 1
    if (status == noErr)
    {
        if (documentPrintInfoPtr->pageFormat == kPMNoPageFormat)    // 2
        {
            status = PMCreatePageFormat(&pageFormat);               // 3
            if ((status == noErr) && (pageFormat != kPMNoPageFormat))
            {
                status = PMSessionDefaultPageFormat(                // 4
                        printSession,
                        pageFormat);
                if (status == noErr)
                    documentPrintInfoPtr->pageFormat = pageFormat;  // 5
            }
            else
            {
                if (status == noErr)                                // 6
                    status = kPMGeneralError;
            }
        }
        else
        {
            status = PMSessionValidatePageFormat(                   // 7
                    printSession,
                    documentPrintInfoPtr->pageFormat,
                    kPMDontWantBoolean);
        }
    }
    if (status == noErr)
    {
        documentPrintInfoPtr->printSession = printSession;          // 8
    }
    else                                                           // 9
    {
        if (pageFormat != kPMNoPageFormat)
            PMRelease(pageFormat);
        if (printSession != NULL)
            PMRelease(printSession);
    }
    return status;
}
```

Here's how the `MTPSetupPageFormatForPrinting` function works:

1. It calls the Carbon Printing Manager (CPM) function PMCreateSession to create a printing session object.

2. If the previous step succeeds, it checks whether the print information structure pointed to by the documentPrintInfoPtr parameter already has a reference to a page format object. The constant kPMNoPageFormat is defined by the Carbon Printing Manager to specify that a page format object (one of type PMPage-Format) has not yet been specified.

3. If no format object exists, it calls the CPM function PMCreatePageFormat to create a page format object.

4. If no error occurred in creating the page format object, it calls the CPM function PMSessionDefaultPageFormat to set default values (such as 100 percent scaling and portrait orientation) for a page format object.

5. If no error occurs in setting default values, it assigns the page format object to the page format field in the print information structure pointed to by the documentPrintInfoPtr parameter.

6. If the function PMCreatePageFormat didn't return an error in step 3, but was unable to create a page format object, MTPSetupPageFormatForPrinting uses the CPM constant kPMGeneralError to set an error value.

7. If the print information structure pointed to by the passed pointer already has a reference to a page format object, MTPSetupPageFormatForPrinting calls the CPM function PMSessionValidatePageFormat to make sure the page format object is valid within the context of the current printing session.

8. If no error has occurred, it assigns the printing session object to the printing session field in the print information structure pointed to by the document-PrintInfoPtr parameter.

9. If any error has occurred, it releases any local variables it may have created (a printing session object and possibly a page format object).

10. It returns a value indicating whether the function successfully created and initialized a printing session object and prepared a page format object (creating it if necessary). A return value of noErr indicates success.

MTPPageSetupDoneProc

The Carbon Printing Manager calls the MTPPageSetupDoneProc function when the user dismisses the Page Setup dialog, regardless of whether the user accepted the dialog or canceled it. This function merely frees the current printing session object, which needn't be saved after the user dismisses the Page Setup dialog. However, applications with more complicated printing needs may wish to perform other operations here. For example, an application may wish to change the displayed margins when a user changes the paper size in the Page Setup dialog.

Copy the code shown in Example 9-3 to the main.c file, below the MTPSetupPage-FormatForPrinting function.

Example 9-3: Function Called When Page Setup Dialog Is Dismissed

```
pascal void MTPPageSetupDoneProc (
                    PMPrintSession printSession,
                    WindowRef documentWindow,
                    Boolean accepted)
{
    OSStatus    status = noErr;                                // 1
    UInt32   infoSize = sizeof (MTPDocumentPrintInfoPtr),
             actualSize;
    MTPDocumentPrintInfoPtr documentPrintInfoPtr = NULL;

    status = GetWindowProperty(documentWindow,                 // 2
             kMTPApplicationSignature,
             kMTPPrintInfoProperty,
             infoSize, &actualSize,
             &documentPrintInfoPtr);

    if ((status == noErr) && (documentPrintInfoPtr != NULL))   // 3
    {
        if (documentPrintInfoPtr->printSession != NULL)
        {
            PMRelease(documentPrintInfoPtr->printSession);
            documentPrintInfoPtr->printSession = NULL;
        }
    }
}
```

Here's how the MTPPageSetupDoneProc function works:

1. It declares and initializes local variables for getting stored print information from the passed window.

2. It calls the Window Manager function GetWindowProperty, passing the constants kMTPApplicationSignature and kMTPPrintInfoProperty to specify the window property to retrieve (a pointer to a Moon Travel Planner print information structure).

3. If it can get a pointer to the print info structure and if the printing session field in the structure is not NULL, it releases the printing session object and sets the field to NULL.

MTPDoPageSetup

The MTPDoPageSetup function displays the Page Setup dialog (shown in Figure 9-1) so the user can specify settings such as paper size and orientation.

Copy the code shown in Example 9-4 to the main.c file, below the MTPPageSetup-DoneProc function.

Example 9-4: The Page Setup Function

```
void MTPDoPageSetup( WindowRef parentWindow )
{
    OSStatus status = noErr;                                         // 1
    UInt32 infoSize = sizeof (MTPDocumentPrintInfoPtr), actualSize;
    MTPDocumentPrintInfoPtr documentPrintInfoPtr = NULL;

    status = GetWindowProperty(parentWindow,                         // 2
                kMTPApplicationSignature,
                kMTPPrintInfoProperty,
                infoSize, &actualSize,
                &documentPrintInfoPtr);

    if ((status == noErr) && (documentPrintInfoPtr != NULL))         // 3
    {
        status = MTPSetupPageFormatForPrinting(                      // 4
                        documentPrintInfoPtr);
        if (status == noErr)
        {
            Boolean accepted;
            PMSessionUseSheets (                                     // 5
                    documentPrintInfoPtr->printSession, parentWindow,
                    documentPrintInfoPtr->pageSetupDoneUPP);

            status = PMSessionPageSetupDialog(                       // 6
                    documentPrintInfoPtr->printSession,
                    documentPrintInfoPtr->pageFormat, &accepted);
        }
    }
    else if (status == noErr)                                        // 7
        status = memFullErr;
    if (status != noErr)                                            // 8
    {
        if (documentPrintInfoPtr != NULL)
        {
            if (documentPrintInfoPtr->printSession != NULL)         // 9
            {
                PMRelease(documentPrintInfoPtr->printSession);
                documentPrintInfoPtr->printSession = NULL;
            }
        }
        MTPPostPrintingError(status);                               // 10
    }
}
```

Here's how the `MTPDoPageSetup` function works:

1. It declares and initializes local variables for getting stored print information from the passed window.

2. It calls the Window Manager function `GetWindowProperty`, passing the constants `kMTPApplicationSignature` and `kMTPPrintInfoProperty` to specify the window property to retrieve (a pointer to a Moon Travel Planner print

information structure).

3. It verifies that `GetWindowProperty` returned a non-null pointer to a print information structure.

4. It calls the function `MTPSetupPageFormatForPrinting` to make sure the print information includes a valid page format object. This function also creates a printing session object for the print information pointer.

5. If no error occurs, it calls the Carbon Printing Manager function `PMSession-UseSheets`, passing the current printing session, the window to be printed, and a pointer to a function the Printing Manager calls when the user dismisses the Page Setup dialog. The pointer points to the `MTPPageSetupDoneProc` function. Calling the `PMSessionUseSheets` function specifies that a printing dialog (in this case the Page Setup dialog) should be displayed as a sheet; that is, attached to the window of the document being printed.

6. To display the Page Setup dialog, it calls the Carbon Printing Manager function `PMSessionPageSetupDialog`, passing the current printing session, the page format object that was set up in a previous step, and a pointer to a Boolean value. When the user dismisses the Page Setup dialog, the Printing Manager calls the function specified by `documentPrintInfoPtr->pageSetupDoneUPP` in the previous call to `PMSessionUseSheets`. When using sheets, the `PMSessionPageSetupDialog` function returns immediately and the Boolean value returned in the `accepted` variable always has the value `false`. If your application needs to perform additional tasks after the user dismisses the Page Setup dialog, it can do so in the `MTPPageSetupDoneProc` function, which is called when the user dismisses the Page Setup dialog. If the user clicks the OK button in the Page Setup dialog, the page format object is updated with the user's changes (if any) and the value `true` is returned to the `MTPPageSetupDoneProc` function. If the user clicks the Cancel button, the page format object is unchanged and the value `false` is returned to the `MTPPageSetupDoneProc` function.

7. If the previous call to `GetWindowProperty` was unsuccessful in creating a pointer to a print information structure, but did not return an error value, `MTPDoPageSetup` sets an error value.

8. It checks the status variable—if there is an error, the Page Setup dialog was not displayed. The `MTPDoPageSetup` function will display an error message and may have some cleaning up to do as well.

9. If an error occurred after getting a pointer to a print information structure and the structure has a pointer to a session object, it releases the object and sets the pointer to `NULL`.

10. It displays an error message to the user.

MTPPrintDialogDoneProc

The Carbon Printing Manager calls the MTPPrintDialogDoneProc function when the user dismisses the Print dialog, regardless of whether the user accepts the dialog or cancels it. This function initiates printing if the user accepted the Print dialog and frees the printing session and print settings object if the user canceled the dialog.

Copy the code shown in Example 9-5 to the main.c file, below the MTPDoPageSetup function.

Example 9-5: Function Called When Print Dialog Is Dismissed

```
pascal void MTPPrintDialogDoneProc (PMPrintSession printSession,
    WindowRef documentWindow, Boolean accepted)
{
    OSStatus    status = noErr;                              // 1
    UInt32    infoSize = sizeof (MTPDocumentPrintInfoPtr),
            actualSize;
    MTPDocumentPrintInfoPtr documentPrintInfoPtr = NULL;

    status = GetWindowProperty(documentWindow,              // 2
            kMTPApplicationSignature,
            kMTPPrintInfoProperty,
            infoSize, &actualSize,
            &documentPrintInfoPtr);

    if ((status == noErr) && (documentPrintInfoPtr != NULL))
    {
        if (accepted)
            MTPDoPrintLoop(documentPrintInfoPtr);          // 3
        else
        {
            if (documentPrintInfoPtr->printSettings          // 4
                        != kPMNoPrintSettings)
            {
                PMRelease(documentPrintInfoPtr->printSettings);
                documentPrintInfoPtr->printSettings = kPMNoPrintSettings;
            }
            if (documentPrintInfoPtr->printSession != NULL)
            {
                PMRelease(documentPrintInfoPtr->printSession);
                documentPrintInfoPtr->printSession = NULL;
            }
        }
    }
}
```

Here's how the MTPPrintDialogDoneProc function works:

1. It declares and initializes local variables for getting stored print information from the passed window.

2. It calls the Window Manager function GetWindowProperty, passing the constants kMTPApplicationSignature and kMTPPrintInfoProperty to specify the window property to retrieve (a pointer to a Moon Travel Planner print information structure).

3. If step 2 succeeded and the user accepted the Print dialog (accepted has the value true), MTPPrintDialogDoneProc calls the MTPDoPrintLoop function to print each page in the selected range. Applications with more complicated printing needs can perform additional operations before commencing printing.

4. If step 2 succeeded and the user canceled the Print dialog (accepted has the value false), MTPPrintDialogDoneProc calls the Carbon Printing Manager function PMRelease to release the print information structure's printing session object and print settings object, if any, and sets the fields for these objects to values indicating they are no longer valid. Releasing an object decrements its reference count, causing it to be deallocated when the count reaches 0. Other applications may need to perform additional operations here in the case that the user cancels the dialog.

MTPDoPrint

The MTPDoPrint function displays the Print dialog (shown in Figure 9-2) so the user can specify such settings as page range and number of copies before printing.

Copy the code shown in Example 9-6 to the main.c file, below the MTPPrintDialogDoneProc function.

Example 9-6: The Print Function

```
void MTPDoPrint( WindowRef parentWindow )
{
    PMPrintSettings printSettings = kPMNoPrintSettings;
    UInt32    minPage = 1,
              maxPage = 1;
    OSStatus status = noErr;                                        // 1
    UInt32 infoSize = sizeof (MTPDocumentPrintInfoPtr), actualSize;
    MTPDocumentPrintInfoPtr documentPrintInfoPtr = NULL;

    status = GetWindowProperty( parentWindow,                       // 2
                            kMTPApplicationSignature,
                            kMTPPrintInfoProperty,
                            infoSize,
                            &actualSize,
                            &documentPrintInfoPtr);

    if ((status == noErr) && (documentPrintInfoPtr != NULL))
    {
```

Example 9-6: The Print Function (continued)

```
    status = MTPSetupPageFormatForPrinting(documentPrintInfoPtr);    // 3
    if (status == noErr)
    {
        status = PMCreatePrintSettings(&printSettings);              // 4

        if ((status == noErr) && (printSettings != kPMNoPrintSettings))
        {
            CFStringRef windowTitleRef;
            status = CopyWindowTitleAsCFString(parentWindow,         // 5
                        &windowTitleRef);
            if(status == noErr)
            {
                status = PMSetJobNameCFString(printSettings,         // 6
                        windowTitleRef);
                CFRelease(windowTitleRef);
            }
            if (status == noErr)
                status = PMSessionDefaultPrintSettings(              // 7
                        documentPrintInfoPtr->printSession,
                        printSettings);
            if (status == noErr)
            {
                documentPrintInfoPtr->printSettings = printSettings;// 8
                printSettings = kPMNoPrintSettings;
            }
        }
        if (status == noErr)
        {
            maxPage = MTPPagesInDoc(documentPrintInfoPtr);           // 9
            status =
                PMSetPageRange(documentPrintInfoPtr->printSettings, // 10
                            minPage, maxPage);
        }

        if (status == noErr)
        {
            Boolean accepted;
            PMSessionUseSheets (                                     // 11
                        documentPrintInfoPtr->printSession,
                        parentWindow,
                        documentPrintInfoPtr->printDialogDoneUPP);

            status = PMSessionPrintDialog(                           // 12
                        documentPrintInfoPtr->printSession,
                        documentPrintInfoPtr->printSettings,
                        documentPrintInfoPtr->pageFormat,
                        &accepted);
        }
    }
}
else
{
```

Example 9-6: The Print Function (continued)

```
        if (status == noErr)                                    // 13
            status = memFullErr;
    }
    if (status != noErr)                                        // 14
    {
        if (documentPrintInfoPtr != NULL)
        {
            if (printSettings != kPMNoPrintSettings)            // 15
                PMRelease(printSettings);
            else if (documentPrintInfoPtr->printSettings        // 16
                              != kPMNoPrintSettings)
            {
                PMRelease(documentPrintInfoPtr->printSettings);
                documentPrintInfoPtr->printSettings = kPMNoPrintSettings;
            }
            if (documentPrintInfoPtr->printSession != NULL)     // 17
            {
                PMRelease(documentPrintInfoPtr->printSession);
                documentPrintInfoPtr->printSession = NULL;
            }
        }
        MTPPostPrintingError(status);                           // 18
    }
}
```

Here's how the MTPDoPrint function works:

1. It declares and initializes local variables for getting stored print information from the passed window.

2. It calls the Window Manager function GetWindowProperty, passing the constants kMTPApplicationSignature and kMTPPrintInfoProperty to specify the window property to retrieve (a pointer to a Moon Travel Planner print information structure).

3. If GetWindowProperty successfully returns a valid pointer to a print information structure, MTPDoPrint calls the MTPSetupPageFormatForPrinting function to make sure the print information structure has a valid page format object for this printing session. That function also creates a printing session object for the session.

4. If no error occurs, it calls the Carbon Printing Manager (CPM) function PMCreatePrintSettings to create a print settings object for this print job. By not saving print settings between calls to the Print dialog, you ensure that the dialog will display with the current default settings, which is the recommended behavior.

5. If no error occurs, it calls the Core Foundation function CopyWindowTitleAsCFString to get the window title as a **CFStringRef** (or reference to a string object).

6. If no error occurs, it calls the CPM function `PMSetJobNameCFString` to set the job name for this print job. This is the name that will be used by the printing system, such as in the print queue. After setting the title, it calls the Core Foundation function `CFRelease` to release the string.

7. If no error occurs in the previous step, it calls the CPM function `PMSessionDefaultPrintSettings` to set default values (such as printer, number of copies, and page range) for the print settings object.

8. If no error occurs in the previous step, it assigns the print settings object to the print settings field in the print information structure and sets the local settings variable to a value indicating it is no longer in use.

9. It calls the function `MTPPagesInDoc` so the Moon Travel Planner can specify the maximum number of pages to print.

10. It calls the CPM function `PMSetPageRange` to set the valid range of pages that can be printed.

11. If no error has occurred, it calls the CPM function `PMSessionUseSheets`, passing the current printing session, a reference to the window to be printed, and a pointer to a function the Carbon Printing Manager calls when the user dismisses the Print dialog. The pointer points to the `MTPPrintDialogDoneProc` function. Calling the `PMSessionUseSheets` function specifies that a printing dialog (in this case the Print dialog) should be displayed as a sheet; that is, attached to the window of the document being printed.

12. To display the Print dialog, `MTPDoPrint` calls the CPM function `PMSessionPrintDialog`, passing the current printing session, the print settings object, the page format object, and a pointer to a Boolean value. When the user dismisses the Print dialog, the Carbon Printing Manager calls the function specified by `documentPrintInfoPtr->printDialogDoneUPP` in the previous call to `PMSessionUseSheets` (in this case, `MTPPrintDialogDoneProc`, which takes care of printing the page if the user accepts the dialog). When using sheets, the `PMSessionPrintDialog` function returns immediately and the Boolean value returned in the `accepted` variable always has the value `false`. If your application needs to perform additional tasks after the user dismisses the Print dialog, it can do so in the `MTPPrintDialogDoneProc` function. If the user clicks the OK button in the Print dialog, the print settings object is updated with the user's changes (if any) and the value `true` is returned to the `MTPPrintDialogDoneProc` function. If the user clicks the Cancel button, the print settings object is unchanged and the value `false` is returned to the `MTPPrintDialogDoneProc` function.

13. If the earlier call to `GetWindowProperty` was unsuccessful in creating a pointer to a print information structure, but did not return an error value, `MTPDoPrint` sets an error value.

14. It checks for any error. At this point, if an error has occurred, you know the Print dialog was never displayed. If an error occurred after getting a pointer to a print information structure, you may have some cleaning up to do—otherwise, you'll just display the error number.

15. If the local print settings variable has a reference to a print settings object, MTPDoPrint calls the CPM function PMRelease to release it. Releasing an object decrements its reference count, causing it to be deallocated when the count reaches 0.

16. If the print information structure has a print settings object, MTPDoPrint calls the CPM function PMRelease to release it and sets the field for this object to a value indicating it is no longer valid.

17. If the print information structure has a printing session object, MTPDoPrint calls the CPM function PMRelease to release it and sets the field for this object to a value indicating it is no longer valid.

18. It calls the function MTPPostPrintingError to display the error to the user.

MTPDrawMoonFactsPage

The MTPDrawMoonFactsPage function draws the specified page in the location specified by the page format object. Copy the code shown in Example 9-7 to the main.c file, below the MTPDoPrint function.

Example 9-7: Function to Draw One Page of the Moon Facts Window

```
OSStatus MTPDrawMoonFactsPage(
    MTPDocumentPrintInfoPtr documentPrintInfoPtr, UInt32 pageNumber)
{
    OSStatus    status = noErr;
    Rect bounds;
    CFStringRef text;
    PMRect    pageRect;

    status = PMGetAdjustedPageRect(
                    documentPrintInfoPtr->pageFormat, &pageRect);      // 1
    if (status == noErr)
    {
        text = CFCopyLocalizedString(CFSTR(kMTPMoonFactsTextKey),NULL);// 2

        if (text != NULL)
        {
            SetRect(&bounds, pageRect.left, pageRect.top,              // 3
                        pageRect.right, pageRect.bottom);

            TXNDrawCFStringTextBox (text, &bounds, NULL, NULL);        // 4
            CFRelease(text);                                          // 5
        }
        else
```

Example 9-7: Function to Draw One Page of the Moon Facts Window (continued)

```
        status = coreFoundationUnknownErr;                          // 6
    }

    return status;                                                  // 7

}
```

Here's how the `MTPDrawMoonFactsPage` function works:

1. It calls the Carbon Printing Manager function `PMGetAdjustedPageRect` to obtain the page size (the imageable area), in points, taking into account orientation, application drawing resolution, and scaling settings.

2. It calls the Core Foundation string function `CFCopyLocalizedString` to get the text that is displayed in the moon facts window.

3. If no error occurs, it sets a drawing location using the previously obtained page size information. This sample code sticks to printing one page, so it always prints the same text regardless of the specified page number. Applications that print more complicated documents would determine the correct material to print for the specified page.

4. It calls the Multilingual Text Engine (MLTE) function `TXNDrawCFStringTextBox` to draw the text from the moon facts window in the specified rectangle.

5. It calls the Core Foundation function `CFRelease` to release the string created by the call to `CFCopyLocalizedString`.

6. If it was unable to obtain the text string in the previous call to `CFCopyLocalizedString`, it sets an error value, using the constant `coreFoundationUnknownErr` (for an unknown Core Foundation error).

7. It returns a status value, indicating whether it succeeded in drawing the page.

The moon facts window has very simple printing needs and only draws one page of text. More complex applications are likely to require more complex drawing and page range calculations. Related issues are described in the next section on the `MTPPagesInDoc` function.

MTPPagesInDoc

The `MTPPagesInDoc` function returns the maximum number of pages to print in the document. Copy the code shown in Example 9-8 to the `main.c` file, below the `MTPDrawMoonFactsPage` function.

Example 9-8: A Function to Supply the Number of Pages in a Document

```
UInt32     MTPPagesInDoc(MTPDocumentPrintInfoPtr documentPrintInfoPtr)
{
    PMRect    paperRect, pageRect;
    UInt32    numPages = 1;
    OSStatus status = noErr;

    status = PMGetAdjustedPaperRect(
                    documentPrintInfoPtr->pageFormat, &paperRect);// 1
    if (status == noErr)
    {
        status = PMGetAdjustedPageRect(
                    documentPrintInfoPtr->pageFormat, &pageRect); // 2
        if (status == noErr)
            numPages = 1;                                         // 3
    }
    return numPages;                                             // 4
}
```

Here's how the `MTPPagesInDoc` function works:

1. It calls the Carbon Printing Manager (CPM) function `PMGetAdjustedPaperRect` to obtain the paper size, taking into account orientation, application drawing resolution, and scaling settings. Applications that print more complicated documents could use this information in determining the number of pages in the document based on the current print settings.

2. If no error occurred, it calls the CPM function `PMGetAdjustedPageRect` to obtain the page size (the imageable area), in points, taking into account orientation, application drawing resolution, and scaling settings. Again, some applications may need to use this information to compute the number of pages in the document.

3. If no error occurred, it sets a hard-coded value of one for the number of pages. For most applications, your page count may vary.

4. It returns the computed number of pages to print in the document.

Of course, most applications will need to do more work than shown here. The number of pages in a document is likely to depend on a number of factors, including document-specific changes by the user (such as adding text or changing font size), as well as Page Setup and Print dialog settings. Some applications might require a separate version of this function for each kind of document they print. If so, you might add a field to the print information structure (described in the section "Define Data Types for Working with Printing") to specify the page count function to be called from the main printing function (in this case, `MTPDoPrint`).

MTPPostPrintingErrors

The `MTPPostPrintingErrors` function displays an alert to notify the user that a printing error has occurred. The alert message includes a localized string and the error number. Copy the code shown in Example 9-9 to the `main.c` file, below the `MTPPagesInDoc` function.

Example 9-9: A Function to Post a Printing Error Alert

```
void      MTPPostPrintingError(OSStatus status)
{
    CFStringRef formatStr = NULL, printErrorMsg = NULL;
    SInt16     alertItemHit = 0;
    Str255     stringBuf;

    // Display any error except user cancelled.
    if ((status != noErr) && (status != kPMCancel))          // 1
    {
        formatStr =  CFCopyLocalizedString(                  // 2
                    CFSTR(KMTPPrintFormatStrKey), NULL);
        if (formatStr != NULL)
        {
            printErrorMsg = CFStringCreateWithFormat(        // 3
                    NULL, NULL,
                    formatStr, status);
            if (printErrorMsg != NULL)
            {
                if (CFStringGetPascalString(printErrorMsg,    // 4
                            stringBuf, sizeof(stringBuf),
                            kCFStringEncodingASCII))
                    StandardAlert(kAlertStopAlert, stringBuf, // 5
                            NULL, NULL, &alertItemHit);
                CFRelease(printErrorMsg);                      // 6
            }
            CFRelease(formatStr);                             // 7
        }
    }
}
```

Here's how the `MTPPostPrintingErrors` function works:

1. It checks whether the passed error should be displayed. Any error except `kPM-Cancel`, indicating the user cancelled printing, should be displayed.

2. It calls the Core Foundation string function `CFCopyLocalizedString` to get a localized formatting string that indicates how the error should be formatted for display.

3. If no error occurs, it calls the Core Foundation string function `CFStringCreate-WithFormat` to get a copy of the string that includes the error number.

4. If no error occurs, it calls the Core Foundation string function CFStringGetPas-
   calString to get a copy of the string that it can display in a standard alert dialog.

5. It calls the Carbon function StandardAlert to display the error message,
   including the error number.

6. It calls the Core Foundation function CFRelease to release the string (printEr-
   rorMsg) created by the call to CFCopyLocalizedString.

7. It calls the Core Foundation function CFRelease to release the string (format-
   Str) created by the call to CFStringCreateWithFormat.

MTPDoPrintLoop

The MTPDoPrintLoop function loops over the specified page range, calling your
draw page function for each page. This function is the Saturn V rocket of printing
functions—it does a lot of heavy lifting. But because it does most of its work by
calling Carbon Printing Manager functions, passing information obtained from a
document print information structure you defined, you should be able to adapt
this print loop code for applications with more sophisticated printing requirements.

Copy the code shown in Example 9-10 into the main.c file, below the MTPPost-
PrintingErrors function.

Example 9-10: A Print Loop Function

```
void MTPDoPrintLoop(MTPDocumentPrintInfoPtr documentPrintInfoPtr)
{
    OSStatus status = noErr,
             tempErr = noErr;
    UInt32   realNumberOfPagesinDoc, pageNumber, firstPage, lastPage;
    GrafPtr  currentPort, printingPort;

    realNumberOfPagesinDoc = MTPPagesInDoc(documentPrintInfoPtr);  // 1

    status = PMGetFirstPage(
                documentPrintInfoPtr->printSettings, &firstPage);  // 2

    if (status == noErr)
        status = PMGetLastPage(
                documentPrintInfoPtr->printSettings, &lastPage);   // 3

    if (status == noErr)
    {
        if (realNumberOfPagesinDoc < lastPage)                     // 4
            lastPage = realNumberOfPagesinDoc;

        status = PMSetFirstPage(                                   // 5
                documentPrintInfoPtr->printSettings,
```

Example 9-10: A Print Loop Function (continued)

```
                    firstPage, false);
        if (status == noErr)
            status = PMSetLastPage(                              // 6
                    documentPrintInfoPtr->printSettings,
                    lastPage, false);
    }
    if (status == noErr)
    {
        status = PMSessionBeginDocument(                         // 7
                documentPrintInfoPtr->printSession,
                documentPrintInfoPtr->printSettings,
                documentPrintInfoPtr->pageFormat);

        if (status == noErr)
        {
            pageNumber = firstPage;
            while ((pageNumber <= lastPage) && (status == noErr)   // 8
                 && (PMSessionError(documentPrintInfoPtr->printSession) == noErr))
            {
                status = PMSessionBeginPage(                     // 9
                        documentPrintInfoPtr->printSession,
                        documentPrintInfoPtr->pageFormat,
                        NULL);

                if (status == noErr)                            // 10
                {
                    GetPort(&currentPort);                      // 11

                    status = PMSessionGetGraphicsContext(       // 12
                            documentPrintInfoPtr->printSession,
                            kPMGraphicsContextQuickdraw, (void**)
                            &printingPort);

                    if (status == noErr)
                    {
                        SetPort(printingPort);                  // 13


                        if (documentPrintInfoPtr->drawDocPageProc) // 14
                            status = (*(documentPrintInfoPtr->drawDocPageProc))
                                    (documentPrintInfoPtr, pageNumber);

                        SetPort(currentPort);                   // 15
                    }
                    tempErr =                                   // 16
                        PMSessionEndPage(documentPrintInfoPtr->printSession);
                    if (status == noErr)
                            status = tempErr;

                    pageNumber++;                               // 17
                }
            }
        }
```

Example 9-10: A Print Loop Function (continued)

```
           tempErr =                                             // 18
             PMSessionEndDocument(documentPrintInfoPtr->printSession);
           if (status == noErr)
               status = tempErr;
       }
   }
   tempErr = PMSessionError(documentPrintInfoPtr->printSession);  // 19
   if (status == noErr)
       status = tempErr;

   if (status != noErr)
       MTPPostPrintingError(status);                             // 20

   if (documentPrintInfoPtr->printSettings != kPMNoPrintSettings) // 21
   {
       PMRelease(documentPrintInfoPtr->printSettings);
       documentPrintInfoPtr->printSettings = kPMNoPrintSettings;
   }

   if (documentPrintInfoPtr->printSession != NULL)               // 22
   {
       PMRelease(documentPrintInfoPtr->printSession);
       documentPrintInfoPtr->printSession = NULL;
   }
}
```

The `MTPDoPrintLoop` function assumes it has been passed a valid pointer to a properly initialized print information structure for the document to print. Here's how the function works:

1. It calls the function `MTPPagesInDoc` so the Moon Travel Planner can specify the maximum number of pages to print.

2. It calls the Carbon Printing Manager (CPM) function `PMGetFirstPage` to obtain the number of the first page to be printed.

You must use 32-bit unsigned containers to obtain the first page and last page values because in some cases the `PMGetFirstPage` and `PMGetLastPage` functions may return very large values from the print settings data structure. You should not use the constant `kPrintAllPages` in your print loop. That constant is used only with the `PMSetLastPage` and `PMSetPageRange` functions to specify a last page. It is not returned by the `PMGetLastPage` function and your code should not look for it here.

---

3. It calls the CPM function PMGetLastPage to obtain the number of the last page to be printed.

4. If the user specified a last page greater than the number of pages in the document, MTPDoPrintLoop sets the last page to the real last page in the document.

5. It calls the CPM function PMSetFirstPage to set the first page of the page range in the print settings object for this print job.

6. It calls the CPM function PMSetLastPage to set the last page of the page range in the print settings object for this print job. Setting the first and last page provides information to the progress dialog that is shown during printing.

7. It calls the CPM function PMSessionBeginDocument to establish a new print job. Note that if no error results from this call, the ensuing code will always call PMSessionEndDocument to end the print job.

8. It sets up a while loop to loop over the range of pages selected for printing. Note that the loop will terminate if any function returns an error (that is, if the variable status has a value other than noErr) or if the CPM function PMSessionError returns an error.

9. It calls the CPM function PMSessionBeginPage to inform the printing system that the drawing that follows is part of a new page.

10. It checks the return status after calling PMSessionBeginPage. Note that in the case that no error occurs, the ensuing code will always call PMSessionEndPage to finish printing the current page.

11. It calls the QuickDraw function GetPort to save the current graphics port.

12. It calls the CPM function PMSessionGetGraphicsContext to obtain the Quick-Draw graphics port for the page being printed.

13. It calls the QuickDraw function SetPort to set the graphics port to the port obtained in the previous step. You must do this before calling the document's function to draw one page.

14. If the print information pointer has a valid drawDocPageProc field, MTPDoPrint-Loop calls that function to draw the current page.

15. It calls the SetPort function again to set the current port back to the saved port after drawing one page.

16. It calls the CPM function PMSessionEndPage to finish printing the current page. It uses a temporary variable to get the status for this function; then, if an error occurs, and there was no previous error, it sets the status variable to that error value. This approach ensures that the current page is always finished and that if any error occurs the loop terminates.

17. It increments the page count within the page-printing loop.

18. On completion of the page-printing loop, MTPDoPrintLoop calls the CPM function PMSessionEndDocument to complete the print job.

19. It calls the CPM function PMSessionError to determine if any printing error has occurred. It again uses a temporary variable to get the status for this function to ensure that the print job is always completed and that if any error occurs, it is reported to the user.

20. If the previous step detects a printing error, MTPDoPrintLoop calls the MTPPost-PrintingErrors function to display the error to the user.

21. Regardless of whether any error has occurred, it releases the print information structure's print settings object, if any, and sets the field for this object to a value indicating it is no longer valid.

22. Regardless of whether any error has occurred, it releases the print information structure's printing session object, if any, and sets the field for this object to a value indicating it is no longer valid.

Add a Print Format String to the Localized Strings

In the section "Define Constants for Working with Printing," you defined the constant KMTPPrintFormatStrKey to obtain a localized format string for use in displaying error strings. You saw how that constant was used in the MTPPostPrintingError function. In this section you'll add the format string to Moon Travel Planner's Localizable.strings file, which you learned about in Chapter 8.

To add a format string to the Localizable.strings file, you perform these steps:

1. Open the Resources folder in the Moon Travel Planner project.

2. Click on the Localizable.strings file.

3. After the last current key/value entry and before the closing right bracket (}), type a semicolon (;).

4. Insert the following line after the semicolon; the characters %ld are C formatting instructions for a long decimal value to display the error number:

```
"Error format" = "Printing error: %ld"
```

Add Printing Code to the Main Function

To set up the Moon Travel Planner to print the text from the moon facts window, you add code to the main function in several places. First, add the following variable declaration at the top of the function with the other variables:

```
PMSheetDoneUPP     pageSetupDoneUPP, printDialogDoneUPP;
```

The **PMSheetDoneUPP** data type is defined by the Carbon Printing Manager (CPM) as a pointer to a sheet done function. The CPM calls your sheet done function when the user dismisses a printing dialog that is being shown as a sheet (that is, attached to the window of the document being printed).

Next you'll use these function pointer variables to set up printing information for the moon facts window. Add the code shown in Example 9-11 to the main function after the code to install the various window event handlers.

Example 9-11: Code to Initialize a Print Information Structure for a Window

```
pageSetupDoneUPP = NewPMSheetDoneUPP(&MTPPageSetupDoneProc);      // 1
   if (pageSetupDoneUPP == NULL)
       goto CantSetUpPrinting;
   printDialogDoneUPP = NewPMSheetDoneUPP (&MTPPrintDialogDoneProc); // 2
   if (printDialogDoneUPP == NULL)
       goto CantSetUpPrinting;

   err = MTPCreatePrintInfoForWindow(gMoonFactsWindow,              // 3
           (MTPDrawDocPageProc) MTPDrawMoonFactsPage,
           pageSetupDoneUPP, printDialogDoneUPP);
   require_noerr (err, CantSetUpPrinting );
```

Here's what the code in Example 9-11 does:

1. It calls the Carbon Printing Manager function NewPMSheetDoneUPP to create a universal procedure pointer (a type of function pointer) to the MTPPageSetup-DoneProc function, which is described in the section "MTPPageSetupDone-Proc." If the call is unsuccessful, the code branches to a failure exit label, CantSetUpPrinting.

2. It calls NewPMSheetDoneUPP again to create a universal procedure pointer to the MTPPrintDialogDoneProc function, which is described in the section "MTPPrint-DialogDoneProc." If the call is unsuccessful, the code branches to a failure exit label, CantSetUpPrinting.

 The Moon Travel Application creates these universal procedure pointers for printing and keeps them throughout the life of the application. In many cases, however, an application creates a universal procedure pointer, uses it, then disposes of it. To dispose of a universal procedure pointer of type **PMSheetDoneUPP**, you call the Carbon Printing Manager function DisposePMSheetDoneUPP.

3. It calls the `MTPCreatePrintInfoForWindow` function to create a print information structure and attach a pointer to it as a property of the moon facts window. It passes the following values:

- `gMoonFactsWindow`. A pointer to the moon facts window

- `(MTPDrawDocPageProc) MTPDrawMoonFactsPage`. A pointer to the function to draw one page of the moon facts window

- `pageSetupDoneUPP`. A pointer to the function to call when the user dismisses the Page Setup dialog

- `printDialogDoneUPP`. A pointer to the function to call when the user dismisses the Print dialog

If the `MTPCreatePrintInfoForWindow` function returns an error, the code branches to a failure exit label, `CantSetUpPrinting`. The macro `require_noerr` is described in Chapter 3, *Project Builder Projects*. You use it to check for "show stopping" errors and jump to a label to exit the application.

Finally, you'll add a failure label to branch to if there is an error while initializing printing. Copy the following line below `CantGetNibRef`:

```
CantSetUpPrinting:
```

Adjust Code in the Moon Facts Window Event Handler

In Chapter 8 you added code to the `MTPMoonFactsWindowEventHandler` function to handle the Page Setup and Print commands, but that code was commented out because you hadn't written the functions yet. Now you can remove the comment characters so that the code looks like this:

```
case kMTPPrintCommand:
    MTPDoPrint (gMoonFactsWindow);
    result = noErr;
    break;
case kMTPPageSetupCommand:
    MTPDoPageSetup (gMoonFactsWindow);
    result = noErr;
    break;
```

Test the Page Setup and Print Commands

To test the Page Setup command from the moon facts window, you perform the following steps. These steps assume you have a printer available and have already selected a default printer. If you haven't selected a default printer, Mac OS X will prompt you to do so.

1. Click the Build button in the upper-left corner of the Moon Travel Planner project window.

2. Click the Run button in the upper-left corner of the project window.

3. Choose Facts for the Traveler in the Moon menu or press Command-F.

4. To open the Page Setup dialog, choose Page Setup in the File menu or press Command-Shift-P. The resulting Page Setup dialog is shown in Figure 9-1.

5. Change any setting in the Page Setup dialog and close the dialog by clicking the OK button. For example, you might click one of the icons for landscape paper orientation.

6. Open the Page Setup dialog as before. You should see that any changes you made are still present.

7. To open the Print dialog, choose Print in the File menu or press Command-P. The resulting Print dialog is shown in Figure 9-2.

8. Change any setting in the Print dialog. For example, you might change the printer or change the number of copies from 1 to 2.

9. Click either the Preview button to get a preview of the printed document, or the Print button to send it to the printer. Any changes you made in the Page Setup or Print dialogs should be reflected in the resulting printed or previewed document.

10. If you repeat the previous steps to open the Page Setup dialog, it should still reflect the changes you made. The Print dialog, however, should still reflect the original (default) settings.

Recap

In this chapter, you learned about the Carbon Printing Manager, which allows your Carbon application to take advantage of printing features available in Mac OS X, while still supporting printing in earlier versions of the Mac OS. You took a look at printing sessions (to perform one printing task), print loops (to print a range of pages), and print function sequence and scope (which determine the order in which you must call certain printing functions).

You saw that the Carbon Printing Manager provides opaque data types for key objects—the printing session, page format, and print settings objects—as well as functions for creating, modifying, extending, and saving these objects.

Finally, you added printing code to the Moon Travel Planner application to print the Facts for the Traveler window. Printing code can be a little daunting, but the code in this chapter should provide a good template for leveraging the support provided by the Carbon Printing Manager.

10

Property Lists

Property lists offer a uniform and architecture-independent means to organize, store, and access data for your application. They are used frequently in Mac OS X, particularly by the *Finder* to determine what to do when it encounters an application or one of its documents. (The Finder is the application that manages the user's desktop and mediates access to applications, documents, and other items in the file system.) Some of the most common data included in a property list are application name, version, type, creator code, and icon filename.

There are a number of reasons why you'll need to modify your application's property list. Property lists store essential configuration information that your program code or the operating system can access at runtime. Application name and version properties are used to display information to the user in an About window or a Finder Info window. If your application opens documents, you need to set up properties to let the Finder know which documents can be opened by your application.

You've already seen in Chapter 3, *Project Builder Projects*, that a property list (the Info.plist file) is part of every Mac OS X application bundle. In Chapter 8, *Text and Localization*, we discussed localizing properties that will be seen in the interface and putting them in an InfoPlist.strings file. We actually haven't looked at the contents of an Info.plist file or taken a look at the default properties associated with a Carbon application. So, in this chapter, we'll:

- See what Project Builder provides in the default information property list
- Modify the information property list for the Moon Travel Planner application
- Look at what an About window can display from a property list

- Create an About window for the Moon Travel Planner application using Interface Builder to create the window, and write code to display property list information in the window

The Information Property List: Info.plist

The information property list (`Info.plist`) is a special form of property list that has predefined keys for specifying application properties of interest to the Finder and other applications. The `Info.plist` is stored inside the application's bundle, as you saw in Chapter 3.

Like all property lists, `Info.plist` is a text file that contains key-value pairs in XML syntax. (A collection of key-value pairs is referred to as a *dictionary*.) For example, the following entry in the information property list sets a key named `CFBundlePackageType` to the string `APPL`. It signifies the bundle is an application:

```
<key>CFBundlePackageType</key> <string>APPL</string>
```

 XML stands for Extensible Markup Language and was developed in 1996 as an outgrowth of SGML (Structured Generalized Markup Language). XML is a popular format for data because it is platform-independent, well-supported, and relatively easy to use.

XML is an HTML-like language for structuring data with custom-defined tags. XML looks similar to HTML in that it uses tags to enclose data. Unlike HTML, the tags in XML are simply delimiters; they do not have any standard meaning as they do in HTML.

For more information about XML, see *Learning XML* and *XML in a Nutshell*, both available through O'Reilly & Associates.

You don't need to learn XML to read or modify the information property list. You can view and modify the information property list using Project Builder or the Property List Editor application provided with Mac OS X. In fact, it is not safe to edit the XML data by hand unless you are very familiar with XML syntax.

There are two categories of predefined keys for an application's properties:

- **Standard keys.** Used for basic configuration information, such as the name of the executable and the version number of the application.

- **Finder keys.** Used by the Mac OS X Finder to store important information about a bundle.

You will need to know the key for any property whose value you want to retrieve programmatically. (You'll do this in the section "Moon Travel Planner: Modifying and Using Properties"). The header file CFBundle.h defines constants for many common property list keys. Although you can define your own properties, you should use the predefined property keys where appropriate rather than define your own.

Table 10-1 lists the default information properties supplied by Project Builder when you create a project. The first five are Standard keys; the rest are Finder keys.

Table 10-1. Default Information Properties Provided for a Project Builder Project Named Sample Application

Key	Value
CFBundleInfoDictionaryVersion	6.0
CFBundleExecutable	Sample Application
CFBundleVersion	0.1
CFBundleDevelopmentRegion	English
CFBundleName	Sample Application
CFBundlePackageType	APPL
CFBundleSignature	????
CFBundleShortVersionString	Sample Application version 0.1
CFBundleGetInfoString	Sample Application version 0.1, copyright 2000 My Great Software.

Standard Keys

There are five standard keys available to a Carbon application. Four of them are included in the default information property list. They are:

- CFBundleInfoDictionaryVersion. This key supports future versioning of the dictionary format. (The key-value pair format used in an Info.plist file is called a dictionary.) You shouldn't modify this value.

- CFBundleExecutable. The name of the main executable for the bundle. For an application, this is the application's executable file. For a loadable bundle, it is the binary that will be loaded dynamically by the bundle. For a framework, it is the shared library for the framework (in the case of a framework, the executable must have the same name as the framework). The executable name should not include an extension.

- CFBundleIdentifier. The unique identifier string for the bundle, with a Java-style package name (think of it as a reverse URL). For example, com.mycompany.mysoftware. The identifier locates the bundle at runtime.

- `CFBundleVersion`. The application version number. The value should be a string; used internally for version identification.

- `CFBundleDevelopmentRegion`. The language or region in which the application was developed.

Finder Keys

These keys are used by the Finder to store important information about a bundle. Among other things, the Finder uses these properties to locate and display an application's icon and recognize document types associated with the application:

- `CFBundleName`. The short name of the bundle suitable for displaying in the user interface, such as in the Application menu and the About window. This key is usually in the `InfoPlist.strings` file because it needs to be localized.

- `CFBundlePackageType`. A four-character code that specifies the bundle's type. For applications, use `APPL`.

- `CFBundleSignature`. A four-character code that specifies the creator, sometimes referred to as the application signature.

- `CFBundleShortVersionString`. A description of the bundles's version that can be displayed to users in the Finder's Info window. (See the version information shown in Figure 10-1 for an example.) This does not have to be the same string you supply for the `CFBundleVersion` key. You should put this in the `InfoPlist.strings` file so it can be localized.

- `CFBundleGetInfoString`. A text string displayed to users in the Finder's Info window. You should include this property in the `InfoPlist.strings` file for localization.

- `CFBundleIconFile`. The filename of the bundle resource that contains the icon the Finder (or other applications) should use to display this bundle. It's optional for filename to have an extension. If it doesn't have one, the operating system appends an appropriate extension.

- `CFBundleGetInfoHTML`. An HTML string that's displayed in the Finder's Info Window. This property is usually included in the `InfoPlist.strings` file for localization. You can use this if you want a richer representation than that provided by the `CFBundleGetInfoString` property. If you define both properties, `CFBundleGetInfoHTML` supersedes `CFBundleGetInfoString`.

- `CFBundleDocumentTypes`. An array of type definitions for the document types an application can recognize. Each document type for a Carbon application can be specified using the following keys:

Figure 10-1. Version information in the Finder's Info window

— CFBundleTypeName. The abstract name for the document type.

— CFBundleTypeIconFile. The name of the icon file, without the extension, that contains the icon the Finder should display for the type.

— CFBundleTypeRole. Defines the application's role with respect to the type; the role can be Editor, Viewer, or None.

— CFBundleTypeOSTypes. An array of four-character codes that map to this type.

— CFBundleTypeExtensions. An array of filename extensions that map to this type.

• CFBundleURLTypes. An array of URL schemes the application can handle. Each URL scheme can be specified using these keys:

— CFBundleURLName. The abstract name for this URL type.

— CFBundleURLIconFile. The name of the icon file, minus the extension, that contains the icon the Finder should display for the type.

— CFBundleURLSchemes. An array of URL schemes handled by this type (http, ftp, and so forth).

Viewing and Modifying Property Lists in Project Builder

Project Builder provides a set of default properties when you create your project. You'll need to view the default list and modify the values to suit your application. You may also need to add properties.

There are three ways you can view and modify property lists in Project Builder: simple or expert views in the Application Settings pane and by opening the Info-Plist.strings file. The method you choose depends on your level of expertise and whether you want to access properties that should be localized.

The Application Settings pane in Project Builder provides access to properties in the Info.plist file. Recall this is the master list of information properties, and can include those that should be localized as well as those that don't need to be localized. You can view the properties in Simple or Expert views. The Simple mode is shown in Figure 10-2. To view the simple mode:

1. Click the Targets tab, then click a target in the Targets list.
2. Click the Application Settings tab.

The keys are listed in a more "readable" form than the CFBundle property names. For example, the CFBundleExecutable key is listed as Executable, and so forth. The simple listing lets you see the core group of information properties that you should set up for your application. If you want to add properties, you'll need to use the Expert view.

The Expert view, shown in Figure 10-3, lets you view Standard, Finder and user-defined keys: the property's key, class (that is, data type), and current value. You can add new properties by clicking New Sibling, then typing a key, class, and value. To modify a property, double-click its value and type the new value.

Any changes you make in the Simple mode are reflected in the Expert view. Any change you make in Expert view is shown in Simple view as long as the property is one of the core properties listed in the Simple view.

The third way you can view and modify properties is to open the Info-Plist.strings file. This is the subset of the information property list—it should contain those properties that need to be localized. Figure 10-4 shows the default InfoPlist.strings file you get when you create a Project Builder project.

To view this file, click the Files tab, then click InfoPlist.strings in the Resources group of the Groups & Files list. Note the syntax; string values must be enclosed by straight quotation marks:

```
<key> = <value>;
```

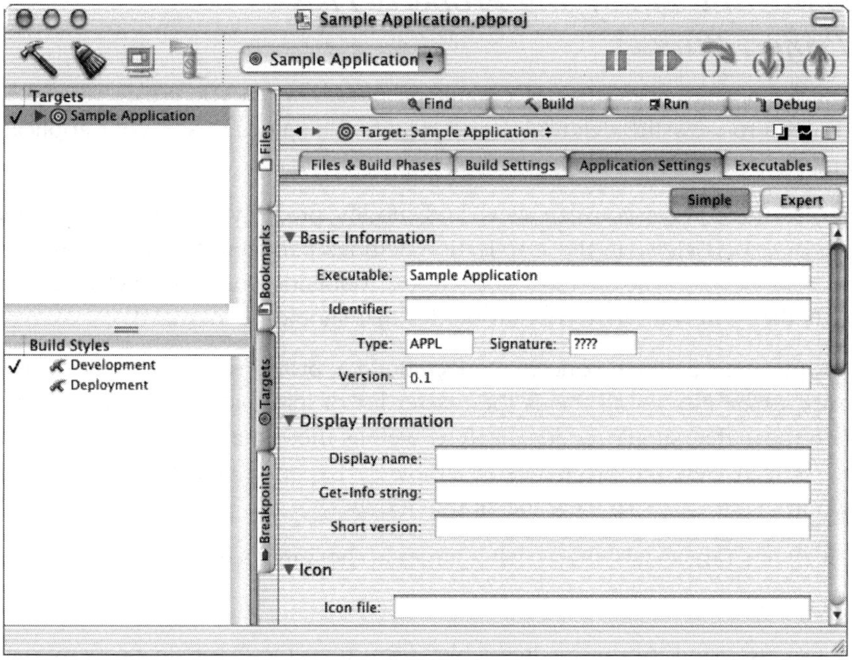

Figure 10-2. Information properties in the Application Settings pane, Simple mode

There are two important things to remember about information properties:

- Project Builder does not coordinate the properties in the `Info.plist` file (those you can see in the Application Settings pane) with those in the `Info-Plist.strings` file. In other words, a change made to one file is not reflected in the other. You may need to make an entry in each file.

- If a property exists in both places (`Info.plist` and `InfoPlist.strings`), the value of the localized version is always used. Any function from the Carbon programming interface that gets property list information first looks for the localized version. If one isn't found, the function looks for the property in the `Info.plist` file.

The About Window

An *About window* is a modeless window (the user can leave it open and perform other tasks in the application) that contains your application's version and copyright information. Figure 10-5 shows two typical About windows. The numbers in the bottom window denote pixel spacing.

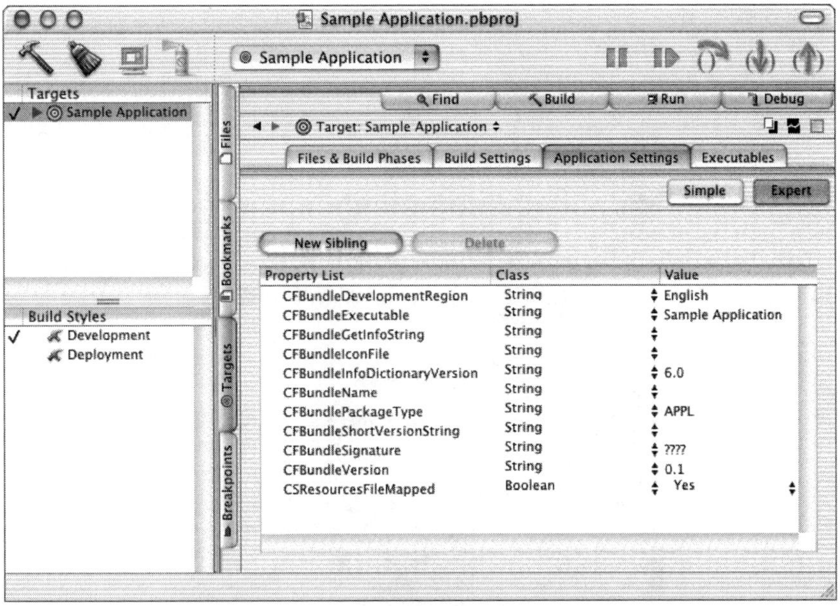

Figure 10-3. Information properties in the Application Settings pane, Expert mode

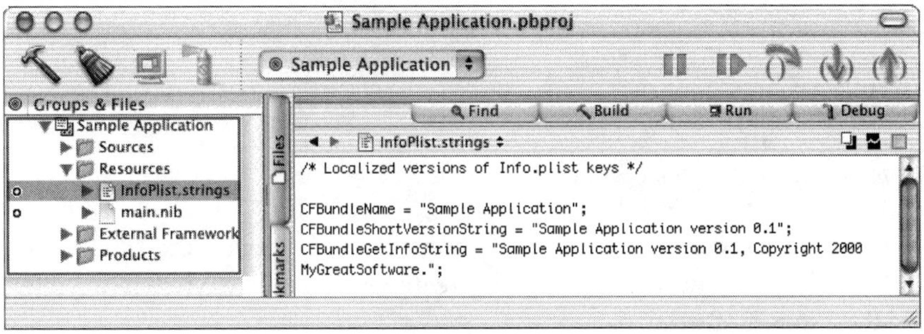

Figure 10-4. The default InfoPlist.strings file

As you might guess from looking at the window, you can get most of the information from the application's information property list. Using the property list assures that the About window displays current information; when the version or copyright information changes, you only need to change it in the property list. It also makes localization easy, because the localized property list values are always returned to your application if they are available.

Items in the window should be centered with the spacing from the bottom of one element to the top of another as indicated in the figure. An application's About

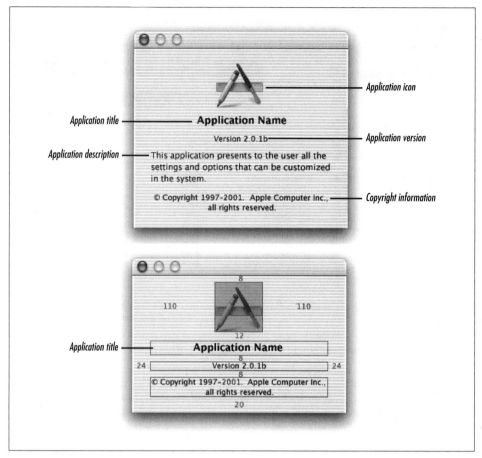

Figure 10-5. Typical About windows

window should have a title bar and be movable, and provide the Close button as
the only active window control. You'll create one in the next section, after you
modify the property list.

Moon Travel Planner: Modifying and Using Properties

There are a few properties that you should set for your application to configure it
properly for the Finder and the operating system. These include the bundle identifier (CFBundleIdentifier) and the application's creator code (CFBundleSignature).
There are other properties you need to set so you can display version and copyright information to the user. You'll set these properties, then create an About window that accesses the property list from within your application.

Besides modifying the property list, there are a number of steps you'll need to follow to actually create the window and get it to function in the Moon Travel Planner we've worked on so far. In this section you'll:

1. Modify the property list.

2. Create a new window.

3. Write code that opens and displays the About window.

4. Write an event handler for the About window.

Modify the Property List

You'll set the bundle identifier first. The bundle identifier is used to locate the application bundle at runtime (see the section "Standard Keys)." It must be unique, so define it as a Java-style package name; for example `com.mycompany.myapp` or `edu.ABCSchool.myapp`.

1. Open the Moon Travel Planner project if it is not already open.

2. Click the Targets tab, then click Moon Travel Planner in the Targets list.

3. Click Application Settings, then click Expert.

4. Click New Sibling, type **CFBundleIdentifier** as the property name, and press Return.

5. Double-click the Value column, type **com.apple.moontravelapp** as the property value, and press Return.

Next you'll modify the property list so the creator code (`CFBundleSignature`) is MTPP. As you saw in Table 10-1, the default value is ????. In Chapter 5, *Interface Builder: Tools and Controls*, we mentioned MTPP has already been registered with Apple as the creator code for Moon Travel Planner. In fact, we used the creator code to set up control IDs in Chapter 5 and declared a constant (`kMTPApplicationSignature`) in Chapter 6, *Carbon Events*, to represent the creator code. We need to add the creator code to the property list so the Finder is aware of Moon Travel Planner's existence.

In the Expert mode property list, double-click ????, the value that's listed for `CFBundleSignature`, then type **MTPP**.

The properties the application displays in the About window should be localized. So you'll modify the default properties in the `InfoPlist.strings` file:

1. Click the Files tab, then click `InfoPlist.strings` in the Resources group of the Groups & Files list. You should see three strings that Project Builder added for you automatically.

```
/* Localized versions of Info.plist keys */
CFBundleName = "Moon Travel Planner";
CFBundleShortVersionString = "Moon Travel Planner version 0.1";
CFBundleGetInfoString = "Moon Travel Planner version 0.1, Copyright 2000
MyGreatSoftware.";
```

2. Modify the keys in the files so they have the following values:

```
CFBundleShortVersionString = "Moon Travel Planner version 1.0.1";
CFBundleGetInfoString = "version 1.0.1, copyright 2001, Lunar Software, Inc.";
```

Create a New Window

You'll use Interface Builder to create a new window. As you recall from the section "The About Window," the window needs to be movable, have a close control, and show a title in the title bar.

1. Click main.nib in the Resources group of the Groups & Files list.

2. Create a new window. Click the Windows button in the Carbon palette, then drag the icon of the window on the left to the desktop.

3. Name the window object. In the Instances pane of the main.nib window, double-click the word "Window" that's under the icon of the window you just created, type **AboutWindow**, and press Return.

4. Assign a title to the window. With the window active, choose Show Info from the Tools menu, choose Attributes from the pop-up menu, type **About Moon Travel** in the Title text field, and press Return. We need to shorten the name to Moon Travel, because the window will be too small to fit About Moon Travel Planner.

5. Set the window's controls in the Control group. Make sure Close Box is the only option selected.

6. Set the window's attributes in the Attribute group. Make sure Standard Handler is the only option selected.

7. Set the window class as Document.

8. Set the Theme Brush setting as Dialog.

9. Resize the window to 264 by 165 pixels. This allows for the application icon, application title, two lines of configuration information, and takes into account the spacing suggested in *Inside Mac OS X: Aqua Human Interface Guidelines.* Choose Size in the pop-up menu, choose Width/Height from the right Content Rect pop-up menu, and type **264** for width and **165** for height.

10. Add the Moon Travel Planner application icon to the interface. You can use the same PICT you used for the main window. Follow the instructions in Chapter 5 for adding an image to the interface. Make sure you use the dimensions 64 by 64 when you size the PICT control.

11. Choose Show Layout Rectangles from the Layout menu. You can align items more precisely using the edges of the layout rectangles.

12. Adjust the spacing of the Moon Travel Planner application icon so it follows the recommendations in *Inside Mac OS X: Aqua Human Interface Guidelines.* The current guidelines call for a spacing of 8 pixels from the top icon to the bottom of the title bar. With the icon selected, choose Show Info from the Tools menu, then choose Size from the pop-up menu. Choose Top/Left from the Bounds pop-up menu and type **8** for the y-value.

13. Center the Moon Travel Planner application icon. With the application icon selected, choose Alignment > Make Centered Column from the Layout menu.

14. Add a static text field below the application icon. This is the application title. From the Controls palette, drag the object named Static Text to the area below the icon.

15. Enter **Moon Travel Planner** as the static text field's value. Double-click the field so a blinking insertion point appears. Type **Moon Travel Planner** and press Return.

16. Adjust the spacing of the Moon Travel Planner text so it follows the recommendations in *Inside Mac OS X: Aqua Human Interface Guidelines.* The current guidelines call for the top of the Moon Travel Planner text's layout rectangle to be 12 pixels from the bottom of the Moon Travel Planner application icon. You actually need to calculate the spacing from the top of the window to the top of the Moon Travel Planner text layout rectangle. That spacing is 8 + 64 + 12, or 84. Eight pixels for the space between the top of the window and the top of the application icon, 64 pixels for the height of the application icon, and 12 pixels for the space between the bottom of the application icon and the top of the Moon Travel Planner text layout rectangle. With the Moon Travel Planner static text field selected, choose Size from the Info window pop-up menu. Choose Top/Left from the Bounds pop-up menu and type **84** for the y-value.

17. Center the Moon Travel Planner text and adjust the spacing. With the Moon Travel Planner static text field selected, choose Alignment > Make Centered Column from the Layout window.

18. Add a static text field below the application name. You'll display the version information in this field.

19. Delete the title of the static text item. The static text field needs to be blank so you can write version information to it. In the Static Text Info window, choose Attributes from the pop-up menu, then delete "Static Text" from the Title text field.

20. Enter **MTTP** as the static text field's signature and **132** as its ID. Choose Control from the pop-up menu in the Static Text Info window. In the Control ID section, type **MTTP** in the Signature field and **132** in the ID field. You'll use these values later to access the static text field when you display the version information.

21. Turn off the Alignment rectangles. Choose Hide Alignment Rectangles from the Layout menu.

22. Position the About window where you'd like it to appear when the user opens it. Where you position the window in Interface Builder determines its position when the user opens it.

23. Choose Save from the File menu.

Create the About Window from the nib File

In Chapter 3 we saw that Project Builder automatically included code to create the main window from the main.nib file. Now that you've added a third window to the main.nib file—the About window-you need to add code to your main function to create the About window from the one you added to the main.nib file. You need to use the function CreateWindowFromNib. You must pass it three parameters, the nib reference from which to get the window description, the name of the window object, and a pointer to a window reference. You already have this code in your main function to create a nib reference from your main.nib file:

```
err = CreateNibReference (CFSTR ("main"), &nibRef);
```

You'll pass nibRef as the first parameter to CreateWindowFromNib.

The second parameter must be a CFString object. For this you need to pass the name of the window object, which you named "AboutWindow" in the section "Create a New Window." You must convert "AboutWindow" to a CFString object using the function CFSTR. So for the second parameter, you'll pass CFSTR("AboutWindow").

The third parameter needs to be a pointer to a window reference. After you call the function, this will refer to the About window. First you must declare the window reference. You can modify the global declaration in the main.c file so it includes the About window. It should look like this once it has been modified:

```
// Global window references.
WindowRef       gMainWindow,
                gMoonFactsWindow,
                gAboutWindow;
```

Now that you have all the parameters in place, you can add the code to create the About window. You should also check for an error, and if the window can't be created, jump to a label that causes the application not to launch. Add this code to the main function, just after the code that creates the main window:

```
err = CreateWindowFromNib (nibRef, CFSTR ("AboutWindow"), &gAboutWindow);
require_no_err(err, CantCreateWindow);
```

Write a Function to Handle the About Command

You assigned a command to the About menu item in Chapter 7, *Interface Builder: Menus*. Now it's time to write a function that handles the command by showing the About window, getting version information from the property list, and writing the version information to the window.

The first thing we need to do is add constants used in the function. You need a constant to represent the command you assigned to the About menu item, and a constant to represent the control ID you assigned to the static text field.

Add the constants shown in Example 10-1 to the main.c file, at the top, just after the statement #include <Carbon/Carbon.h>:

Example 10-1: Constants Needed for the About Window

```
#define kMTPOpenAboutWindowCommand 'aBtb'
#define kMTPVersionInfoID 132
```

Before we write the function, you'll declare its prototype. It takes a window reference to the About window as a parameter. You can put the following function prototype in the main.c file, along with the other function prototypes you've declared so far.

```
pascal void MTPAboutWindowCommandHandler (WindowRef window);
```

Now we can add the function. It shows the About window, gets the Get Info string from the InfoPlist.strings file, and displays the string in the About window. Copy the AboutWindowCommandHandler function in Example 10-2 to the main.c file.

Example 10-2: A Function That Shows the About Window

```
pascal void MTPAboutWindowCommandHandler (WindowRef window)
{
    CFStringRef             text;
    CFBundleRef             appBundle;
    ControlID  versionInfoID = { kMTPApplicationSignature,
                                  kMTPVersionInfoID };
    ControlRef              versionControl;
    ControlFontStyleRec     controlStyle;

    appBundle = CFBundleGetMainBundle ();                        // 1
    text = (CFStringRef) CFBundleGetValueForInfoDictionaryKey (appBundle,
```

Example 10-2: A Function That Shows the About Window (continued)

```
                                CFSTR("CFBundleGetInfoString"));  // 2
if ((text == CFSTR(" ") ) || (text== NULL))
        text = CFSTR("Nameless Application.");               // 3
GetControlByID( window, &versionInfoID, &versionControl );   // 4
SetControlData ( versionControl, kControlLabelPart,
                        kControlStaticTextCFStringTag,
                        sizeof(CFStringRef), &text);         // 5
controlStyle.flags = kControlUseJustMask;                    // 6
controlStyle.just = teCenter;                                // 7
SetControlFontStyle( versionControl, &controlStyle );        // 8
ShowWindow (window);                                         // 9
SelectWindow (window);
}
```

Here's what the function does:

1. The Core Foundation Bundle Services function CFBundleGetMainBundle returns the bundle associated with the Moon Travel Planner application. You need to pass the bundle as a parameter to the function in the next statement.

2. The Core Foundation Bundle Services function CFBundleGetValueForInfoDictionaryKey returns the string associated with the key CFBundleGetInfoString. This is the string you modified in the section "The Information Property List: Info.plist." The function CFBundleGetValueForInfoDictionaryKey takes a CFString object as a parameter, so you must use the function CFSTR to convert the Get Info string to a CFString object.

3. To catch possible errors, if the string CFBundleGetInfoString doesn't exist, then set the value of text to "Nameless Application."

4. The Control Manager function GetControlByID gets the control handle associated with the text field in which you'll display the version information.

5. The Control Manager function SetControlData sets the text field to the value of the string returned by the function CFBundleGetValueForInfoDictionaryKey.

6. The flag kControlUseJustMask specifies that the justification field of the controlStyle data structure should be applied to the control.

7. The Text Edit constant teCenter specifies that text in the control should be centered.

8. The Control Manager function SetControlFontStyle sets the font style for the static text field to the values passed in the controlStyle data structure.

9. Now that the text you want to display is written to the control, you need to show the window using the Window Manager function ShowWindow. Then, make it active using the SelectWindow function.

So far, nothing in our Moon Travel Planner application calls the MTPAboutWindow-CommandHandler function. When the user chooses About Moon Travel Planner from the application menu, the About command is issued, but nothing in our program captures that command. We need to add another case to the switch statement in the main window event handler you wrote in Chapter 6. Recall that handler takes care of the Compute Travel Time and Show Facts commands. We need to add a statement so it also handles the About command. Modify the switch statement in the function MTPMainWindowEventHandler so it now looks like the code shown in Example 10-3.

Example 10-3: The Modified Switch Statement in the Main Window Event Handler

```
switch (command.commandID)

    {
    case kMTPComputeCommand:
            MTPComputeCommandHandler ((WindowRef) userData);
            result = noErr;
            break;
    case kMTPShowMoonFactsCommand:
            MTPShowMoonFactsWindow(gMoonFactsWindow);
            result = noErr;
            break;
    case kMTPOpenAboutWindowCommand:
            MTPAboutWindowCommandHandler(gAboutWindow);
            result = noErr;
            break;
    }
```

Once the window is open, the Moon Travel Planner application needs to handle any events associated with it. We need to write an event handler for the window next.

Writing an Event Handler for the About Window

You've already written two event handlers—one for the main window and another to handle the Facts for the Traveler window—so writing a third should be fairly routine for you.

In this section, you'll declare an event type specifier associated with the About window event handler, then install the event handler for the About window.

The handler only needs to take care of a window close event. Copy the following to the main function, after the declaration for the Facts for the Travelers window event specifier:

```
EventTypeSpec aboutSpec = { kEventClassWindow, kEventWindowClose };
```

Declare the event handler. Copy the following declaration to the main.c file, just after the constants and global variable declarations:

```
pascal OSStatus MTPAboutWindowEventHandler (
                            EventHandlerCallRef handlerRef,
                            EventRef event, void *userData);
```

Install the event handler. After the line DisposeNibReference(nibRef), add the following code:

```
InstallWindowEventHandler (gAboutWindow,
        NewEventHandlerUPP (MTPAboutWindowEventHandler),
        1, &aboutSpec, (void *) gAboutWindow, NULL);
```

Copy the function in Example 10-4 to the main program, after the function MTP-MoonFactsWindowEventHandler.

Example 10-4: The About Window Event Handler

```
pascal OSStatus MTPAboutWindowEventHandler (EventHandlerCallRef handlerRef,
                                EventRef event, void *userData)
{
    OSStatus        result  = eventNotHandledErr;
    UInt32          eventKind;

    eventKind = GetEventKind (event);                           // 1
    if ( eventKind == kEventWindowClose)                        // 2
    {
            HideWindow ( (WindowRef) userData);                 // 3
            result = noErr;
    }
    return result;
}
```

Here's what the function does:

1. The Carbon Event Manager function GetEventKind returns the kind of the event.

2. If the event is a close window event, then it handles it; otherwise, it returns the result code eventNotHandledErr to indicate the Carbon Event Manger should handle the event.

3. The Window Manager function HideWindow hides the About window.

Build, run, and test the application

Let's build and run the application to make sure the About window opens and looks as it should:

1. Click the Build button in the upper-left corner of the Moon Travel Planner project window.

2. Click the Run button in the upper-left corner of the project window.

3. Choose About Moon Travel Planner from the application menu. Does the window open? It should look like the one shown in Figure 10-6.

Figure 10-6. The About window for the Moon Travel Planner application

4. Click the Close box. Does the About window close?

5. Click the Quit button.

If everything worked, you're ready to move on!

Recap

We took a look at the property list and the default properties that Project Builder provides when you create a new project. We also discussed the Standard and Finder keys available to your application and showed how you can add your own custom keys. Finally we created an About window for the Moon Travel Planner application and used the property list as the source of information to display in the About window. In the next chapter, you'll see how to use Navigation and File services to open and save files.

11

Files

In any application that you write, you'll probably manipulate data. Some of this data you may want, or need, to keep—even after your application quits or the system restarts. Perhaps it is data that your application needs to run, or perhaps it is data that your users create and may wish to return to at a later time. If you want that data to be there when your application quits and is later restarted, you'll have to store that information in a persistent form—that is, as a file.

In this chapter, you will learn some of the concepts that you'll need to store and retrieve data in files in Mac OS X. You'll also learn the tasks every application that stores and retrieves data should perform. As a final step, you'll add code to the Moon Travel Planner application to open, display, save, and close an itinerary file for planning a trip to the moon.

Managing Files on the Mac

In our discussion of opening and saving files, we will focus on storing and retrieving user data, which most applications must do at some time or another. To store and retrieve user data on a physical storage device, there are two things that you must do:

- Communicate with the physical storage device to transfer the data and organize it on disk.

- Allow users to choose the data to retrieve and the locations in which to store data, and to make other, similar choices about the data that you are storing for the users.

If your application needs to store its own data that doesn't need to be visible to users, you can use the file management tasks that you learn here; you simply don't have to interface with the user.

The Mac OS provides APIs that help you to manage these tasks. These are:

- The File Manager, which helps your application manage the transfer of your data to the physical storage device

- Navigation Services, which provides the interface for users to navigate through the file system and choose the destination or source of the information that they are saving or retrieving

The File Manager

The File Manager is that part of the operating system that handles the organization and transfer of data located on physical data storage devices. All of the operations that you perform to implement basic opening and saving functionality in your application are based on the most fundamental file system object: the file.

Files

A *file* is a named, ordered sequence of bytes stored on a volume. A *volume* is a portion of a physical storage device that is formatted to contain files. A volume can be the entire disk or just part of the disk. For instance, a CD is formatted as a single volume. The hard drive of your computer can be formatted to contain multiple volumes.

All computer users have encountered files. The average user is probably most familiar with documents, which are files that a user can open and edit (for example, the text of a term paper, written in an application that handles word processing, such as AppleWorks). Nonetheless, there are many other types of files. An email browser can store information about a given user's network connection and email account in a preferences file, and a computer game can store information about the state of the game for a particular session. The executable for your application is also a file.

You should know the following before you start working with files:

- How files are organized
- How to identify a file

- How to access a file

- The size of a file

The organization of the file system.   Let's take a brief look at how files are arranged into a coherent system of data storage. Although your application does not, for the most part, need the information in this section to perform its basic file management chores, it provides some background for the file handling about which you will learn in later sections.

A *file system* is a way of organizing files and the information necessary to access them. Mac OS X uses a hierarchical file system to organize files on a volume. In the hierarchical file system used by Mac OS X, files are grouped into directories. These directories are also referred to as folders. A *directory* is a named collection of files and other directories. Each directory can contain any combination of files and other directories. The directory in which a file is located is that file's *parent directory*. This holds true for directories as well; for each subdirectory, the directory within which it is located is known as the parent directory.

Each volume has a single root directory, which serves as the base of the directory hierarchy on that volume; all other directories are subdirectories of the root directory. In the example shown in Figure 11-1, the folder titled "MyVolume" is the root directory of a volume named "MyVolume".

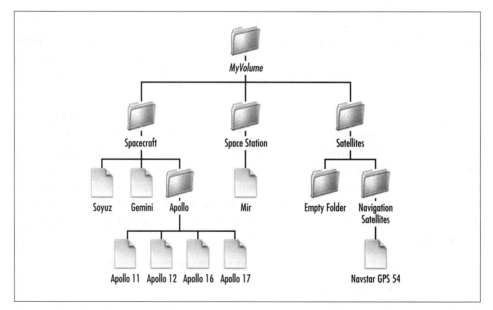

Figure 11-1. The hierarchical file system

The root directory of a volume is not the same as the volume itself. Although they may appear to be the same to the user (for instance, a user can double-click a volume in the Finder to navigate through the hierarchy on that volume), the root directory of a volume and the volume itself are represented and handled differently by the file system.

A volume appears on the desktop only after it has been mounted. For nonejectable drives, this occurs automatically at system startup. For CDs (and similar ejectable media), this occurs after the CD is inserted into the computer's CD drive. When a volume is mounted, the File Manager assigns the volume a volume reference number. You can use this volume reference number to refer to the volume only for as long as it is mounted.

There are two different ways in which the hierarchical organization of the file system is represented:

- The way in which the file system is represented to the user
- The way in which the file system is represented on the physical storage media

The Finder and the file system.   The Finder is responsible for representing the file system to the user. The Finder reflects the basic characteristics of the hierarchical file system. Volumes are represented by icons of disks, directories are represented by folder icons, and user-created files are represented by document icons. A given directory can contain any combination of directories and files; files cannot contain other files or directories. Volumes, directories, and files are identified explicitly by their names (which are displayed next to their icons) and identified implicitly by their location within the directory hierarchy. Thus, to a user and to the file system, the file named `main.c` in the folder MoonTravelPlanner is different from the file named `main.c` in the folder MyMTPProject. No two files or subdirectories within a given directory may have the same name. Figure 11-2 shows a typical Finder window in Mac OS X, representing one part of the file system hierarchy on the volume "Flower Power".

On HFS Plus and HFS volumes, the File Manager is not case-sensitive when comparing names, so, within a given directory, `main.c` and `Main.c` would both refer to the same file. On UFS volumes (available on Mac OS X), file names are case-sensitive, so `main.c` and `Main.c` would be different files. You will learn more about these volume types in the next section.

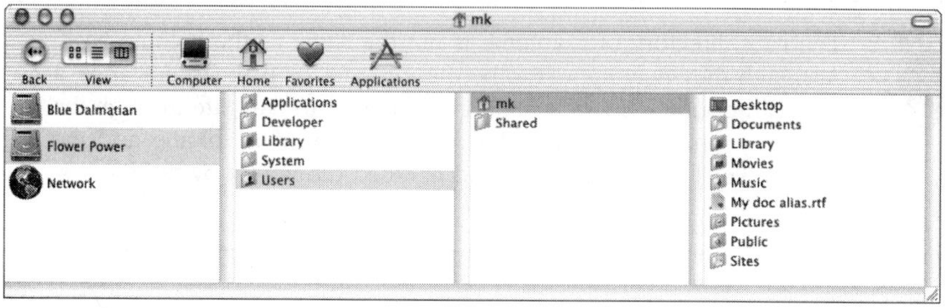

Figure 11-2. The file system, as portrayed by the Finder

The volume format.   The *volume format* is the physical representation of the file system organization on the data storage device. It defines the way that information is laid out on the volume. The default volume format used by the Mac OS is HFS Plus (HFS stands for Hierarchical File System). Mac OS X supports other volume formats, too; namely:

- Universal File System (UFS); similar to the standard volume format of most Unix operating systems

- HFS, which was the default volume format for Macintosh systems before Mac OS 8.1

- UDF (Universal Disk Format), for DVD volumes

- ISO 9660, for CD-ROM volumes

The two volume formats that you will encounter most frequently on Mac OS X are HFS Plus and UFS. The volume format not only specifies how all of the user files and folders are arranged on the volume, it also includes all of the structures needed to retrieve the data.

For the most part, unless you are writing a disk-checking utility or some other application that requires low-level access to the volume, you do not need to know the details of how the volume format represents this information; the File Manager takes care of interpreting this information and locating the appropriate structures on the volume. There are some cases, however, in which you may want to know about the particular volume format used by the system on which your application is running; for instance, that filenames on HFS Plus volumes are case-insensitive, but filenames on UFS volumes are not. If you try to create a file named `MyFile` in the same directory that contains the file `myfile` on an HFS Plus volume, the File Manager returns a duplicate filename error. The same attempt will succeed on a UFS volume, however.

If you're still curious and would like to learn more about the volume formats available on Mac OS X, see the File Manager documentation in Carbon Help (available in the Project Builder Help menu).

Identifying a file. If you want to manipulate files, you need to know how to refer to them. When your application needs to open a particular file, you have to tell the File Manager which file you are referring to, in a way that the File Manager understands. The File Manager uses the FSRef data type to represent a file; therefore, you use FSRefs to specify files to the File Manager.

An FSRef structure uniquely identifies a file. The FSRef data type is an opaque structure that contains the identity of the volume on which the file resides, as well as the information that the File Manager needs to locate the file on that volume. Because this structure is opaque, its information is private to the File Manager; you cannot access the structure directly. To create a new FSRef or to access the information contained in an FSRef, you must use File Manager functions provided for that purpose.

You can use the File Manager function FSMakeFSRefUnicode to create an FSRef structure for a file. If you are creating a new file, you can also get an FSRef directly from the function that you use to create the file, FSCreateFileUnicode. To create an FSRef structure (or to create a new file), you must know:

- The file's name. Filenames consist of any sequence of 1 to 255 characters and are represented by the HFSUniStr255 data type. By default, the File Manager uses a Unicode encoding for filenames. Files located within the same directory must have unique names. If you try to create a file in a directory that uses the same name as a file that already exists within that directory, the File Manager will return an error.

You shouldn't use non-printing characters in a filename. Non-printing characters in a filename can be very confusing when the filename is displayed to the user. The null character is illegal in filenames on Mac OS X. You've already seen that HFS Plus and HFS treat the case of names differently from UFS volumes. There may be constraints on filenames other than those imposed by the File Manager, depending upon the volume format.

- The file's location. A file's location has two parts: the volume on which the file resides, and the file's location on that volume. You specify the location of a file on a volume by specifying the directory in which it resides. The directory in which a file is located is called the file's *parent directory.* In most cases, you specify the location of a file by the FSRef of the file's parent directory.

Because the `FSRef` already contains information about the volume on which the directory (and therefore the file) resides, you do not have to specify the volume separately.

In some cases, you may not have an `FSRef` for the file's parent directory, but you may have other information that you can use to specify its location. For instance, there are a number of programming interfaces (such as AppleScript, the Keychain Manager, and QuickTime, to name a few) that still refer to files with an `FSSpec` data type.

The `FSSpec` data type is the structure that the File Manager previously used to represent files and directories, prior to Mac OS 9.0. If your application interfaces with a part of the operating system that uses `FSSpec` structures, you can create an `FSRef` from the `FSSpec` by using the function `FSpMakeFSRef`. If you need to convert your `FSRef` into an `FSSpec` to pass to another part of the operating system, you can call the File Manager function, `FSGetCatalogInfo`.

Note, however, that an `FSSpec` may refer to a file that has not yet been created, but an `FSRef` cannot. If you know the volume on which a file is located and the directory ID (a number that uniquely identifies the directory) of the file's parent directory, you can use the File Manager function `PBMakeFSRefSync` to create an `FSRef` for the file or its parent directory. For more information on these two functions, see the File Manager documentation in Carbon Help (available in the Project Builder Help menu).

The combination of a file's name and its location uniquely identifies a file. Of course, you're probably still wondering how you go about getting the name and location of the file. Most applications will do file handling while working with user files and will use Navigation Services to interface with the user for operations performed on these files. Navigation Services returns an `FSRef` for the file or directory chosen by the user. For an open operation, Navigation Services returns an `FSRef` to the file to open. For a save operation, Navigation Services returns the `FSRef` of the file's parent directory. You will learn more about Navigation Services in the section "Navigation Services."

You should note that an `FSRef` is used to refer to a file or directory only while the volume on which the file resides is mounted. To create a persistent reference to a file, which remains valid when the volume is unmounted, use the Alias Manager. For more information, see the Alias Manager documentation in Carbon Help.

File access.   To transfer information between your application and file, you need to access the file through an *access path*. When you open a file, the File Manager creates an access path to the file. This path specifies the route to be followed when accessing the file on the volume. This access path is described by a *file reference number*. The file reference number is a number greater than 0 that uniquely identifies the path that you have opened. You use this reference number to specify the path when you read data from, and write data to, the file. Multiple paths to the same file can be opened simultaneously; each path has a different file reference number.

For each open access path to a file, the File Manager also maintains certain information that you need to know about. Specifically, it maintains the file mark and the permissions. The *file mark* identifies the current position within the file. The file mark is the number of the next byte in the file that will be written or read; each time a byte is written or read, the file mark is moved. Unless you have just opened the access path (which automatically sets the file mark to the beginning of the file), you should set the position of the file mark before you begin to access data in a file, to ensure that the read or write operation begins where you actually want it to begin. For instance, before you read in a user's moon travel itinerary, you probably want to set the file mark to the beginning of the file. If you don't, the File Manager will begin reading data from the current position of the file mark, which may not be the file's beginning.

As you create more complicated applications and you begin to save different types of data in a file (for example, you may choose to allow your users to store pictures of their destination spots with their moon travel itineraries), knowing where in the file your current operation will begin is even more important. If you start from an unknown spot, you run the risk of missing the boundaries between different types of data and improperly interpreting the contents of the file.

You should also be aware of the permissions associated with an access path to a file. The permissions specify which operations you can perform on the file via that access path. There are three basic types of permission you can have: permission to read the file, permission to write to the file, and permission to read and write the file. When you open a file, you request the type of permissions that you will need to get your job done. For instance, if you are opening a file that is editable by the user, you should ask for read and write permission; you should be able to read data from the file to display it to the user and write data to the file when the user wants to save the changes that he has made. On the other hand, if you are opening a document that the user should be able to read, but not change, you can request read-only permission, to display the information to the user.

While more than one access path can read a file at one time, only one path at a time may have write access. If you try to open a file and another access path is already open to the file that has conflicting permissions, your request for access to the file will be denied. Thus, if you ask for read/write permission to a file that is already being written to via another access path, the File Manager will return an error and an invalid reference number.

File size.   Knowing how to identify and access a file is crucial to any type of file handling that you do; knowing how to express the size of a file is less critical, but still important. Although the simple file handling that you will do later in this chapter doesn't really require that you know the file's size, as your application becomes more complex and the amount of data that you wish to store grows, you will want to know how to measure a file's size.

The maximum file size has several constraints. One constraint is the size of the volume on which it is located. Another possible constraint is the size of the value used by the File Manager to specify file sizes. On Mac OS X, this is a signed 64-bit value; if it were up to the File Manager alone, you could create a file that was 2^{63} bytes, or 8 million terabytes.

 There may be additional constraints on the size of a file, depending upon the type of the volume on which the file resides. For more information, see the File Manager documentation in Carbon Help.

Not only do you need to know how large your file can be, you also need to know how to express the size of the file. The basic measure of a file's size is the number of bytes that it contains. A file actually has two different sizes. These are the logical size and the physical size. This comes about because the File Manager allocates space to a file in chunks called *allocation blocks*, which contain multiple bytes. (It wouldn't be very efficient to allocate space one byte at a time.) The size of an allocation block is variable from one volume to another and is determined at the time of the volume's initialization.

The physical size (or physical end-of-file) is the number of bytes currently allocated to the file. The logical size (or logical end-of-file) is the number of allocated bytes in the file that currently contain data. The difference between physical and logical size is illustrated in Figure 11-3. The file that is shown fills up only 509 bytes of its last allocation block, but all 1024 bytes are allocated to the file. For the most part, you will be concerned with the file's logical size; it is the file's logical size that the File Manager returns when you call the function FSGetForkSize to determine the size of a file.

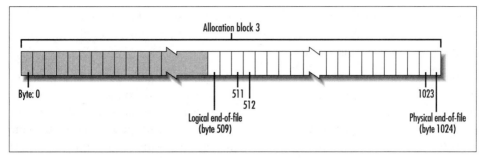

Figure 11-3. Physical and logical end-of-file

The typical tasks of file management

Although there are many, many ways in which you can manipulate files (you can make copies of them, move them, open them remotely.... there are all sorts of things you can do), most applications really need to perform only a handful of tasks. These are:

- Creating new files

- Opening files

- Reading files

- Writing files

Creating a new file. To create a new file, you use the File Manager function FSCreateFileUnicode. As you discovered in the section "Identifying a file," you need the name and location of the file that you wish to create in order to identify it to the File Manager. (Remember, since the file does not yet exist, you don't yet have an FSRef for the file). You pass the new file's name and an FSRef structure identifying the parent directory of the file (that is, identifying the folder where the file will be created) to FSCreateFileUnicode. The File Manager then creates this file on the volume, in the directory which you specified, and returns an FSRef for the new file.

For the most part, you will need to create a new file when:

- The user chooses the Save As command from the File menu to save the current document as a new file.

- The user chooses the Save command from the File menu, but the document that she wishes to save does not yet have a file associated with it on the volume.

In both cases, you should use Navigation Services to ask the user for the name that she wishes to give to the file and for the location where she wishes to save the file. Navigation Services then returns an FSRef for the directory in which to place the new file (that is, an FSRef for the file's parent directory) and the file's name, which you can use to create the file. You will learn more about Navigation Services later in this chapter.

Opening a file. Before you can access or change the data that a file contains, the file must be open. To open a file, use the File Manager function FSOpenFork. When you call FSOpenFork, you must tell the File Manager which file you wish to open, the name of the file fork that you wish to open, and the type of access that you want (that is, the permissions). The File Manager returns the file reference number that identifies the access path that it has created to the file.

A file on HFS Plus volumes, and on volumes of certain other formats, can have multiple parts, called *forks*, that store various types of information. Traditionally, Macintosh files have had two file forks: the data fork and the resource fork.

Although the File Manager (beginning with Mac OS 9.0) allows files to have any number of named forks on volumes that support them, Apple recommends that you store your data in the data fork of your file, for compatibility with file systems that may not recognize multiple file forks. In this book, all of the file handling that you perform is done on the data fork.

You do not have to explicitly create the data fork of the file; it is automatically created for you when you create a file (as is the resource fork). To get the name of the data fork, call the File Manager function FSGetDataForkName. The function returns a constant for the data fork name.

To specify the file to open, pass an FSRef structure identifying the file. If you recently created the file (for example, if the user chose the Save As command to create a copy of the file with a different name, you would generally open the newly created copy into the existing document window, so that it becomes the active file), you can use the FSRef that you obtained from FSCreateFileUnicode. If the user chooses the Open command from the File menu, you should use Navigation Services to ask the user to identify the file to open; Navigation Services returns to your application an FSRef that identifies the file chosen by the user.

The permissions that you request depend upon the file I/O operations that you wish to perform. If you need to write to the file, you should pass the constant fsRdWrPerm to the FSOpenFork function. This requests read and write privileges for the file. If another access path is already open to the file, your request for read and write permission will be denied. If reading the file is better than nothing, you can retry the request, calling FSOpenFork again with less restrictive permissions, using the constant fsRdPerm. This constant requests read access only.

Reading and writing data .   Once you have an open path to the file, you can get down to the real nitty-gritty: reading the data stored in the file on disk, and writing data to the file on disk. To read data from the file, use the File Manager function FSReadFork. To write data to the file, use the function FSWriteFork. Both functions work in a similar manner. Given a file reference number to an open file, the functions read or write the specified number of bytes into or out of a buffer that you are responsible for providing. If you are writing to a file, the buffer that you provide should contain the data that you wish to write to the file. If you are reading from the file, the File Manager places the specified number of bytes into the buffer that you provide; you are then responsible for interpreting that information. In both cases, the File Manager returns the actual number of bytes read or written. This number will match the number of bytes requested, unless an error condition was encountered. The most common error result that you will encounter while reading a file is the end-of-file error, which tells your application that there are no more bytes to be read from the file. If you are reading from the file in chunks (rather than all at once), you can use the end-of-file error to determine that you have read all of the information from the file.

You can read and write bytes to and from the file one by one, all at once, or in any amount in between. The size of the buffer that you use is up to you; however, an I/O size of 4 KB or more is recommended for local volumes. Disk accesses are time consuming; having a larger I/O size reduces the number of disk accesses that your application has to make and improves the efficiency of your file handling. When you read and write itinerary files in the section "Read the itinerary file" and the section "Write the save data," you will notice that we use a smaller I/O size. Our itineraries are small files, and the inefficiency of our file handling isn't even noticeable. As you develop more complex applications and manipulate larger files, however, the efficiency of your file handling code will become increasingly important. Your users don't want to sit around waiting for your application to open a 6 MB file that you read in increments of 256 bytes.

For improved file handling efficiency, it is also recommended that you "align" your read and write requests. This means that, whatever the size of your buffer, it should be a multiple of 4 KB and that the starting position of the read or write operation (that is, the byte number at which the operation begins) is also a multiple of 4 KB. For more information on improving the efficiency of your file accesses, see the File Manager documentation in Carbon Help.

For both `FSReadFork` and `FSWriteFork`, you can also specify the position in the file from which the operation should begin. You specify a position by providing a base location and an offset into the file from that base location. You can tell the File Manager to start counting the offset from the beginning of the file, from the logical end-of-file, or from the current position of the file mark. If you specify the constant `fsAtMark` in the `positionMode` parameter of either `FSReadFork` or `FSWrite-Fork` or if you do not specify a starting position, the operation begins at the current file mark.

When writing a file, the File Manager transfers the data from your application's buffer and writes it to the disk cache in memory. Similarly, when reading a file, the File Manager transfers data from the disk to the disk cache in memory. The File Manager uses the disk cache as an intermediate buffer when reading from and writing to a file. This is useful, for instance, when certain bits of information are going to be accessed frequently. In this case, it is more efficient for the File Manager to read this information from the disk cache than to read it off of the disk itself. The same holds true for writing data to the disk. If your application is performing numerous writes, it is more efficient for the File Manager to store the data in the disk cache until it has amassed a certain number of bytes. If you know that certain information is going to be accessed often, you can tell the File Manager to cache that data by setting the `pleaseCacheBit` bit in the permissions parameter to either of these functions. Similarly, if you know that certain information won't be accessed very frequently, you can request that the File Manager refrain from caching the data by setting the `noCacheBit` bit.

Navigation Services

If you want to provide users with the ability to save and open documents, you'll need to do more than just save and retrieve data from a physical storage device. You'll need to provide a way for the user to specify which file to open and where to save a document. Navigation Services is the part of the operating system that provides the user interface for opening and saving documents.

When a user wants to open a file or save a new file, your application will use Navigation Services to display a dialog that requests information about the location and identity of the file to open or save. When the user responds to the dialog, Navigation Services returns to your application the information that it needs to identify the file to File Manager functions. Navigation Services uses a structure called the *reply record* to return this information.

The programming model

When you use Navigation Services to create and display dialogs, there are six major steps that you need to take. You will use the same basic steps for any of the dialogs that you can create with Navigation Services. Using the Save dialog as an example, you will perform the following steps, which are illustrated in Figure 11-4:

1. Create the type of dialog that you need. In the example shown in Figure 11-4, you call the `NavGetDefaultDialogCreationOptions` function to set up the default dialog features and then call the `NavCreatePutFileDialog` function to create a Save dialog. (Navigation Services provides a different dialog creation function for each type of dialog)

2. Display the dialog by calling the `NavDialogRun` function.

3. Respond to the Navigation Services event. You handle this event with a callback function, called a navigation event handler, that you register with Navigation Services when you create the dialog. When an event occurs, Navigation Services calls your handler and passes it a constant that identities the type of event. There are several types of event that your event handler may receive, but the event that signifies that the user has responded to the dialog is the user action event (identified by the `kNavCBUserAction` constant, passed to your navigation event handler). In the example in Figure 11-4, the event is a user action event. We will take a closer look at the navigation event handler in the next section.

4. After your navigation event handler receives the user action event (signifying that the user has dismissed the dialog, by clicking one of its buttons or pressing Return to select the default button), you process the dialog session information from your callback function. You get the session information from the reply record that you obtain by calling the `NavDialogGetReply` function, and you take the action appropriate to the user's response. For example, if you obtain the `kNavUserActionSave` constant from the reply record, your application should save the appropriate file.

5. After you are finished processing the dialog session, dispose of the reply record by calling the `NavDisposeReply` function.

6. When Navigation Services calls your navigation event handler with the `kNavCBTerminate` event, indicating that it is finished with the dialog, dispose of the dialog reference by calling the function `NavDisposeDialog`.

The navigation event handler

You've seen the steps involved in creating and displaying a dialog using Navigation Services. A lot of the work is done by the navigation event handler that your application defines. Let's take a closer look at the navigation event handler.

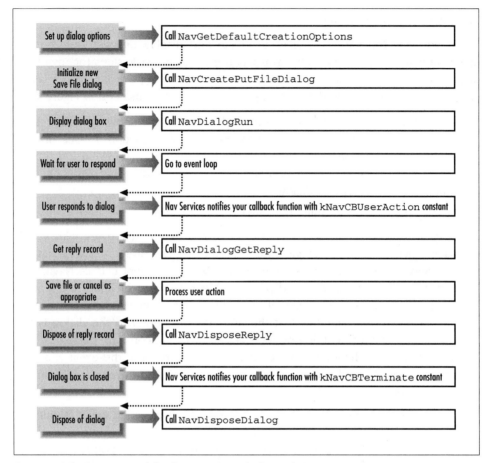

Figure 11-4. Creating and displaying a Save dialog with Navigation Services

When you create a dialog with Navigation Services, you call the NavDialogRun function to display the dialog. NavDialogRun returns after its displays the dialog. Even though the function has returned, that does not mean that the dialog has been dismissed by the user. So, how do you know when the user has, in fact, responded to the dialog? Navigation Services notifies you when the user takes an action (or when another event that you may want to know about occurs) by calling your navigation event handler. You must tell Navigation Services which event handler to use, by passing a pointer to your event handler function when you create the dialog.

The navigation event handler that you define must have the following form:

```
void NavEventProcPtr (NavEventCallbackMessage callBackSelector, NavCBRecPtr
callBackParms, void *callBackUD);
```

When Navigation Services calls your navigation event handler, it will pass your handler the following information:

- `callbackSelector`. The event that triggered the call to your navigation event handler.

- `callbackParms`. A structure of type `NavCBRec` that contains more detailed information about the particular dialog and the event. For instance, it contains the dialog reference of the dialog being displayed, information about the event in a `NavEventData` structure, information about the user action (if any), and other information that you may need to respond to the event.

- `callbackUD`. Application-specific data that you specify when you create the dialog. If there is any information not already provided by Navigation Services that your navigation event handler needs to respond to events, you can pass a pointer to this information in the function that you use when you create the dialog. Navigation Services passes this information back to you when it calls your navigation event handler.

There are various events that your navigation event handler may receive, although it is not obligated to handle all of them. For example, the `kNavCBCustomize` event notifies your application that it can prepare any custom control information that it wishes to display with the dialog. This particular event and others like it are beyond the scope of this book; instead, we will focus on the events that you have to handle to get the information necessary for opening and saving documents. For more information on the other events that your navigation event handler may handle, see the Navigation Services documentation in Carbon Help (available in the Project Builder Help menu).

There are two events that you will always want to handle. First, your navigation event handler should handle the `kNavCBUserAction` event. This event signifies to your application that the user has responded in some way to the dialog. When your event handler receives the `kNavCBUserAction` event, you can get the kind of action that the user took by calling the `NavGetUserAction` function. The value that you get back tells your application exactly what action to take. For instance, if your application had called Navigation Services to put up a Save dialog and the user response generated a `kNavUserActionSaveAs` user action, your application could go ahead and retrieve the data from the session (by calling `NavGetReply`) and then save the document.

If the user chose to cancel the operation, the user action returned would be `kNavUserActionCancel` and your application should take no further action. If you put up the dialog in response to a user request to close the window or quit the application, you should respond to `kNavUserActionCancel` by halting the close or quit operation and returning to your application's normal state. There are user actions for each of the different responses that a user may give; the particular responses that you may get from any given dialog depend upon the type of dialog.

The other event that your application should handle is the kNavCBTerminate event. Navigation Services calls your event handler with this event after the dialog has been dismissed by the user and is no longer needed. This gives your application a chance to do any cleaning up that it may need to do (such as freeing any memory that it has allocated) before disposing of the dialog itself.

Persistence

Before we look at the individual types of dialogs that you can display with Navigation Services, let's take a look at an important feature of the Navigation Services API: persistence. Persistence is the ability of Navigation Services to store information, such as the last directory location visited by the user and the size and position of dialogs. This information is maintained on a per-application basis. Navigation Services separates preferences for Open and Save dialogs so that each dialog's preferences are unique for each application. For example, the first time that your application brings up a Save dialog, the user may click the disclosure button to show the column view browser, allowing the user to navigate through the file system. (We'll see more of this browser in the section on dialogs.) This browser is not shown by default. The next time that the application brings up the Save dialog, however, Navigation Services remembers that the user has revealed the column view browser. Navigation Services displays the column view browser without the user having to click the disclosure button again.

Navigation Services can also save different sets of preferences for the same type of dialog within an application. For instance, if your application uses an Open dialog for more than one purpose—say, to open a browser to go to a given URL and to open a local HTML file—you can request that Navigation Services use different preferences for each dialog by specifying preferences keys in the dialog creation options that you pass to the dialog creation function.

Navigation Services also remembers the last document opened for a given type of dialog and makes this the default selection the next time the dialog is used. If no location has been stored for a dialog or if the directory itself is not available (if its volume is unmounted, for example), the Documents folder becomes the default location.

If a dialog's position has not been previously set, either by the user or your application, or if the dialog's position otherwise can't be shown, the dialog is displayed in the center of the main screen.

The Navigation Services dialogs

Now that we've discussed how creating and displaying dialogs with Navigation Services works, we'll take a look at the dialogs that you use to solicit information from the user for opening and saving documents.

Standard user interface elements in Navigation Services dialogs. All Open, Save, and Choose dialogs share some basic user interface elements. By default, they appear in almost any dialog that you display using Navigation Services. These elements include:

- A column view browser
- A Where pop-up menu button
- A default button
- A Cancel button
- A size box

The size box allows the user to resize the dialog. The Cancel button allows the user to cancel the operation, and the default button specifies the action that will be taken if the user presses Return. This is generally the action that is expected of the user, given the type of dialog that is being displayed. The Save button is the default for a Save dialog, for instance. The other two interface elements in the list above are more complex and require a bit more explanation.

The column view browser. The column view browser provides the primary user access to the file system from a Navigation Services dialog. An example of the browser list is shown in Figure 11-5.

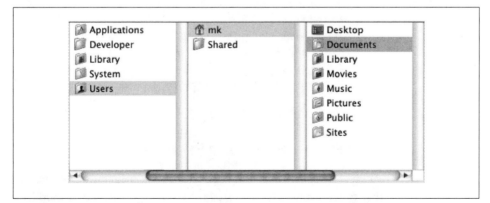

Figure 11-5. The column view browser in a Navigation Services dialog

When your application first displays a Navigation Services dialog, your application can specify a default location for opening, saving, or locating files. If you do not specify a default location, the column view browser shows the Documents folder. For each type of dialog that is opened afterwards, the browser defaults to the directory location in use when the user last closed that particular dialog.

Users can select multiple files from within an Open dialog by Shift-clicking within the column view browser or using the Select All command. For discontiguous selection, the user can Command-click within the browser.

The Where pop-up menu. The Where pop-up menu displays the current location and allows the user to navigate the file system hierarchy. The Where pop-up menu includes Favorite Places and Recent Places. This menu is shown in Figure 11-6.

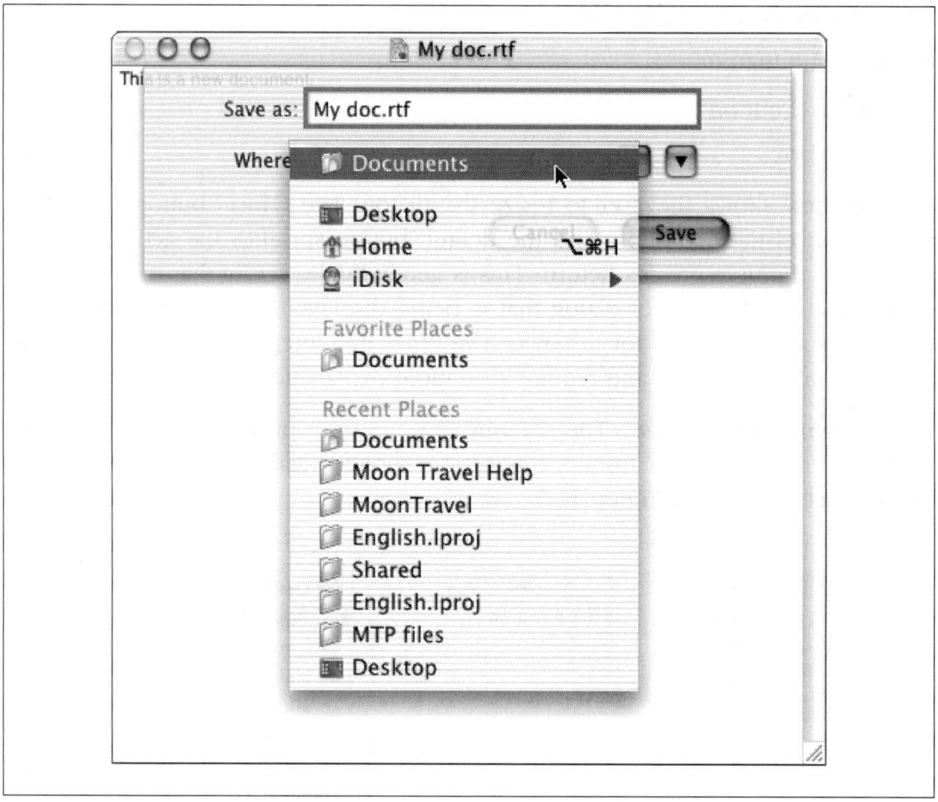

Figure 11-6. The Where pop-up menu of a Navigation Services dialog

Favorite Places includes all folders in the user's Favorites folder; Recent Places contains the last five folders into which the user saved files. Navigation Services does not display files in the Where pop-up menu.

The Add to Favorites button allows the user to add the item or items currently selected in the browser list to the Favorite Places menu. Items may be folders, volumes, or servers.

Open dialog. Your application should display an Open dialog when the user selects the Open command from the File menu or when the user types the command-key equivalent, Command-O. The Open dialog allows the user to navigate to the file or files that he wishes to open. An example of the Open dialog is shown in Figure 11-7.

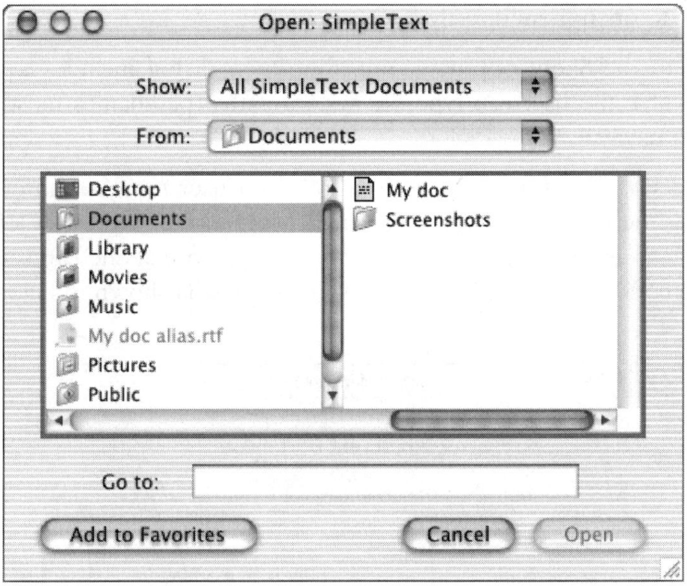

Figure 11-7. An Open dialog

In addition to the browser list, the Open dialog also includes a Show pop-up menu. The Show pop-up menu allows the user to choose the file types displayed by the column view browser. The list of available file types is built from information provided by your application when it calls the NavCreateGetFileDialog function. The Show pop-up menu is optional; you can specify that Navigation Services leave it out when you create the dialog.

The first section of the Show pop-up menu contains an item called "All Readable Documents." If the user selects this item, the browser displays all files that match the types that your application can open. You will learn how to specify the types of documents that your application can open in Chapter 13, *Desktop Icons*.

The second section of the Show pop-up menu contains an item called "All <app name> Documents" followed by your application's "native" file types. Native file types are those types you provide in the typeList parameter of the NavCreateGet-FileDialog function.

If you choose not to specify file types in the typeList parameter, you can show all files of a particular type in the browser list by using an application-defined filter function. Using a filter function would, for example, allow you to show all text files, regardless of which application created them.

The last section of the Show pop-up menu is reserved for the "All Documents" menu item. This option allows the display of all files, regardless of your application's ability to open them directly.

In addition to the Show pop-up menu, the Open dialog includes a Go to: text field, into which the user can type file system paths (pathnames must begin with "/" or "~") to navigate in the dialog.

The Open dialog also supports previews. When a user navigates through the file system using the column view browser and selects a file, a preview of the document is shown, using the actual document contents, so that she can see if she has selected the correct file. An Open dialog with preview is shown in Figure 11-8.

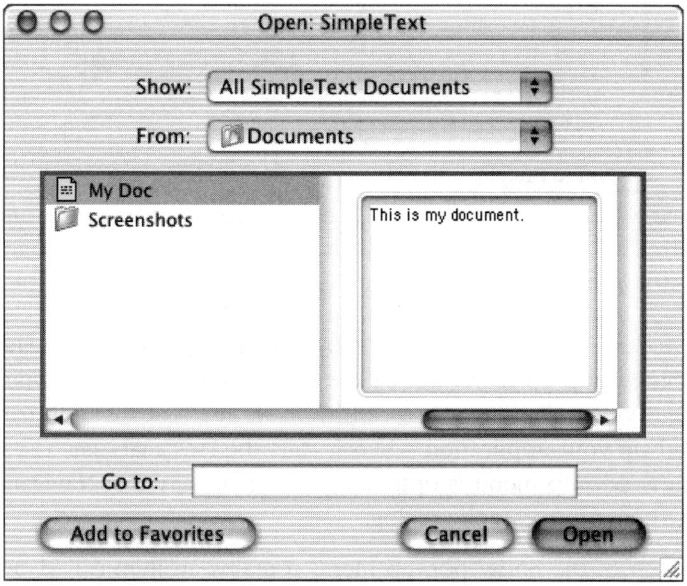

Figure 11-8. An Open dialog with preview

When the user selects a file to open and clicks the Open button (or presses Return), Navigation Services notifies your navigation event handler of the user action. Your event handler retrieves the user's selection in the reply record, just as in the example shown in Figure 11-4. Your application can use the FSRef structure returned in this reply record to call the File Manager and open the file.

If the user action shows that the user clicked the Cancel button, your application should return to its previous state.

For further guidelines on setting up an Open dialog, see *Inside Mac OS X: Aqua Human Interface Guidelines* (listed in Appendix A, *Additional Resources.*)

Save Changes. Your application should display a Save Changes dialog when a document has unsaved changes and the user closes the document window, selects the Quit command from the application menu, or types the command key equivalent of either command. The Save Changes dialog allows users to save changes or discard changes to a particular document or application. A Save Changes dialog is shown in Figure 11-9.

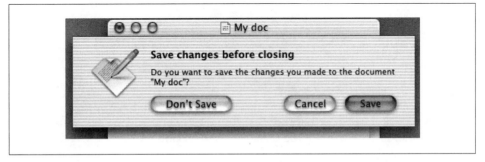

Figure 11-9. A Save Changes dialog

The default button for the Save Changes dialog is the Save button. When the user clicks this button, Navigation Services notifies your navigation event handler, and your event handler retrieves the user action. If the document has been previously saved, your application should call the File Manager to save the changes to the existing file. If the document has not been saved, your application should bring up a Save Location dialog (described in the next section), to allow the user to specify where to save the document and what name to use for the file.

The Cancel button cancels the operation; if the user action that your navigation event handler retrieves indicates that the user has clicked the Cancel button, your application should return to its previous state. If the user clicked the Don't Save button, on the other hand, your application should close the document without saving changes.

For further guidelines on setting up a Save Changes dialog, see the *Inside Mac OS X: Aqua Human Interface Guidelines.*

Save Location. When the user chooses the Save As command from the File menu, chooses the Save command for a document that has not yet been saved, or types the command key equivalent of either command, your application should bring up a Save Location dialog. The Save Location dialog allows the user to specify a name and location for a document. The Save Location dialog should also appear if the user clicks Save in a Save Changes dialog for a previously unsaved document.

The Save Location dialog has two states, collapsed and expanded. The collapsed Save Location dialog is shown in Figure 11-10.

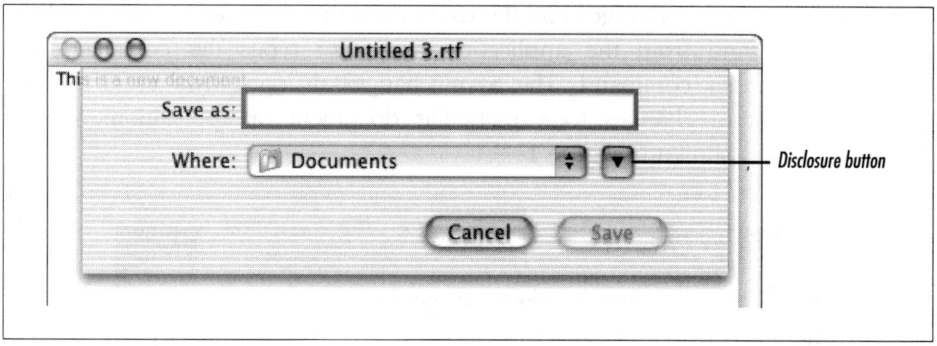

Figure 11-10. A collapsed Save Location dialog

When the dialog is collapsed, the user can enter a name and choose a frequently accessed location. The parts of the collapsed Save dialog are:

- The "Save as" text field for the document name. The user specifies the file-name for the new file in this field. This field can also act as a "Go to" field: if a user enters a pathname by typing "/" or "~" as the first character, the current location in which to save the file will become the location specified by the path when the user presses Return. The user cannot specify the name of the new file in the path; he must first clear the field and then type in the filename.

- The Where pop-up menu, which we discussed in the section "The Where pop-up menu."

- The Cancel and Save buttons. The Save button is the default.

Clicking the disclosure button in the collapsed dialog expands the dialog and displays:

- The column view browser, which we discussed in the section "The column view browser."

- The Add to Favorites button.

- The New Folder button. If the user clicks this button, Navigation Services displays a dialog that queries the user for the new folder's name.

The expanded version of the Save Location dialog is shown in Figure 11-11.

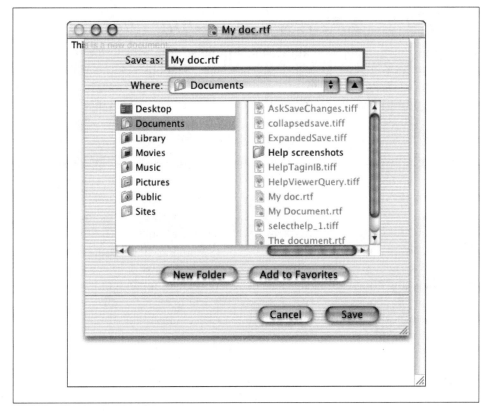

Figure 11-11. An expanded Save Location dialog

When the user clicks a button in the dialog, Navigation Services notifies your navigation event handler, which then retrieves the user action. If the user has selected a folder in which to save the file, using either the Where pop-up menu or the column view browser, and has clicked the Save button, your application should retrieve the reply record. From the reply record, your application can get the FSRef structure that specifies the folder in which to save the new file. You can then use this FSRef to create the save file, as explained in the section "Creating a new file," and save the document.

If the user action shows that the user clicked the Cancel button, your application should return to its previous state.

For further guidelines on setting up a Save Location dialog, see *Inside Mac OS X: Aqua Human Interface Guidelines*.

Moon Travel Planner: Handling Files

You've now built an application that allows users to plan trips to the moon. Planning *how* to get somewhere is helpful, but what do tourists do once they get to the moon? To make your application truly useful as a moon travel planner, you should help users plan their itineraries once they're moon-side. In this section, you will add a new window to your application: the itinerary window, which will display a traveler's vacation event schedule for the duration of a stay on the moon.

You will also save the contents of the itinerary window in a file, and retrieve the contents of existing itinerary files. If you were creating a fully featured, robust application, you would make the text of the itinerary file editable by the user; however, that would involve creating a text editor. Since we do not show you how to handle text editing in this book, we will use a read-only itinerary file. Using a read-only file, we can still implement the Open and Save As commands. Once your application can handle these commands, you will have implemented most of the file handling code that you would need in order to implement the other standard File menu commands, Save and New. We will note in the chapter the places where you would normally implement these other commands.

 To get a quick start on supporting text editing capabilities in your application, read the Multilingual Text Engine documentation in Carbon Help.

To add an itinerary to your Moon Travel application, you will:

1. Create a new itinerary window.
2. Define the constants and variables needed to create an itinerary file.
3. Write the window event handler for the itinerary window.
4. Write the functions to open an itinerary file.
5. Write the functions to save an itinerary file.
6. Write the function to close the itinerary window.
7. Add code to the main window event handler to open an itinerary.
8. Build, run, and test the application.

Create a Window to Display the Itinerary

The first step in creating itineraries that your users can actually use is creating an interface for the itinerary. Before we do anything else, we need a window in which we can display the itinerary. By now, you're an old pro at creating windows. This time, however, we'll do things a bit differently. In Chapter 8, *Text and Localization*, we created a new window by adding a window to the existing `main.nib` file. Now we'll create a new nib file and then put a window in it.

As you write more sophisticated and complex applications, you may find you need a large number of interface resources (document windows, tool palettes, message boxes, and so forth), but the resources don't need to be available all the time. For example, in an editing application, a user may sometimes need one document window, but at other times needs multiple document windows along with several tool palettes.

Although you can define all interface resources in the `main.nib` file, it's more memory efficient to create one or more auxiliary nib files. A good strategy is to limit what you put in the `main.nib` file to the menu bar and perhaps one window—the minimum number of items that must be open when your application launches. Then create auxiliary nib files for other interface resources.

A document window, such as the itinerary window, is a perfect candidate for an auxiliary nib file. You'll create a new nib file for a window that you'll use to display the contents of the itinerary file your users open:

1. Double-click the `main.nib` file in the Moon Travel Planner project to activate Interface Builder. (If you are already in Interface Builder, you don't need to do this.)

2. Choose New from the File menu.

3. Select a Carbon window from the Starting Points dialog, as shown in Figure 11-12. When you click New, an untitled nib file opens along with a new window.

4. Choose Save As from the File menu. Name the nib file `itinerary.nib`. You should save the nib file to the `English.lproj` folder.

5. Name the window object `Itinerary`, as shown in Figure 11-13. In the Instances pane of the `itinerary.nib` window, double-click the word "Window," type **Itinerary**, and press Return. This is the name by which you'll refer to the window in your code. You'll use this name to create the window from the nib file.

6. Use the Show Info window to enter **Itinerary** as the window's title. The title is the text users see in the title bar at the top of the window. With the window active, choose Show Info from the Tools menu, choose Attributes from the

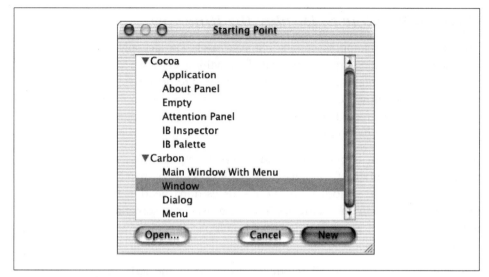

Figure 11-12. The Starting Points dialog in Interface Builder

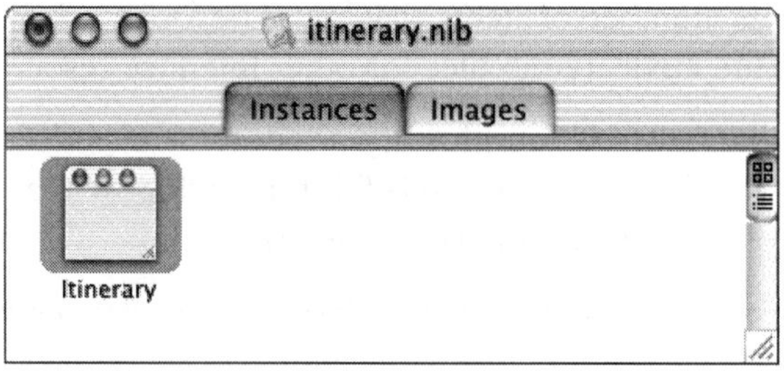

Figure 11-13. Naming the window object Itinerary

pop-up menu at the top of the Info window, type **Itinerary** in the Title text field, and press Return.

7. Choose Document from the Window Class pop-up menu.

8. Set the window's controls. In the Controls group, make sure Close Box and Collapse Box are the only checkboxes selected.

9. Set the window's attributes. In the Attributes group, make sure Standard Handler and Resizable are selected.

10. Resize the window to 500 by 600 pixels. Choose Size from the pop-up menu at the top of the Show Info window, choose Width/Height from the right Content Rect pop-up menu, and type **500** for width and **600** for height. Then press Return.

11. Choose Save from the File menu. You're done with the window. Now you need to add the `itinerary.nib` file to your project.

12. Click the Project Builder icon in the Dock to make it active.

13. Choose Add Files from the Project menu and select the `itinerary.nib` file.

14. When the dialog shown in Figure 11-14 opens, click Open, select "Copy into group's folder," and click Add.

Figure 11-14. Adding the nib file to your project

15. If necessary, in the project window, drag the `itinerary.nib` file reference to the Resources group.

Define Constants and Variables for Creating Itinerary Files

Before you begin adding the code to your Moon Travel Planner application to open and save itinerary files, you need to define the constants and global variables that you will need later. Copy the code shown in Example 11-1 to the `main.c` file, after the `kPrintInfoPtrProperty` constant that you defined in Chapter 9, *Printing*.

Example 11-1: Constants for Opening and Saving Itinerary Files

```
#define kMTPOpenItineraryCommand      'oPit'
#define kMTPSaveAsItineraryCommand    'sAit'
#define kMTPDocType                   'iTin'
#define kMTPCFStringProperty          'cfst'
```

Here's what the constants represent:

- `kMTPOpenItineraryCommand` (the Open command). In Chapter 7, *Interface Builder: Menus*, you defined the commands for opening and saving itineraries in Interface Builder. To make it easier to refer to the Open and Save commands, you should define constants for the four-character codes that represent the commands.

- `kMTPSaveAsItineraryCommand` (the Save As command). Just as with the Open command, it is easier to refer to the four-character code for the Save As command if we define a constant for it.

- `kMTPDocType`. The file type of the documents that the Moon Travel Planner application creates. You will learn more about file types and how to provide them in Chapter 13.

- `kMTPCFStringProperty`. A constant that you will use to store and retrieve information about the itinerary text, as a "property" of the itinerary window. You stored printing information in a similar manner in Chapter 9.

Finally, let's define a global variable. Paste the following line into the `main.c` file after the declaration for `MTPDocumentPrintInfoPtr`:

```
NavEventUPP gEventProc;
```

You will use this variable to hold a pointer to the navigation event handler that you will define in the section "Open an Itinerary File."

Write the Itinerary Window Event Handler

You've already created the definition for the itinerary window's appearance using Interface Builder; now you need to implement the itinerary window's behavior. For the itinerary window, we will define an event handler for the window events (events of class `kEventClassWindow`) and command events (events of class `kEventClassCommand`) that we wish to handle. Back in Chapter 7, when you created the Moon Travel Planner application's menu bar, you selected the menu commands for opening, saving, and closing an itinerary, and you assigned them four-character code constants to identify them. In this section, you will write the `MTPItineraryWindowEventHandler`, which responds to those commands.

First, let's declare the itinerary window event handler. Copy the following lines into the `main.c` file, after the declaration for the `MTPDoPrintLoop` function:

```
OSStatus MTPItineraryWindowEventHandler (EventHandlerCallRef handlerRef,
                      EventRef event, void *userData);
```

Now implement it. Copy the `MTPItineraryWindowEventHandler` function in Example 11-2 into the `main.c` file, after the body of the `MTPDoPrintLoop` function:

Example 11-2: The Event Handler for the Itinerary Window

```
OSStatus MTPItineraryWindowEventHandler (EventHandlerCallRef handlerRef,
                                          EventRef event, void *userData)
{
    OSStatus err;
    HICommandcommand;
    UInt32 eventKind;
    UInt32 eventClass;

    eventClass = GetEventClass(event);                             //1
    eventKind = GetEventKind (event);                              //2
    err = eventNotHandledErr;                                      //3
    if ((eventClass == kEventClassWindow) && (eventKind == kEventWindowClose))
        {
            SelectWindow (gMainWindow);                            //4
            err = MTPDoCloseItinerary((WindowRef)userData);        //5
        }
    else if (eventClass == kEventClassCommand)
        {
            GetEventParameter (event, kEventParamDirectObject, typeHICommand,
                   NULL, sizeof (HICommand), NULL, &command);      //6
            switch (command.commandID)
            {
            case kMTPOpenItineraryCommand:
                err = MTPDoOpenItinerary((WindowRef)userData);     //7
                break;
            case kMTPSaveAsItineraryCommand:
                err = MTPDoSaveItineraryAs((WindowRef)userData);   //8
                break;
            case kMTPCloseCommand:
                SelectWindow (gMainWindow);
                err = MTPDoCloseItinerary((WindowRef)userData);    //9
                break;
            }
        }
    return err;
}
```

Here is what the itinerary window command event handler does:

1. The Carbon Event Manager function `GetEventClass` returns the class of the
   event that triggered the call to the itinerary window event handler.

2. The Carbon Event Manager function `GetEventKind` returns the particular type
   of event that triggered the call to the itinerary window event handler.

3. The event handler initializes the error message to `eventNotHandledErr`. If the
   handler does not handle the event that was passed to it, the Carbon Event
   Manager will handle the event if it can.

4. If the event was a window close event—that is, if the user clicked the
   itinerary window's close button—the Window Manager function `SelectWindow`
   makes the Moon Travel Planner main window the active window.

5. If the event was a window close event, the `MTPDoCloseItinerary` function, which you will write in the section "Close the Itinerary," closes the itinerary window.

6. If the event was a command event, the Carbon Event Manager function `GetEventParameter` retrieves the command that triggered the call to the handler.

7. If the command was the Open command, the handler calls the function `MTPDoOpenItinerary` to open an itinerary from an existing file. You will write the `MTPDoOpenItinerary` function in the section "Open an Itinerary File." The `MTPDoOpenItinerary` function, along with the other Moon Travel Planner functions called by the event handler, takes a window reference (`WindowRef`) as its argument. When you install the window event handler in the section "Create a new itinerary window," you will specify a pointer to the itinerary window as an argument to the `InstallWindowEventHandler` function. The Carbon Event Manager passes this reference back to the event handler in the `userData` parameter when it calls the handler.

8. If the command was the Save As command, the handler calls the function `MTPDoSaveItineraryAs`, which displays a Save dialog that allows the user to specify a new name and location for the file, and then saves the file. You will write this function in the section "Save the Itinerary."

9. If the command was the Close command, the handler makes the same function calls as it did for the window close event in steps 4 and 5. It first makes the Moon Travel Planner main window the active window by calling `SelectWindow`, and then calls the `MTPDoCloseItinerary` function to close the window.

Open an Itinerary File

When a user selects the Open command from the File menu in the Moon Travel Planner application, the application needs to provide an interface for the user to select the file to open and then to open the itinerary file chosen by the user. To open a previously created itinerary file, you need to do six things:

1. Configure and display an Open dialog that lets the user locate the file to open.

2. Respond to the user's action.

3. Retrieve the file to open.

4. Create a new itinerary window in which to display the contents of the file.

5. Read the data in from the itinerary file.

6. Display the contents of the itinerary file in the itinerary window.

Configure and display an Open dialog

The first step in opening the itinerary file is to create and display a dialog that allows the user to choose the itinerary file to open. In the section "Write the Itinerary Window Event Handler," you wrote your itinerary window event handler to respond to the Open Itinerary command by calling the MTPDoOpenItinerary function. Now, you will implement that function.

First, let's declare the function. Copy the following lines into the main.c file, after the declaration for the MTPItineraryWindowEventHandler function:

```
OSStatus MTPDoOpenItinerary();
```

Now implement the function. Copy the MTPDoOpenItinerary function in Example 11-3 into the main.c file.

Example 11-3: A Function that Creates and Displays an Open Dialog

```
OSStatus MTPDoOpenItinerary()
{
    OSStatus err = noErr;
    NavDialogRef theOpenDialog;
    NavDialogCreationOptions dialogOptions;
    if (( err = NavGetDefaultDialogCreationOptions(
                      &dialogOptions)) == noErr ) {          //1
    dialogOptions.modality = kWindowModalityAppModal;        //2
    gEventProc = NewNavEventUPP( MTPNavEventCallback );      //3
    if ((err = NavCreateGetFileDialog( &dialogOptions, NULL,
            gEventProc, NULL,
            NULL, NULL, &theOpenDialog )) == noErr) {        //4
        if ( theOpenDialog != NULL ) {
            if (( err = NavDialogRun( theOpenDialog )) != noErr) {  //5
                NavDialogDispose( theOpenDialog );           //6
                DisposeNavEventUPP( gEventProc );
            }
        }
    }
    }
    return err;
}
```

Here's what the MTPDoOpenItinerary function does:

1. The Navigation Services function NavGetDefaultDialogCreationOptions fills out a NavDialogCreationOptions structure with default values for configuring the Open dialog. The dialog options structure tells Navigation Services how to set up such features as the size, location, and modality of the Open dialog.

2. The function specifies that the dialog should be application modal by setting the `modality` field of the `NavDialogCreationOptions` structure to `kWindowModal-ityAppModal`. An application modal dialog takes over the application until the user responds to the dialog. For more information on modality, see *Inside Mac OS X: Aqua Human Interface Guidelines.*

3. The Navigation Services function `NewNavEventUPP` creates a pointer to the Moon Travel Planner navigation event handler, `MTPNavEventCallback`. When the user dismisses the Open dialog, Navigation Services calls the navigation event handler with information about the event that triggered the call. You will write the navigation event handler in the section "Respond to the user's action."

4. The Navigation Services function `NavCreateGetFileDialog` creates the Open dialog, with the characteristics specified by the `NavDialogCreationOptions` structure. Passing the pointer to the navigation event handler in the third parameter tells Navigation Services which callback function to call when the user takes an action.

5. The Navigation Services function `NavDialogRun` displays the Open dialog to the user. If there is no error in displaying the dialog, the navigation event handler performs the next step in opening the itinerary file.

6. If there was an error displaying the Open dialog, the Navigation Services function `NavDialogDispose` disposes of the dialog reference, and the Navigation Services function `DisposeNavEventUPP` disposes of the pointer to the navigation event callback.

Respond to the user's action

In the previous section, you implemented the `MTPDoOpenItinerary` function, which creates the dialog that allows the user to select which file to open. When displaying a dialog using Navigation Services, the `NavDialogRun` function may return before the user has responded to the dialog. How, then, do you know when the user has taken an action? Furthermore, how do you know what that action is, once it has been taken? The answer: through a navigation event handler.

As we discussed in the section "The programming model," Navigation Services calls your navigation event handler when a navigation event occurs. For the most part, the type of event that you will be interested in is a user action event, although there are other types of events that you can choose to handle. However, the Moon Travel Planner application only has to handle the user action event. When you receive the user action event, you can retrieve the user's response to the dialog and perform whatever operations are appropriate for the user's action.

In this section, you'll write the MTPNavEventCallback function and handle the user action for opening a file. When you created the Open dialog, you specified the navigation event handler, MTPNavEventCallback. When the user responds to the Open dialog, by clicking either the Cancel or Open button, Navigation Services calls MTPNavEventCallback with information about the user's response. You can then proceed with opening the file, if the user has indeed selected a file to open.

First, let's declare the navigation event handler. Copy the following lines into the main.c file, after the declaration for the MTPDoOpenItinerary function:

```
pascal void MTPNavEventCallback(
NavEventCallbackMessage callBackSelector,
NavCBRecPtr callBackParms, void* callBackUD);
```

To implement the MTPNavEventCallback function, copy the MTPNavEventCallback function in Example 11-4 into the main.c file.

Example 11-4: The Navigation Event Handler

```
pascal void MTPNavEventCallback( NavEventCallbackMessage callBackSelector,
                                 NavCBRecPtr callBackParms, void* callBackUD)
{
    OSStatus err = noErr;
    switch (callBackSelector) {
        case kNavCBUserAction: {                                    //1
            NavReplyRecord reply;
            NavUserAction userAction = 0;
            if ((err = NavDialogGetReply (callBackParms->context,
                                    &reply )) == noErr ) {          //2
                userAction = NavDialogGetUserAction (
                                callBackParms->context);            //3
                switch (userAction) {
                    case kNavUserActionOpen: {
                        MTPOpenTheFile (&reply);                    //4
                        break;
                    }
                }
                err = NavDisposeReply (&reply);                     //5
            }
            break;
        }
        case kNavCBTerminate: {                                     //6
            NavDialogDispose (callBackParms->context);             //7
            DisposeNavEventUPP (gEventProc);                        //8
            break;
        }
    }
}
```

The callback selector passed as an argument to your navigation event handler tells it what type of event triggered the call. Here's what the navigation event handler does:

1. The function tests for a user action event. If the event was a user action, you should handle this event, because information about the user's response to the dialog is described by this type of event.

2. The Navigation Services function NavGetDialogReply retrieves information about the user's response in the form of a NavReplyRecord structure. If the dialog is an Open dialog, the reply record should hold the information necessary to identify the file to open. If it was a Save dialog, the reply record would contain the information necessary to identify the location where the file should be saved and the name that the file should be given.

3. The Navigation Services function NavDialogGetUserAction determines exactly what type of action the user took. The user action that you should respond to is the action represented by the kNavUserActionOpen constant. If this is the action returned by Navigation Services, then you can go ahead and open the file.

4. If the user chose a file to open (that is, if the last step returned the kNavUser-ActionOpen constant), then the callback function calls the MTPOpenTheFile function to finish opening the file.

5. The Navigation Services function NavDisposeReply disposes of the reply record after the function MTPOpenTheFile has exited.

6. If the event that triggered the call to the callback function was kNavCBTerminate, then the dialog has been terminated, and the callback should tidy up.

7. The function NavDisposeDialog disposes of the open dialog.

8. The function DisposeNavEventUPP releases the memory associated with the pointer to the navigation event callback function.

Retrieve the file to open

In the last section, you wrote the navigation event handler, which retrieves the user's reply from Navigation Services. If the user has indeed selected a file to open, the handler calls the MTPOpenTheFile function to finish opening the itinerary file. In this section, you will implement the MTPOpenTheFile function.

Declare the MTPOpenTheFile function. Copy the following lines into the main.c file, after the declaration for the MTPNavEventCallback function:

```
void  MTPOpenTheFile(NavReplyRecord *reply);
```

Now implement the function. Copy the MTPOpenTheFile function in Example 11-5 into the main.c file.

Example 11-5: A Function that Retrieves the File to Open

```
void MTPOpenTheFile(NavReplyRecord *reply)
{
    AEDesc actualDesc;
    FSRef fileToOpen;
    HFSUniStr255 theFileName;
    CFStringRef fileNameCFString;
    WindowRef newWindow;
    OSStatus err;

    if ((err = AECoerceDesc(&reply->selection,
                typeFSRef, &actualDesc)) == noErr)              //1
    {
        if (&actualDesc != NULL) {
        if ((err = AEGetDescData (&actualDesc,
                (void *)(&fileToOpen),
                sizeof(FSRef)) == noErr))                       //2
        {
            err = FSGetCatalogInfo ( &fileToOpen, kFSCatInfoNone,
                    NULL, &theFileName,
                    NULL, NULL );                               //3
            fileNameCFString = CFStringCreateWithCharacters (NULL,
                    theFileName.unicode,
                    theFileName.length );                       //4
            newWindow = MTPDoNewItinerary( fileNameCFString);   //5
            ShowWindow(newWindow);                              //6
            err = MTPReadFile(&fileToOpen, newWindow);          //7
        }
        }
        AEDisposeDesc(&actualDesc);                             //8
    }
}
```

Here's what the `MTPOpenTheFile` function does:

1. The Apple Event Manager function `AECoersceDesc` coerces the data returned by Navigation Services in the `NavReplyRecord` structure to validate that it is indeed an `FSRef`.

2. If the coercion succeeds, the Apple Event Manager function `AEGetDescData` retrieves the `FSRef` identifying the file to open.

3. The File Manager function `FSGetCatalogInfo` returns the name of the file. You will use the filename to set the title of the itinerary window. The `FSCatalogInfo` call can return much more information about the file, such as its creation date, size, permissions, and so forth. However, all you need for the Moon Travel Planner is the name, so you specify `kFSCatInfoNone` to indicate that you do not wish to retrieve any additional information.

4. The Core Foundation String Services function `CFStringCreateWithCharacters` converts the Unicode filename returned by the File Manager into a `CFString` representation. The File Manager uses the `HFSUniStr255` data type to store

Unicode filenames; the function that you will use in the next section to set the window title expects a `CFStringRef` data type.

5. The `MTPDoNewItinerary` function creates a window in which to display the itinerary and returns that window. You will write the `MTPDoNewItineray` function in the next section.

6. The Window Manager function `ShowWindow` shows the itinerary window, which is created to be initially hidden.

7. The `MTPReadFile` function reads in the itinerary data from the file. You will write the `MTPReadFile` function in the section "Read the itinerary file."

8. The Apple Event Manager function `AEDisposeDesc` disposes of the Apple Event descriptor that you used to retrieve the `FSRef` for the file to open.

Create a new itinerary window

The last function that you wrote, `MTPOpenTheFile`, gets all of the information that you need in order to identify the file to open. You're still not ready to read the itinerary data from the file, however. Before you can do that, you need to create the itinerary window in which you will display the information that you read from the itinerary file. It might seem as if you've already done just that. However, in the section "Create a Window to Display the Itinerary," you defined only the appearance and characteristics of the itinerary window. In this section, you'll create an actual instance of an itinerary window to hold the itinerary text. The `MTP-DoNewItinerary` function creates and initializes a new itinerary window.

First, declare the `MTPDoNewItinerary` function. Copy the following lines into the `main.c` file, after the declaration for the `MTPOpenTheFile` function:

```
WindowRef MTPDoNewItinerary(CFStringRef inName);
```

Now implement the function. Copy the `MTPDoNewItinerary` function in Example 11-6 into the `main.c` file.

Example 11-6: A function that creates a new itinerary window

```
WindowRef MTPDoNewItinerary(CFStringRef inName)
{
    IBNibRef itineraryNib;
    EventTypeSpec itinerarySpec[2] = {
            {kEventClassCommand,kEventCommandProcess},
            {kEventClassWindow, kEventWindowClose}};           //1

    OSStatus err;
    WindowRef theWindow;

    err = CreateNibReference(CFSTR("itinerary"), &itineraryNib);     //2
    require_noerr( err, CantGetNibRef );
    err = CreateWindowFromNib(itineraryNib,
```

Example 11-6: A function that creates a new itinerary window (continued)

```
                CFSTR("Itinerary"), &theWindow);                    //3
    require_noerr( err, CantCreateWindow );
    DisposeNibReference(itineraryNib);                              //4
    err = InstallWindowEventHandler (theWindow,
            NewEventHandlerUPP (MTPItineraryWindowEventHandler),
            2,
            itinerarySpec,
            (void *) theWindow, NULL);                              //5
    err =  SetWindowTitleWithCFString ( theWindow, inName);         //6
    return theWindow;                                               //7

    CantCreateWindow:
    CantGetNibRef:
        return NULL;
}
```

Here's what the MTPDoNewItinerary function does:

1. MTPDoNewItinerary initializes an event specification, identifying the events that the itinerary window handles. You use this specification to register the itinerary's window event handler in step 5. The itinerary window handles two types of events: command events and window close events.

2. The function CreateNibReference finds and opens the itinerary.nib file that you created in the section "Create a Window to Display the Itinerary."

3. The function CreateWindowFromNib creates the itinerary window, using the definition in the itinerary.nib file.

4. The function DisposeNibReference disposes of the nib reference, which we no longer need now that the window has been created.

5. The Carbon Event Manager function InstallWindowEventHandler registers the itinerary event handler that you wrote in the section "Write the Itinerary Window Event Handler." You pass a reference to the newly created itinerary window to the InstallWindowEventHandler function. When the Carbon Event Manager calls MTPItineraryWindowEventHandler, the Carbon Event Manager passes the reference to the itinerary window back to your application.

6. The Window Manager function SetWindowTitleWithCFString sets the title of the itinerary window to the name of the file, which is passed as an argument in the inName parameter.

7. The MTPDoNewItinerary function returns a reference to the new window that it creates.

Read the itinerary file

Finally, now that you have an itinerary window in which to display the itinerary text, you are ready to read the data from the itinerary file on disk. The MTPRead-File function opens the itinerary file and reads data from the itinerary's data fork.

First, declare the MTPReadFile function. Copy the following lines into the main.c file, after the declaration for the MTPDoNewItinerary function:

```
OSStatus MTPReadFile(FSRef *inFSRef, WindowRef theWindow);
```

Now implement the function. Copy the MTPReadFile function in Example 11-7 into the main.c file.

Example 11-7: A Function that Reads Data from an Itinerary File

```
OSStatus MTPReadFile(FSRef *inFSRef, WindowRef theWindow)
{
    ByteCount count, actualCount;
    SInt16 forkRefNum=0;
    UniChar buffer[256];
    OSStatus err = noErr;
    CFMutableStringRef theText;
    HFSUniStr255 forkName;

    theText = CFStringCreateMutable (NULL, 0);                       //1
    err = FSGetDataForkName (&forkName);                             //2
    err = FSOpenFork (inFSRef, forkName.length,
                    forkName.unicode, fsRdPerm,  &forkRefNum);       //3
    if (err == noErr) {
        do {
            count = 256 * sizeof(UniChar);                          //4
            err = FSReadFork (forkRefNum, fsAtMark,
                            0, count, &buffer, &actualCount);       //5
            actualCount/= sizeof (UniChar);                         //6
            CFStringAppendCharacters (theText, buffer, actualCount);//7
        } while (err == noErr);
        if (err == eofErr) {                                        //8
            err = noErr;
            MTPDisplayFile (theText, theWindow);                    //9
            err = SetWindowProperty (theWindow,
                        kMTPApplicationSignature,
                        kMTPCFStringProperty,
                        sizeof (CFStringRef),
                        (void *)&theText);                          //10
        }
        err = FSCloseFork(forkRefNum);                              //11
    }
    return err;
}
```

Here's what the MTPReadFile function does:

1. The Core Foundation String Services function CFStringCreateMutable creates a new, changeable, CFString object. You will use this CFString object to hold the text that you read from the itinerary file.

2. The File Manager function FSGetDataForkName returns the name of the data fork of the file where the itinerary text is stored.

3. The File Manager function FSOpenFork opens the data fork of the itinerary file. We request read permission by specifying the fsRdPerm constant. The FSOpenFork function returns a fork reference number that identifies the access path to the itinerary file that the File Manager has created. You will use this fork reference number to read the file.

4. At the beginning of the do loop, the MTPReadFile function initializes the count variable to the size of 256 Unicode characters, the size of the buffer that it has allocated to receive the data read in by the File Manager.

5. While data still remains to be read from the file, the File Manager function FSReadFork reads data from the file into the buffer that you have provided. Specifying fsAtMark to the FSReadFork function indicates that the read operation should begin at the current position of the file mark. Since the file mark gets moved with each read we make, on the next call to FSReadFork, we pick up right where we left off. When you opened the file with the FSOpenFork function, the File Manager automatically set the file mark to the start of the file. Therefore, when you read the file, you automatically start reading at the beginning. If you were accessing the file via an access path that had not just been opened or if you wished to start reading from elsewhere in the file, you would call the File Manager function FSSetForkPosition to ensure that you began reading the file from the intended position.

6. The MTPReadFile function divides the number of total bytes read by the size of a Unicode character to get the number of Unicode characters in the buffer.

7. The Core Foundation String Services function CFStringAppendCharacters appends the text that the File Manager read from the file to the CFString object.

Normally, you would not read in the data from the file and store it in a string. Instead, you would typically associate it with some sort of document record that contains the information that your application needs to create, track, and manipulate a document in your application. In this particular case, the itinerary document would be a text editing document, using Multilingual Text Engine (MLTE), to handle text editing. You would then associate the file and the file data with the "text object" that represents a simple MLTE document. However, text editing is beyond the scope of this tutorial, and we use the CFString object simply to allow us to illustrate the tasks of saving data to a file and retrieving data from a file.

8. The MTPReadFile function tests for the end-of-file error. When the FSReadFork function returns an end-of-file error (represented by the eofErr constant), all of the data has been read from the file and the loop terminates. If the loop terminates because of another error, the MTPReadFile function exits.

9. The MTPDisplayFile function displays the text that you've read in from the file in the itinerary window. You will write MTPDisplayFile in the next section, the section "Display the itinerary text."

10. The Window Manager function SetWindowProperty associates the CFString holding the itinerary text with the itinerary window.

11. The File Manager function FSCloseFork closes the data fork of the itinerary file.

Display the itinerary text

Your last task in opening a file is to display the contents of the file that you've just read. To do this, you will write the MTPDisplayFile function.

First, declare the MTPDisplayFile function. Copy the following line into the main.c file, after the declaration for the MTPReadFile function:

```
void MTPDisplayFile(CFStringRef stringToDisplay, WindowRef inWindow);
```

Now implement the function. Copy the MTPDisplayFile function in Example 11-8 into the main.c file.

Example 11-8: A Function that Displays the Contents of an Itinerary File

```
void MTPDisplayFile (CFStringRef stringToDisplay,
                     WindowRef inWindow)
{
  Rect bounds;
  GrafPtr oldPort;
```

Example 11-8: A Function that Displays the Contents of an Itinerary File (continued)

```
GetPort (&oldPort);                                                       //1
SetPortWindowPort (inWindow);                                             //2
EraseRect (GetWindowPortBounds (inWindow, &bounds));                      //3
TXNDrawCFStringTextBox (stringToDisplay, &bounds, NULL, NULL);            //4
SetPort (oldPort);                                                        //5
}
```

Here's what the `MTPDisplayFile` function does:

1. The QuickDraw function `GetPort` gets the current graphics port; you will use this later on to restore the graphics port.

2. The Window Manager function `SetPortWindowPort` sets the graphics port to the itinerary window's port.

3. The QuickDraw function `EraseRect` makes sure that the area bounded by the window is empty. The Window Manager function `GetWindowPortBounds` returns the boundaries of the itinerary window, which the `EraseRect` function uses as the bounds of the area that it erases.

4. The Multilingual Text Engine (MLTE) function `TXNDrawCFStringTextBox` draws the contents of the `CFString` in which we've stored the itinerary text into the window. This is static text. Note that if you were displaying the contents of a real user file, you should allow the user to view and change the document, so you would have to display the text differently. For editable text documents, MLTE does most of the work of displaying the text onscreen for you. For more information, see the Multilingual Text Engine documentation in Carbon Help.

5. The QuickDraw function `SetPort` restores the current graphics port to its original state.

Save the Itinerary

A user who creates an itinerary for the moon trip may wish to save it as a text file. When the user invokes the Save or Save As command, either by selecting them in the File menu or by using the `Command-S` keyboard shortcut, your application needs to save the contents of the itinerary to disk. In this section, we will implement the Save As command, to save a new file. To save a new file you must:

1. Configure and display a Save dialog that lets the user specify the name and location for the file to save.

2. Respond to the user's action.

3. Create the Save file to hold the itinerary text.

4. Write the itinerary contents to the file.

Once you've implemented the Save As command for new files, implementing the Save command is relatively simple. When a user selects the Save command from the File menu, or types **Command-S**, your application should check to see if a file exists for the current document. If not, it's the same as a Save As operation, and you should create a new file. If a file already exists on disk for the document, you can skip right to step 4 in the list above, writing the data to disk. Because we are not implementing an editable itinerary window in this tutorial, there is little point in implementing the Save command (there would be no changes to save!). However, as described here, once you've implemented the Save As command, adding in the handler for the Save command is not difficult.

Configure and display a Save dialog

When the user selects the Save As command or when the user tries to save an itinerary for which a file does not yet exist, you must provide an interface to the user that allows her to choose the location at which to store the file and the name that she wishes to give to the new file. Only then can you proceed with the save operation. In this section, you will write the code to display a Save dialog.

First, declare the MTPDoSaveItineraryAs function. Copy the following lines into the main.c file, after the declaration for the MTPDisplayFile function:

```
OSStatus MTPDoSaveItineraryAs(WindowRef theItineraryWindow);
```

Now implement the function. Copy the MTPDoSaveItineraryAs function in Example 11-9 into the main.c file.

Example 11-9: A Function that Creates and Displays a Save Dialog

```
OSStatus MTPDoSaveItineraryAs (WindowRef theItineraryWindow)
{
    OSStatus err = noErr;
    NavDialogRef theSaveDialog;
    NavDialogCreationOptions dialogOptions;
    if (( err = NavGetDefaultDialogCreationOptions
                    (&dialogOptions )) == noErr ) {               //1
            err = CopyWindowTitleAsCFString( theItineraryWindow,
                    &dialogOptions.saveFileName );               //2
            dialogOptions.parentWindow = theItineraryWindow;     //3
            dialogOptions.modality = kWindowModalityWindowModal; //4
            gEventProc = NewNavEventUPP( MTPNavEventCallback );  //5
            if ((err = NavCreatePutFileDialog(&dialogOptions,
                        kMTPDocType,
                        kMTPApplicationSignature,
                        gEventProc,
                        (void *)(theItineraryWindow),
                        &theSaveDialog)) == noErr) {             //6
                if ( theSaveDialog != NULL ) {
```

Example 11-9: A Function that Creates and Displays a Save Dialog (continued)

```
                  if (( err = NavDialogRun
                        (theSaveDialog)) != noErr) {          //7
                        NavDialogDispose( theSaveDialog );     //8
                        DisposeNavEventUPP( gEventProc );      //9
                        }
                }
            }
        if ( dialogOptions.saveFileName != NULL )
                CFRelease( dialogOptions.saveFileName );       //10
    }
    return err;
}
```

Here's what the MTPDoSaveItineraryAs function does:

1. The Navigation Services function NavGetDefaultDialogCreationOptions fills out a NavDialogCreationOptions structure with standard default values. The dialog options structure tells Navigation Services how to set up such features as the size, location, and modality of the Save dialog.

2. The function CopyWindowTitleAsCFString retrieves the itinerary window's title and assigns it to be the default filename that appears in the Save dialog.

3. The MTPDoSaveItineraryAs function sets the itinerary window as the parent window of the Save dialog; this makes the dialog a sheet belonging to the itinerary window. In the Aqua user interface, *sheets* are dialogs that belong to a particular window and appear to emerge from that window to emphasize the connection between the dialog and the parent window. Save dialogs should be sheets. The Save dialog is only relevant to the window that received the Save command, and the direct correlation between the window to be saved and the Save dialog is made clear by the visual presentation of the dialog.

4. The MTPDoSaveItineraryAs function sets the modality of the dialog creation options to kWindowModalityWindowModal to make the dialog a sheet. A sheet is a window modal dialog, meaning it prevents all further action upon the window until the user addresses the dialog. The sheet does not, however, interfere with other documents within the same application. Window modal is not the default value in the dialog creation options structure, so you must specify the modality before creating the dialog.

5. The Navigation Services function NewNavEventUPP allocates a pointer to the navigation event handler that you wrote in the section "Respond to the user's action." In the next section, you will add code to this handler to handle saving. This navigation event handler is called by Navigation Services when the user responds to the Save dialog.

6. The Navigation Services function `NavCreatePutFileDialog` creates the Save dialog. Passing the pointer to the navigation event handler tells Navigation Services to call this function when the user responds to the dialog. When calling `NavCreatePutFileDialog`, pass a pointer to the itinerary window in the `callBackUD` parameter. When the dialog is dismissed, Navigation Services passes this window reference back to your navigation event handler, so that you may use it in further calls.

7. The Navigation Services function `NavDialogRun` displays the Save dialog.

8. If there was an error displaying the dialog, the `NavDisposeDialog` function disposes of the Save dialog.

9. Also in case of an error displaying the dialog, the `DisposeNavEventUPP` function disposes of the pointer to the save event callback function.

10. When the `NavDialogRun` function returns, the `MTPDoSaveItineraryAs` function checks for a valid `CFString` in the `saveFileName` field of the dialog creation options structure and, if it is valid, releases the `CFString`.

Respond to the user's action

In the previous section, you created and displayed a Save dialog to allow the user to specify the name and location of the new file. Just as in the section "Open an Itinerary File," you do not know when the user has responded to the dialog, or what that response is, until Navigation Services calls your navigation event handler. In this section, you will add a few lines of code to the event handler that you wrote in the section "Open an Itinerary File," so that the navigation event handler responds to save as well as open events.

Modify the second switch statement in the `MTPNavEventCallback` function so it now looks like the code shown in Example 11-10.

Example 11-10: Navigation Event Handler Switch Statement After Adding "Save As" Code

```
switch (userAction) {
    case kNavUserActionOpen: {
        MTPOpenTheFile (&reply);
        break;
    }
    case kNavUserActionSaveAs: {
        err = MTPDoFSRefSave ((WindowRef)(callBackUD), &reply );
        break;
    }
}
```

The navigation event handler works exactly as it did before, except now it handles saving in addition to opening. The new lines of code state that if the user action that triggers the call to the navigation event handler is a Save As action, the navigation event handler calls the Moon Travel Planner function `MTPDoFSRefSave` to save the file. You will write the MTPDoFSRefSave function in the next section.

Create the save file

You have now created and displayed a dialog for the save operation and retrieved the user response. Your navigation event handler, which you created in the section "Respond to the user's action," called the function MTPDoFSRefSave to continue the save operation. The MTPDoFSRefSave function creates the new file from the information that your navigation event handler retrieved from Navigation Services and then prepares the file for saving.

 Normally, if you are implementing the Save As command, you would open the newly created file and display it in the user's current document window. To keep things simple in this book, we've chosen to omit that part.

First, declare the MTPDoFSRefSave function. Copy the following line into the main.c file, after the declaration for the MTPDoSaveItineraryAs function:

```
OSErr MTPDoFSRefSave (WindowRef  theItineraryWindow, NavReplyRecord* reply );
```

Now implement the function. Copy the MTPDoFSRefSave function in Example 11-11 into the main.c file.

Example 11-11: A Function that Creates a Save File

```
OSErr MTPDoFSRefSave (WindowRef theItineraryWindow, NavReplyRecord* reply )
{
    OSErr   err = noErr;
    FSRef   fileRefParent;
    AEDesc  actualDesc;

    if ((err = AECoerceDesc (&reply->selection,
                typeFSRef, &actualDesc )) == noErr) {          //1
        if ((err = AEGetDescData( &actualDesc, (void *)&fileRefParent,
                    sizeof( FSRef ) )) == noErr ) {            //2
            UniChar* nameBuffer = NULL;
            UniCharCount sourceLength = 0;
            sourceLength = (UniCharCount) CFStringGetLength(
                    reply->saveFileName );                     //3
            nameBuffer = (UniChar*)NewPtr (sourceLength *2);   //4
            CFStringGetCharacters ( reply->saveFileName,
                    CFRangeMake( 0, sourceLength),
                    &nameBuffer[0] );                          //5
            if (nameBuffer != NULL) {
                if ( reply->replacing ) {
                    FSRef fileToDelete;
                    if ((err = FSMakeFSRefUnicode (&fileRefParent,
```

Example 11-11: A Function that Creates a Save File (continued)

```
                    sourceLength, nameBuffer,
                    kTextEncodingUnicodeDefault,
                    &fileToDelete )) == noErr) {                    //6
                err = FSDeleteObject( &fileToDelete );              //7
            }
        }
        if ( err == noErr ) {
            FSRef  newFSRef;
            FileInfo *fileInfo;
            FSCatalogInfo catalogInfo;
            fileInfo = (FileInfo *)
                    &catalogInfo.finderInfo[0];                     //8
            BlockZero(fileInfo, sizeof(FileInfo));                  //9
            fileInfo->fileType = kMTPDocType;                       //10
            fileInfo->fileCreator =
                    kMTPApplicationSignature;                       //11
            if ((err = FSCreateFileUnicode (&fileRefParent,
                    sourceLength, nameBuffer,
                    kFSCatInfoFinderInfo,
                    &catalogInfo, &newFSRef,
                    NULL)) == noErr) {                              //12
                MTPWriteFile (&newFSRef,
                    theItineraryWindow);                           //13
            }
        }
    }
    DisposePtr ((Ptr)nameBuffer );                                 //14
    }
    AEDisposeDesc( &actualDesc );                                  //15
    }
    return err;
}
```

Here's what the MTPDoFSRefSave function does:

1. The Apple Event Manager function AECoerceDesc checks for a valid FSRef by coercing the Apple Event descriptor returned by Navigation Services in the reply record.

2. If the coercion succeeds, the Apple Event Manager function AEGetDescData extracts the FSRef from the descriptor. This FSRef does not describe the new file itself, because that file does not yet exist. Rather, the FSRef returned in the reply record describes the parent of the new file; that is, it describes the directory in which the new file will reside.

3. The Core Foundation String Services function CFStringGetLength gets the length of the CFString returned by Navigation Services as the filename of the new file.

4. The `NewPtr` function allocates storage space for a buffer into which the filename will be read.

5. The Core Foundation String Services function `CFStringGetCharacters` retrieves the name specified by the user for the new file. The name is read from the `CFString` into a buffer of Unicode characters, which is the representation that the File Manager expects.

6. If the user has chosen to replace the existing file, the File Manager function `FSMakeFSRefUnicode` makes an `FSRef` for the existing file. The user has the option of replacing an existing file. In that case, the application should delete the old file before saving the new one. `FSMakeFSRefUnicode` identifies the file to delete using the `FSRef` of the file's parent directory and the filename that you've retrieved.

7. If the user has chosen to replace an existing file, the File Manager function `FSDeleteObject` deletes the old file.

8. The function sets the pointer to the `FileInfo` structure to the `finderInfo` field of the `catalogInfo` structure. The `finderInfo` field of the `catalogInfo` structure contains information that the Finder uses to identify the file. When we create the file, we will pass this information to the `FSCreateFileUnicode` function, so that the file is created with the appropriate Finder information. Casting the `finderInfo` field to a `FileInfo` structure makes it easier to fill out the finder information that we wish to set.

9. The `BlockZero` function initializes all of the fields of the `FileInfo` structure to zero.

10. The function sets the file type of the new file to the Moon Travel Planner application's file type.

11. The function sets the file creator of the new file to the Moon Travel Planner application signature.

12. The File Manager function `FSCreateFileUnicode` creates a new file for the itinerary. The file is specified by the name and the identity of the parent directory. The File Manager returns an `FSRef` for the new file. When you create the file, you pass to the `FSCreateFileUnicode` function, the `FSCatalogInfo` structure containing the information that identifies your file to the Finder. You also pass the `kFSCatInfoFinderInfo` constant to notify the File Manager that it should use this information to set the Finder information for the new file.

13. The `MTPWriteFile` function opens the file and saves the itinerary data. You will implement this function in the section "Write the save data."

14. The `DisposePtr` function disposes of the storage allocated to the filename buffer.

15. The Apple Event Manager function `AEDisposeDesc` disposes of the event
descriptor used to retrieve the `FSRef` from the `NavReplyRecord` structure.

Write the save data

The final step in saving a file is writing the data to disk. The `MTPWriteFile` function
opens the file for writing and calls `FSWriteFork` to write the itinerary data to disk.

First, declare the `MTPWriteFile` function. Copy the following lines into the `main.c`
file, after the declaration for the `MTPDoFSRefSave` function:

```
OOSStatus MTPWriteFile (FSRef *inRef, WindowRef theItineraryWindow);
```

Now implement the function. Copy the `MTPWriteFile` function in Example 11-12
into the `main.c` file.

Example 11-12: A Function that Writes the Itinerary Data to Disk

```
OSStatus MTPWriteFile (FSRef *inRef, WindowRef theItineraryWindow)
{
    HFSUniStr255 forkName;
    SInt16 forkRefNum;
    CFIndex length;
    CFStringRef theString;
    OSStatus err;
    UniChar * buffer;

    err = GetWindowProperty (theItineraryWindow,
                    kMTPApplicationSignature,
                    kMTPCFStringProperty,
                    sizeof(CFStringRef), NULL,
                    (void *)&theString);                           //1
    length = CFStringGetLength(theString);                         //2
    buffer = (UniChar*)NewPtr(length * sizeof(UniChar));           //3
    CFStringGetCharacters (theString, CFRangeMake(0, length), buffer); //4
    err = FSGetDataForkName (&forkName);                           //5
    if (( err = FSOpenFork (inRef, (UniCharCount)forkName.length,
                forkName.unicode,
                fsRdWrPerm, &forkRefNum)) == noErr) {              //6
        err = FSWriteFork(forkRefNum, fsFromStart,
                0, length, (void *) buffer, NULL);                 //7
        err = FSCloseFork(forkRefNum);                            //8
    }
    free(buffer);                                                  //9
    return err;
}
```

Here's what the `MTPWriteFile` function does:

1. The Window Manager function `GetWindowProperty` retrieves the `CFString` that
   you associated with the itinerary file in the section "Read the itinerary file."

2. The Core Foundation String Services function CFStringGetLength returns the length of the itinerary text contained in the CFString.

3. The NewPtr function allocates a buffer for the characters to write to disk. In this case, the buffer should be the length of the text in the CFString object.

4. The Core Foundation String Services function CFStringGetCharacters retrieves the text from the CFString object into the buffer that we have provided.

 As we mentioned earlier, in the section "Read the itinerary file," if you were to make the itinerary file user editable, you would normally have some sort of structure that represents the document as a whole (such as an MLTE text object). You would have to retrieve the data associated with that document before writing it to disk.

---

5. The File Manager function FSGetDataForkName retrieves the name of the file's data fork. You should always store your data in the data fork. Currently, the File Manager simply returns a constant for the data fork name, but using the function provided by the File Manager ensures that future changes in implementation won't affect your code.

6. The File Manager function FSOpenFork opens the data fork of the file to save. When you open a file fork, you must specify the type of access you wish to have to the fork. In this case, we pass the constant fsRdWrPerm to the File Manager, requesting read and write privileges. A fork reference number specifying the path to the open fork is returned; a fork can have more than one path open at a time, as long as their permissions don't conflict.

7. The File Manager function FSWriteFork writes the specified number of bytes from the buffer containing the itinerary text to the disk.

8. The File Manager function FSCloseFork closes the file fork.

9. The function frees the memory allocated to the buffer.

Close the Itinerary

At this point, you have one more command and one more event to handle. These are the Close command and the window close event. Luckily, you can use the same function for both of them. You will write that function in this section.

When you close a document, you should perform any clean-up that may be necessary for your program. In our case, this clean-up is quite simple. However, if you were working with a full-fledged editable text document, there would be more to do. For instance, you would want to check for any unsaved changes in the document, and if there are any, you would give the user a chance to save those changes before closing the window, using the Save Changes dialog that you learned about in the section "The Navigation Services dialogs." You would close any fork reference that you may have been using; dispose of text objects, pointers to callback functions, or any other objects for which you've allocated memory; and perform any other clean-up tasks that need to be done.

First, declare the MTPDoCloseItinerary function. Copy the following lines into the main.c file, after the declaration for the MTPWriteFile function:

```
OSStatus MTPDoCloseItinerary(WindowRef inWindow);
```

Now implement the function. Copy the MTPDoCloseItinerary function in Example 11-13 into the main.c file.

Example 11-13: A Function that Closes an Itinerary Window

```
OSStatus MTPDoCloseItinerary(WindowRef inWindow)
{
    CFStringRef theString;
    OSStatus err = noErr;

    err = GetWindowProperty (inWindow, kMTPApplicationSignature,
                kMTPCFStringProperty, sizeof(CFStringRef),
                NULL, (void *)&theString);                        //1
    if (theString != NULL) CFRelease (theString);                //2
    DisposeWindow(inWindow);                                     //3
    return err;
}
```

Here's what the MTPDoCloseItinerary function does:

1. The Window Manager function GetWindowProperty gets the CFString that you associated with the itinerary window in the MTPReadFile function.

2. If the string is not empty, the Core Foundation function CFRelease releases the memory allocated to the CFString.

3. The Window Manager function DisposeWindow disposes of the window.

Handle the Open Command from the Main Window

As a last step, you need to add code to the Moon Travel Planner application to handle the Open Itinerary command. All you need to do to handle the Open Itinerary command from the Moon Travel Planner main window, is add a case to the switch statement in the main window event handler you wrote in Chapter 6, *Carbon Events*. Modify the switch statement in the MTPMainWindowEventHandler function so it now looks like the code shown in Example 11-14.

Example 11-14: The Modified Switch Statement in the Main Window Event Handler

```
switch (command.commandID)
  {
    case kMTPComputeCommand:
        ComputeCommandHandler ((WindowRef) userData);
        result = noErr;
        break;
    case kMTPShowMoonFactsCommand:
        MTPShowMoonFactsWindow(gMoonFactsWindow);
        result = noErr;
        break;
    case kMTPOpenAboutWindowCommand:
        MTPAboutWindowCommandHandler(gAboutWindow);
        result = noErr;
        break;
    case kMTPOpenItineraryCommand:
        result = MTPDoOpenItinerary();
        break;
  }
```

Now, when the user chooses Open Itinerary from the File menu, the Moon Travel Planner main window will process the command and open an itinerary window.

Build, Run, and Test the Application

Now do the following:

1. Click the Build button in the upper-left corner of the Moon Travel Planner project window.

2. Click the Run button in the upper-left corner of the project window.

3. Open an itinerary by using the Open menu command. Select the Open Itinerary command from the Moon Travel Planner File menu. The application will bring up an Open dialog, such as the one shown in Figure 11-7. Use the column view browser or the Where pop-up menu to navigate to the Itineraries folder that was provided with the tutorial. In the column view browser, select the itinerary file "Itinerary" and click the Open button in the Open dialog. You should see the window shown in Figure 11-15.

4. Save an itinerary. Select the Save As command from the Moon Travel Planner File menu. The application will bring up a Save Location dialog, similar to the one in Figure 11-10. In the Save as text box, enter the filename for the new file. Choose the location in which to save the file by navigating through the file system with the column view browser (which you can see by clicking the disclosure button to the right of the Where pop-up menu) or by selecting a folder in the Where pop-up menu.

   Click the Save button. A new file should appear in the location that you specified, with the filename that you provided. Right now this file has a generic

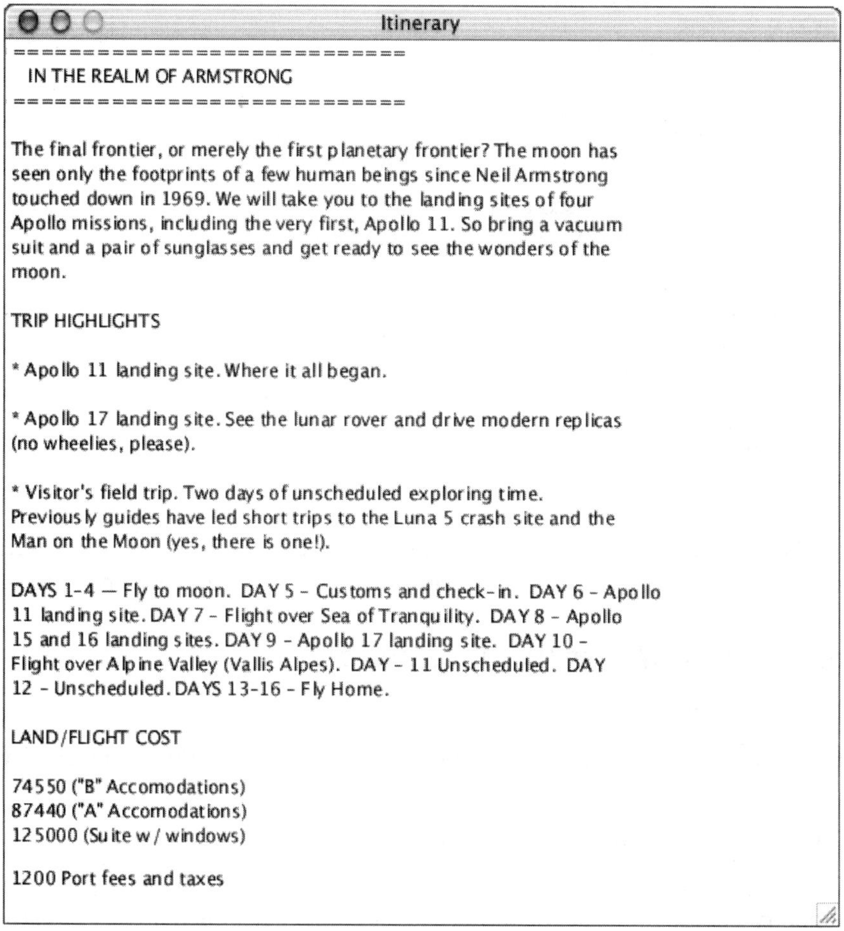

```
  ● ● ○                              Itinerary
  =============================
    IN THE REALM OF ARMSTRONG
  =============================

  The final frontier, or merely the first planetary frontier? The moon has
  seen only the footprints of a few human beings since Neil Armstrong
  touched down in 1969. We will take you to the landing sites of four
  Apollo missions, including the very first, Apollo 11. So bring a vacuum
  suit and a pair of sunglasses and get ready to see the wonders of the
  moon.

  TRIP HIGHLIGHTS

  * Apollo 11 landing site. Where it all began.

  * Apollo 17 landing site. See the lunar rover and drive modern replicas
  (no wheelies, please).

  * Visitor's field trip. Two days of unscheduled exploring time.
  Previously guides have led short trips to the Luna 5 crash site and the
  Man on the Moon (yes, there is one!).

  DAYS 1-4 — Fly to moon. DAY 5 – Customs and check-in. DAY 6 – Apollo
  11 landing site. DAY 7 – Flight over Sea of Tranquility. DAY 8 – Apollo
  15 and 16 landing sites. DAY 9 – Apollo 17 landing site. DAY 10 –
  Flight over Alpine Valley (Vallis Alpes). DAY – 11 Unscheduled. DAY
  12 – Unscheduled. DAYS 13-16 – Fly Home.

  LAND/FLIGHT COST

  74550 ("B" Accomodations)
  87440 ("A" Accomodations)
  125000 (Suite w / windows)

  1200 Port fees and taxes
```

Figure 11-15. The Itinerary window

document icon; in Chapter 13, you will learn how to provide a document icon
that will be displayed for the documents that you create with Moon Travel
Planner. You can open the saved file to make sure the text was actually saved.

Recap

Basic file management is a task that you must perform if you wish to store persistent information on a physical storage medium and retrieve that information at a later time. In this chapter, you learned about files and how they're organized in the file system. You learned how to identify and access files, and you learned the basic tasks necessary to open and save files. You also learned how to create and display dialogs to solicit information from users when opening and saving files.

Finally, you added an itinerary window to the Moon Travel Planner application and wrote the code to open and save itinerary files. In the next chapter, you'll learn how to provide help to your users.

12

Providing Help

No matter how intuitive a user interface for an application may seem to the developer, it's likely some people will need information about using it. To make a complete application, you should provide user help.

Apple's philosophy of help is that users look at it with a specific goal in mind. In other words, users turn to help when they know what they want to do in the application but aren't sure how to do it. The application's help should get users back to their task as quickly as possible. When users open help, chances are that they are already somewhat frustrated and impatient; well-designed help plays a significant part in a user's overall experience with your application.

In Carbon, you can provide two types of help in your application: help books and help tags. A help book provides onscreen documentation about how to perform tasks or troubleshoot problems. A help book is a collection of HTML files that users view in Help Viewer, a simple browser that can open automatically from your application. A help tag provides a brief description of something in the user interface. A help tag appears when the user hovers the mouse pointer over the item in the interface.

To work with help books and integrate them into your application, you use Apple Help, a technology that includes definitions of HTML elements and programming interfaces. To add simple, text-only help tags to your application, you can use Interface Builder. If you want to provide fancier help tags, including graphics or QuickTime movies, for example, use the Carbon Help Manager.

In this chapter you'll:

- Learn about help books and what type of content is appropriate for them

- Look at the basic mechanics for producing searchable help books

- Learn how help tags work and when and how to use them

- Add a help book to Moon Travel Planner and register it

- Add a help tag to Moon Travel Planner

Help on Mac OS X

Help books provide the type of content that probably comes to mind when you think about online help for an application. The information in a help book should answer questions that users have about how to accomplish a task or how to fix something that went wrong. Earlier in this book, you learned how to access developer documents through the Project Builder Help menu. These documents are examples of help books that you view in Help Viewer. Figure 12-1 shows a page in Mac Help, another example of a help book provided by Apple. (Mac Help contains information to answer questions users might have about using the Finder, System Preferences, and other parts of Mac OS X that users interact with.)

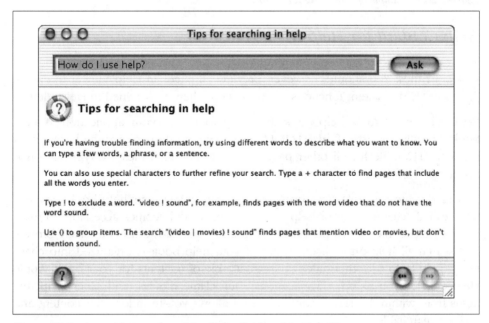

Figure 12-1. A sample page from Mac Help, displayed in Help Viewer

A user can open your help book in Help Viewer by choosing a menu item in the Help menu or by clicking a Help button that's always visible in the application interface. Once your help book is open, a user can type a query or browse a table of contents to get to pertinent information. To open your help book directly to a relevant page, you can also add Help buttons or contextual menus in appropriate places in your user interface.

Help tags provide a type of help that's simpler than that of help books; help tags contain hints about how to use controls and other elements in the user interface. Sometimes a brief description of a control is all a user needs to proceed with a task. Figure 12-2 shows a help tag in the Interface Builder palettes window. By looking at the brief description of each palette, you could quickly get an idea of what elements are in each palette.

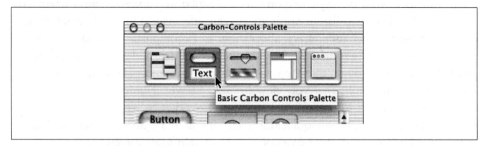

Figure 12-2. Example of a help tag for a control

Help Content for Help Books

You can create content for help books using any authoring tool that generates HTML 3.2 files. You should, however, preview all pages in Help Viewer to ensure that your HTML content functions as you intend when it is opened in Help Viewer.

Place all content for a help book in a help folder for your application. A help book typically consists of an HTML file specifying a title page for the book and a separate HTML file for all other pages of the book. Such files are typically organized into subfolders.

You can create a simple help book, or you can divide your help book into sections called "chapters." Your help book automatically becomes accessible to users via the Help Center, an Apple-provided location that allows users to easily browse and search all help on their computer. If your help book is organized into chapters, Apple Help uses their titles to create a table of contents for your book. Apple Help enables you to open applications, QuickTime movies, and other scriptable items from within the HTML content, and it allows you to index your content and make it searchable.

Guidelines for creating help content

Here are a few suggestions to keep in mind as you write your help books. For more information about Apple's philosophy for help, see *Inside Mac OS X: Aqua Human Interface Guidelines* in Carbon Help (available in the Project Builder Help menu).

- Focus on actual user tasks and troubleshooting. To come up with relevant tasks, imagine people using your application and asking "How do I . . .?" or "Why can't I . . .?".

- Don't document obvious tasks or interface elements. The more topics your help contains, the harder it is for users to find what they're looking for. Focus on behaviors that truly need explanation.

- Be as concise as possible. Remember that the user wants to be doing his or her work, not reading help text.

- Be judicious about including illustrations of the interface. Users may confuse art with the actual interface, and too much art can be distracting. When you do use art, make sure that it truly enhances the help content, and make it obvious that illustrations are not interactive.

The mechanics of creating help book content

To take full advantage of Apple Help and Help Viewer and to make your help book as useful as possible, there are certain basic elements that you may want to include. The following sections describe several of the most important help book components.

Anchors. An anchor is a label that you create with the HTML tag <A NAME>. Your application must use at least one anchor in order for the Help Viewer to be able to locate the application's help. You can also use this HTML tag to label basic tasks or information likely to be looked up frequently. You can provide quick access to information that you label with an anchor yourself by calling the Apple Help function AHLookupAnchor, and you can include anchors in your help's index. (For more information, see the section "Indexing.") The following is an example of an anchor:

```
<A NAME="Creating a Cartoon Character"></A>
```

Segments. You can divide a single HTML file into smaller sections so that each segment is returned as a separate "hit" result when the user searches your help book. Segments differ from chapters. Segments simply focus the results of user searches on your book. An example of the markup for a segment is shown in Example 12-1.

Example 12-1: Dividing an HTML File into Segments

```
<!--AppleSegStart ="Creating a Cartoon Character"-->
<A NAME="Choosing an Expression"></A>
The help content goes here...
<!--AppleSegEnd-->
```

Note that this example also includes an anchor. Also note that every `AppleSegStart` tag must have an `AppleSegEnd` tag.

Descriptions. You can also add descriptions to your help content. These descriptions are displayed with Help Viewer search results, assisting users with determining which topic is most relevant to them. There are two ways to provide descriptions for your help content. You can provide an abstract for an HTML file as a whole, or you can provide descriptions for individual segments within an HTML file.

To create a description for one complete help page you would use this tag in the HTML file for that page:

```
<META NAME="DESCRIPTION" CONTENT="This section describes the tools you can use to
create a cartoon character.">
```

To create a description for a segment within a help page, you would use the `AppleSegDescription` tag. A description for the segment on choosing an expression, for example, added to the segment in the previous listing, is shown in Example 12-2.

Example 12-2: Adding a Description (Search Result Abstract) to an HTML Segment

```
<!--AppleSegStart ="Creating a Cartoon Character"-->
<A NAME="Choosing an Expression"></A>
<!--AppleSegDescription="This section describes the Expression palette and shows how
you can assign an expression to a cartoon character."-->
The help content goes here...
<!--AppleSegEnd-->
```

Keywords. Using anchors, segments, and descriptions makes your help content searchable on a basic level. In many cases, however, users don't know the exact spelling or terminology to use for a query in Help Viewer. That's where keywords come in; keywords enable you to add common misspellings, as well as synonyms for concepts and sections in your HTML help content, so that a user who enters one of these keywords can obtain relevant search results. For example, a user entering the query "How do I give a cartoon character an expression?" would certainly arrive at the appropriate help content. But a user who types "How do I make Mr. Grump have a happy face?" would get no search results. To add the keywords "happy" and "face" to the help content, you would add the following to our HTML content:

```
<!--AppleKeywords="happy, face"-->
```

The following tag would add keywords to the entire HTML file:

```
<META NAME="KEYWORDS" CONTENT="happy, face">
```

Indexing

Help Viewer uses the Sherlock search engine to provide fast, full-text searching of help books. To make your help content searchable in Help Viewer, you must use the Apple Help Indexing Tool. The indexing tool is available in the Apple Help Software Developer's Kit (SDK) (see Appendix A, *Additional Resources*, for information on getting SDKs from Apple).

Before you create an index, make sure your help files are in their final folder locations. The index file stores relative path information, so moving content files after indexing invalidates the index file.

If you put anchors in your index, you must tell the tool to include them before you create the index. To do so, open the Indexing Tool, choose Preferences from the Edit menu, and select the Anchor Indexing checkbox.

To create an index file, simply drag the folder containing your help content onto the Apple Help Indexing Tool. The Indexing Tool scans the folder and creates a file inside the folder you dropped on the tool. This index file must remain in the folder for the index to work correctly.

To learn more about creating help books, see the Apple Help documentation in Carbon Help (available in the Project Builder Help menu).

Help Tags

Whereas a help book allows you to provide detailed help for your application, help tags provide a mechanism for offering users short hints and tips about your application as they move through the application's interface.

A help tag—a small rectangle that displays text—appears when the user hovers the mouse pointer over an interface element. Help tags are useful for providing brief descriptions of controls, such as a button that displays an icon but no text. (See Figure 12-2 for an example of a help tag for a control.)

How does a help tag work?

If the pointer hovers for a specified length of time over an item that has a help tag, the Carbon Help Manager displays the text in a help tag. When the user moves the pointer off the item, the Carbon Help Manager removes the help tag from the screen.

The easiest way to add help tags is to use Interface Builder. If an interface element supports help tags, you can specify the text for it in its Info window in Interface Builder; you don't have to write any code. Creating help tags in this way will be sufficient for most applications. You'll see how to do that later, in the section "Moon Travel Planner: Adding Help."

You can also create help tags with the Carbon Help Manager. You'll need to write code using Carbon Help Manager functions, such as `HMSetControlHelpContent`, `HMSetWindowHelpContent`, and `HMSetMenuItemHelpContent` to associate help tag content with an interface element. If you prefer, you can use the Carbon Help Manager to associate a callback function with the interface element for which you want to provide a help tag. The Carbon Help Manager calls this function to display the help text. If you use this method, you are also responsible for disposing of the help tag content when the tag is removed from the screen. If you want more information, see the Carbon Help Manager documentation in Carbon Help (available in the Project Builder Help menu).

A *callback function* is an application-defined function that is invoked at a specified time or based on criteria established by the application.

Guidelines for writing help tags

Use help tags to help users determine the function of interface elements. Note that help tags should be state-independent: a help tag for an item always displays the same text, even when the item is in an unavailable state. For example, let's say the Forward button in a mail program has this help tag: "Send the selected message to someone else." The word "selected" gives a clue as to why the button may be dimmed (because the user hasn't selected a message yet).

When you write help tags, keep the following guidelines in mind:

- Keep it short. The longer the text, the larger the tag; the larger the tag, the more that it interferes with your application's interface. Help tags are useful for providing additional hints, but they are not suitable for providing comprehensive instructions about the operation of your application; that type of content should be provided through help books. Keep each help tag to a maximum of 75 characters.

- Don't tell users something they already know. Repeating already visible information simply clutters the screen. If the item has an onscreen label, for example, you don't need to repeat the item's name in the help tag. Don't create a tag for a "Send" button that says "Sends mail."

- Make it relevant. The help tag text should tell users what they want to know most about the item, which is usually the task they can perform by using it.

- Don't get tag happy. You don't need to label everything on the screen. Don't create tags for standard operating system elements such as windows, scroll bars, title bars, and menus. For instance, create a tag for a window if the purpose of the window might not be clear (a tool palette, for example); don't create a tag simply to say that it is a window. Assume that anyone using your application already knows interface basics.

Moon Travel Planner: Adding Help

Let's add a help book and a help tag to the Moon Travel Planner application. Since Moon Travel Planner is small and easy to use, a simple help book (without chapters) is sufficient. A help book is included with the materials for this book.

To add the help book and a help tag to the Moon Travel Planner application, you must do the following:

1. Add the Moon Travel Planner help book to the project.

2. Modify the property list so it includes the help book name and folder.

3. Register the help book.

4. Write a help tag.

Add the Help Book to the Project

The Moon Travel Planner help book needs to be added to the language-specific folder, `English.lproj`, and then added as a resource to the Moon Travel Planner application:

1. In the Finder, copy the Moon Travel Planner Help folder to the `English.lproj` folder in the Moon Travel Planner folder. Use the help book provided with the Moon Travel Planner materials (see the the Preface for information on how to obtain the materials).

2. Open the Moon Travel Planner project in Project Builder.

3. Add the Moon Travel Planner Help folder to the Moon Travel Planner project. Choose Add Files from the Project menu, select the Moon Travel Planner Help folder, and click Open. Select "Create Folder References for any added folders" and click Add. Project Builder adds the folder as a resource if you've selected this option.

4. If you need to, drag the Moon Travel Planner Help folder to the Resources group.

Modify the Application's Property List

In this section you'll add two entries to the application's property list so Apple Help can locate the Moon Travel Planner help book. The first entry consists of the CFBundleHelpBookFolder key with a string value identifying the folder for your help book. The second entry consists of a CFBundleHelpBookName key with a string value specifying the help book's title, as defined in your title page file (the help's home page). Together, the entries assure that when the user chooses Moon Travel Planner Help from the Help menu, Help Viewer opens to the title page of the Moon Travel Planner help book.

When you include the CFBundleHelpBookFolder property in your property list, Carbon automatically provides a Help menu for your application. This is why you deleted the Help menu in Chapter 7, *Interface Builder: Menus*. You don't need the Help menu provided by Interface Builder.

Follow these steps to modify the Moon Travel Planner property list:

1. Click the Targets tab, then click Moon Travel Planner in the Targets list.

2. Click the Application Settings tab, then click the Expert button.

3. Create an entry for the help book folder name. Click New Sibling, type CFBundleHelpBookFolder as the property name, and press Return. Then double-click the Value column, type **Moon Travel Planner Help** as the property value, and press Return.

4. Create an entry for the help book name. Click New Sibling, type CFBundle-HelpBookName as the property name, and press Return. Then double-click the Value column, type **Moon Travel Planner Help** as the property value, and press Return.

Register the Help Book

When the Moon Travel Planner application launches, it should call a function to register the help book. Once the help book is registered, it appears in the Help Center. In this section, you'll add code to register the help book.

First, you need to declare the registration function you'll use. In the main.c file in your Moon Travel Planner project, type the following statement before the main function, just after the event and command handler declarations:

```
OSStatus MTPRegisterMoonTravelHelp (void);
```

Next, you'll create the function. The function needs to provide the application bundle to the Apple Help function that does the actual registration. Copy the code shown in Example 12-3 to the bottom of the main.c file.

Example 12-3: The Function for Registering the Help Book

```
OSStatus MTPRegisterMoonTravelHelp (void)
{
    CFBundleRef    myAppsBundle;
    CFURLRef       myBundleURL;
    FSRef          myBundleRef;
    OSStatus       err = 0;

    myAppsBundle = NULL;                                      // 1
    myBundleURL = NULL;

    myAppsBundle = CFBundleGetMainBundle();                  // 2
    if (myAppsBundle == NULL) { err = fnfErr; goto bail;}    // 3
    myBundleURL = CFBundleCopyBundleURL(myAppsBundle);       // 4
    if (myBundleURL == NULL) { err = fnfErr; goto bail;}
    CFURLGetFSRef (myBundleURL, &myBundleRef);               // 5
    if ( ! CFURLGetFSRef(myBundleURL, &myBundleRef) )
    {
         err = fnfErr;
         goto bail;
    }
    err = AHRegisterHelpBook (&myBundleRef);                 // 6
    if (err != noErr) goto bail;
    CFRelease (myBundleURL);                                 // 7
    return noErr;                                            // 8
    bail:
         if (myBundleURL != NULL) CFRelease(myBundleURL);
         return err;
}
```

Here's what the function does:

1. Sets up a known state you can check against when you do error checking throughout the function.

2. The Core Foundation Bundle Services function *CFBundleGetMainBundle* returns a reference to the application's main bundle.

3. This statement, and others like it in this function, check to make sure something other than NULL is returned. If NULL is returned, the err is set to indicate a "not found" error, and the function jumps to the bail statement.

4. The Core Foundation Bundle Services function CFBundleCopyBundleURL returns the location of the bundle.

5. The Core Foundation URL Services function CFURLGetFSRef returns the file specification reference (FSRef) for the bundle URL.

6. The Apple Help function AHRegisterHelpBook registers the help book associated with the application.

7. The Core Foundation Base Services function `CFRelease` releases the memory associated with `myBundleURL`.

8. If all goes well, the function exits here. Otherwise, the `bail` statement executes, the function releases the memory associated with `myBundleURL`, and returns an error.

Your application needs to call the `MTPRegisterMoonTravelHelp` function when the application starts up. You should add this statement just before the statement `RunApplicationEventLoop`:

```
MTPRegisterMoonTravelHelp();
```

Add a Help Tag

Now that you have provided help pages for your Moon Travel Planner application, you will learn how to provide hints to the user through help tags. For the purposes of this tutorial, we will create a tag for the graphic in the Moon Travel Planner window:

1. Make the Moon Travel Planner project window active. Click the Project Builder icon in the Dock.

2. Open the `main.nib` file. Double-click the `main.nib` file in the Resources list.

3. Open the Moon Travel Planner window. Double-click the MainWindow icon in the Instances pane.

4. Open the Picture Info window. Click the graphic in the Moon Travel Planner window, then choose Show Info from the Tools menu.

5. Add a help tag to the graphic. Choose Help from the pop-up menu in the Picture Info window.

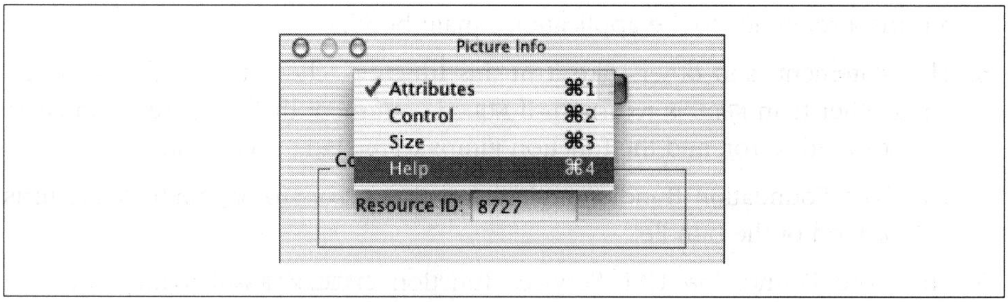

Figure 12-3. Displaying help information for a control

6. Write the help tag content. In the Text field shown in Figure 12-4, type `Luna, satellite of the earth`.

7. Specify the help tag location. Choose Default from the Display Side pop-up menu, as shown in Figure 12-4.

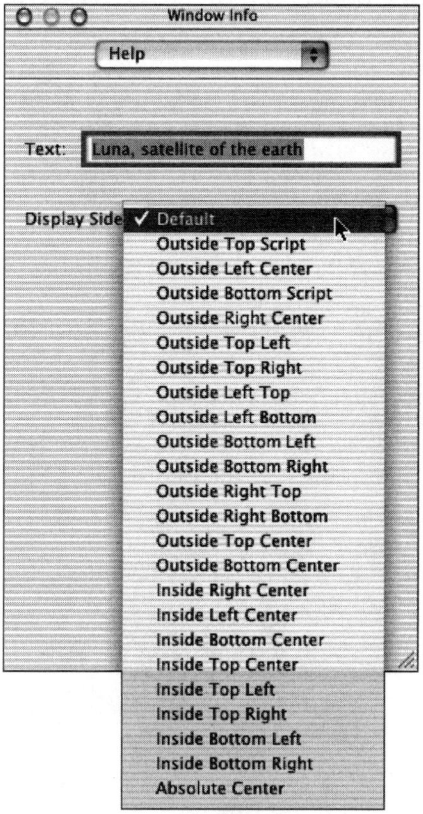

Figure 12-4. Choosing a location for a help tag

Make Sure Help Works Properly

You need to make sure that the Moon Travel Planner help book opens and the help tag you added appears. Let's build, run, and test the application.

1. Click the Build button in the upper-left corner of the Moon Travel Planner project window.

2. Click the Run button in the upper-left corner of the project window.

3. Choose Moon Travel Planner Help from the Help menu. Does Apple Help Viewer open? It should look like the page shown in Figure 12-5.

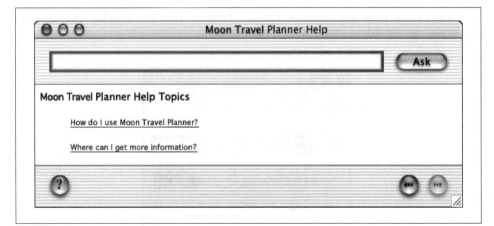

Figure 12-5. The first page of Moon Travel Planner Help

4. Click the Moon Travel Planner main window to make it active.

5. Place the pointer over the graphic. In a few seconds you should see the help tag appear. Does it look similar to the one shown in Figure 12-6?

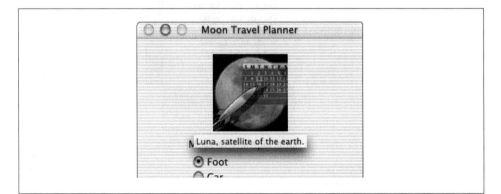

Figure 12-6. The help tag for the moon picture

6. Move the pointer off the picture. The tag should disappear.

7. Click Quit.

If everything worked, you're ready to move on!

Recap

Now that you've added content to the Help menu and provided a help tag, the Moon Travel Planner application is almost complete. The main item it's lacking is a custom icon. Next you'll add application and document icons so users can easily recognize your application and its itinerary files in the Finder.

13

Desktop Icons

The Finder, the application that manages the user interface in Mac OS X, represents the file system to the user through the metaphor of a desktop with folders and documents on it. Those ubiquitous little pictures called icons are the heart of the desktop metaphor because they represent documents, storage media, folders, and applications to the user. By manipulating icons, the user can conduct such operations as launching applications, opening folders, and moving files.

Graphic limitations of earlier operating systems constrained icons to a two-dimensional style. Mac OS X icons, on the other hand, are capable of having depth and a lush look that approaches photo-realism.

When you create an application, the operating system will assign it a generic icon unless you provide your own custom icon. While not entirely unappealing, a generic icon doesn't communicate anything to the user about an application. To make your application complete, you should provide a custom icon. If your application creates documents or uses plug-ins or other files, you should provide icons for those as well. In this chapter, you'll:

- Take a look at the kinds of icon that are used on Mac OS X
- See what goes into icon design
- Look at the technical details of icons, such as sizes and masks
- Find out how to get a file or application to appear with your icon
- Add application and document icons to the Moon Travel Planner application

Icon Basics

Creating icons requires artistic and technical skills. You'll need artistry to design effective and professional-looking icons. You'll need technical skill to package the icon with other application resources, and then to make the necessary changes to get the Finder to display the icons. This section contains information for both the artistic and technical aspects of icons.

Types of Icons

Desktop icons represent a file or folder to the user. Since there are different kinds of files, there are different kinds of icons. Each type of icon has distinguishing characteristics that help the user identify what kind of file the icon represents.

Application icons

Every application, from the simplest utility to the largest productivity suite, should have its own custom icon. The application icon is the single most important way for users to identify and choose a particular application out of the dozens or hundreds in their workspaces, so you should make it easy for them by providing a distinctive application icon. Figure 13-1 shows three examples of custom application icons.

Figure 13-1. Examples of application icons

Note that all the application icons shown in Figure 13-1 share several characteristics. Each icon contains familiar objects, shown as though they might be sitting on a desk or tabletop. The composition of the icon makes use of perspective, color, and shading to provide photo-realistic representation of the objects. Applications are tools for the user, so application icons should always show a picture of a tool that indicates the nature of the task the application is designed to accomplish. In Figure 13-1, for example, the icon on the left shows a pen, the icon in the center shows a pair of glasses, and the icon on the right shows a compass. Using the tools as indicators, it should not be surprising that the icon on the left represents a text editing application, the icon in the center represents a PDF document viewer, and the icon on the right represents a drawing application.

Document icons

If your application creates document files, you should provide icons that identify these files. This helps users avoid the frustration of looking into a folder full of document files with generic icons and being unable to identify which applications created the files. If your application creates several types of document files (such as text and PDF files, for example), you should provide separate icons for each type of file. Figure 13-2 shows several examples of document icons.

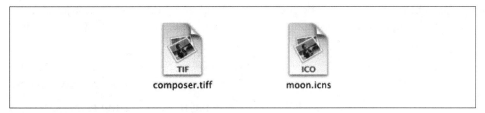

Figure 13-2. Examples of document icons

These icons contain several key indicators that tell the user that these icons represent document files and not applications. For one, these icons don't show pictures of a tool. Another clue (one that should be familiar to longtime Mac OS users) is the icon outline, which forms an image of a piece of paper with a curled-up corner. In addition, these icons contain representations of the kind of documents in the file. For example, in Figure 13-2, the pictures show photographs to indicate that the file contains graphics. Finally, the icons help the user identify which type of document file is represented by using a three-letter abbreviation for the file type.

Icons for plug-ins and other support files

If your application uses files other than document files, you can create icons that identify these files to the user. Many applications use optional components called plug-ins that add specialized enhancements to an application's core functionality. An example of a plug-in is an optional spell-checking component for a word-processing application. Some applications use support files to store settings or user preference information. A web browser's bookmark file is an example of a support file. If your application uses plug-ins or support files, it is helpful to create separate icons for these files so that users do not mistake them for document files.

Design Tips

Unless you are an artist yourself, you'll probably need to have an artist design great-looking icons for your application. The following list of tips will help your artist design an icon whose look is compatible with Aqua:

- Use imagery your users will easily recognize; it should be universal. Avoid focusing on a secondary aspect of an element. For example, for a mail icon, a rural mailbox would be less recognizable than a stamped postcard.

- Avoid using anatomy. Anatomical images are hard to do well and can often detract from the intended meaning.

- Keep it focused. Make sure you include an object that captures the purpose of the application or control.

- Use color judiciously to help the icon tell its story; don't add color just for the sake of making the icon more colorful. A gradient typically looks better than sharp delineations of color.

- Avoid using replicas of Apple hardware products in your icons. Otherwise your icon could be obsolete or meaningless when a hardware design changes.

- Use a single light source with the light coming from above the icon.

You can find more information on icon design in *Inside Mac OS X: Aqua Human Interface Guidelines* in Carbon Help (available in the Project Builder Help menu).

Icon Sizes and Masks

In Mac OS X, icons are displayed at various sizes, from as small as 16 × 16 pixels to as large as 128 × 128 pixels. Application icons, document icons, and other icons that display in the Finder can be viewed at different sizes: they can be magnified in the Dock, they can be previewed at full size, and users can specify a preferred size.

At the very least, you need to provide a *thumbnail icon*, which is an icon that's 128 × 128 pixels. Mac OS uses a sophisticated scaling algorithm to reduce this size when required—for example, when the user sets the Dock to a smaller size. Some intricately detailed icons do not display well when scaled down from thumbnails, so you should provide smaller versions of each icon—64 × 64, 32 × 32, and 16 × 16—if you wish to avoid scaling problems.

Icons need to have a *mask*, an area within which a user clicks the mouse to select the icon. Icon masks are sometimes known as hit areas, since they determine which mouse clicks hit the icon and which don't. The Finder uses the mask to crop the icon's outline into the desktop's background color or pattern.

You can specify a mask area as simple as the square that contains the icon, or design one that follows the contour of an elaborate figure. For example, if you used a rocket-shaped logo in your icon, you could specify the outline of the rocket as the mask area, rather than using the entire 128 × 128 pixel square that encloses the rocket. In general, you should avoid unusually shaped mask areas that can be frustrating to novice users, who may not understand why a mouse click inside the perimeter of the icon does not register as a hit.

Assigning Icons to Applications and Files

Once you've designed and created icons for your application, you'll need to take a few more steps to get the icons to display in the Finder. The image files that contain your application and document icons should be in 'TIFF' or 'PICT' format. Then, you'll need to do the following:

- Import your icons, and any masks you create for them, into an Icon Composer file. You must create one file for each set of icons—the application icons, document icons, and so forth.

- Register the Icon Composer file for the application icon. You do this in Project Builder.

- Add a document type to your project. You do this in Project Builder. You need to set up a document type and indicate which Icon Composer file contains the document's icon images.

Importing icons into Icon Composer

You must import your icons, and any masks you create for them, into Icon Composer. Icon Composer is provided with the Mac OS X Developer CD; you'll find it in the /Developer/Applications/ directory. You need to create an Icon Composer file for each set of icons (application and document).

You import all sizes of an icon into the Icon Composer file. Icon Composer saves the file with a .icns extension, which designates the type of file Mac OS X uses specifically for icons. When you import images that are smaller than the thumbnail, Icon Composer asks if you'd like it to extract a mask for you. Unless you have created a mask, you should let Icon Composer extract one for you.

If you import multiple sizes of an icon to an Icon Composer file, Mac OS X automatically displays the appropriate sizes for a given situation. If you import just the thumbnail size, Mac OS X scales the icon as best it can when a smaller size is needed.

Once you have a .icns files you must still associate the icons in it with specific applications or files. You'll see how that's done in the next two sections.

Register the Icon Composer file for the application icon

The Application Settings pane in Project Builder provides a field in which you can type the name of the Icon Composer file (but without the `.icns` extension). In addition to specifying this file, you should also make sure you've entered a creator code in the Signature setting field in the Application Settings pane. You learned about creator codes in Chapter 5, *Interface Builder: Tools and Controls*. As you may recall, creator codes (often referred to as creators) identify your application to the Finder as well as identify documents created by your application. Each creator code must be unique, so that the Finder can display the correct icons and associate the correct document files for each application.

 When assigned to an application, a creator code is also called an application signature, because it identifies the application. When assigned to a document, it identifies who created the file, hence the name creator code.

When you create your own application, you should register a unique creator code with Apple Developer Technical Support, which maintains a database of creator codes to ensure that there are no duplications. Before you choose a creator code, you should know that codes consisting entirely of lowercase characters (moon, for example) are reserved by Apple. See Appendix A, *Additional Resources*, for information on where to register your creator code.

Adding a Document Type to a Project

You need to inform the Finder of the types of document your project creates by adding each document type in the Document Types section of Project Builder's Application Settings pane. At the minimum, you must provide a creator code, file type, and Icon Composer filename for each document type. You need to supply the creator code you use for the application.

While a creator code identifies the application that created a file, a file type (also sometimes called an OS type) is a four-character code that identifies a document's format. When your application creates a new document, it must specify file type information for the document file. There are two categories of file types, generic and custom.

Generic file types.   There are numerous generic file types, which are well-known file formats that can be parsed by a large number of applications. The most familiar generic file type is `'TEXT'`, which indicates that a file is a simple stream of ASCII characters. Other generic file types include those for graphics formats like `'PICT'` and `'TIFF'`. One advantage of using a generic file type for your documents is that you can usually find well-tested sample code to use in your project, instead of creating file-reading and file-writing functions from scratch.

Custom file types. If your application needs to store information in a document in a way that isn't practical with generic file types, you can design a custom file type. For example, graphics applications often use custom file formats that use compression to reduce the space required to store large amounts of data. In addition to designing the file format, you need to specify a custom file type. Every file type that your application uses for its document files should have a distinctive icon, so that users can quickly distinguish it from other types. As with creator codes, file types consisting entirely of lowercase letters are reserved by Apple.

 Icons can do more than simply represent files in the user interface. By using the Icon Services programming interface, you can change the appearance of your application's icons to reflect changes in a file's condition or the progress of a process. To find out more, see the Icon Services and Utilities documentation in Carbon Help (available in the Project Builder Help menu).

Now that you've gotten an overview of how application and document icons are added to an application, you can get some practice by adding icons to the Moon Travel Planner application.

Moon Travel Planner: Adding Icons

You may have noticed that, after you build and run the Moon Travel Planner application, the Finder uses generic icons to represent the application and its document files. In this section, you'll add icons that inspire an interest in the moon and lunar travel. You won't need to design any icons; just download the materials provided for this book. See the Preface for details.

You'll do the following:

1. Import images into Icon Composer.

2. Add icon files to the Moon Travel Planner project.

3. Register the application file.

4. Add a document type to the Moon Travel Planner project.

5. Make sure the icons display in the Finder.

An important prerequisite to adding icons to your application is adding the application's creator code to the property list. You already entered the Moon Travel Planner creator code, `'MTPP'`, in Chapter 10, *Property Lists.*

Import Images to Icon Composer

Icon Composer creates a file with a `.icns` extension in the format used by Mac OS X to store icons. You'll only import a thumbnail image for the Moon Travel Planner application. You'd use the same procedure to import images of other sizes, if you had them.

Follow these steps to create Icon Composer files for the application and document icons provided with the Moon Travel Planner application. These icons are in the `MTP.tif` and `MTPDoc.tif` files, respectively. See the Preface for details on how to obtain the materials.

You should follow these procedures twice: once to create an Icon Composer file for the application icon, and the second time to create an Icon Composer file for the document icon:

1. Double-click Icon Composer in the `/Developer/Applications` directory. Icon Composer automatically opens an untitled file for your icons.

2. Choose Import Image from the File menu.

3. Select the file that contains the application icon, as shown in Figure 13-3. You can select the `MTP.tif` or `MTPDoc.tif` file provided with the Moon Travel Planner materials. If you created your own icon, you can use it instead of the one provided.

4. Choose a data size from the Import To pop-up menu. The `MTP.tif` and `MTP-Doc.tif` files each contain a thumbnail icon, so you should select "Thumbnail 32 bit data" then click Open. If you have an icon of a different size, choose the appropriate size from the pop-up menu. The `MTP.icns` file appears in the Icon Composer window, as shown in Figure 13-4.

5. Add any icons you've created in other sizes. Mac OS X requires that you add a thumbnail icon; all other sizes are optional. If you have additional smaller

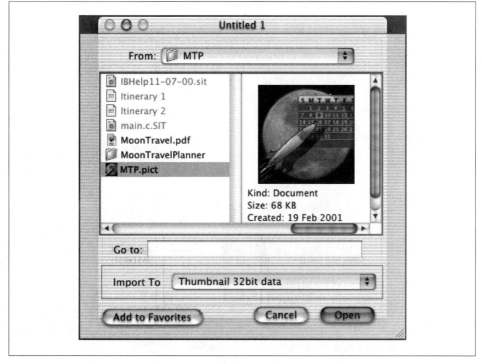

Figure 13-3. Importing an image into Icon Composer

images to import, either repeat steps 2-4 for each image or just drag the desired image from the Finder into the appropriate box in Icon Composer. When you add any icon other than the thumbnail, you'll see a dialog asking if you want Icon Composer to extract a mask for the image. Unless you have special masking needs, you should let Icon Composer extract the mask. Otherwise, you'll need to add a mask for each image (other than the thumbnail) you add.

6. Choose Save from the File menu. Type MTP or MTPDoc as the filename and save the file in the Moon Travel Planner project folder. Icon Composer automatically appends .icns to the filename.

Add the Icon Files

Now that you've created the MTP.icns or MTPDoc.icns file, you need to add it to the Moon Travel Planner project, then make the appropriate settings so the new icon replaces the generic one. For each file, follow these steps:

1. Open the Moon Travel Planner project. If the Moon Travel Planner is already open, click its icon in the Dock to make it active.

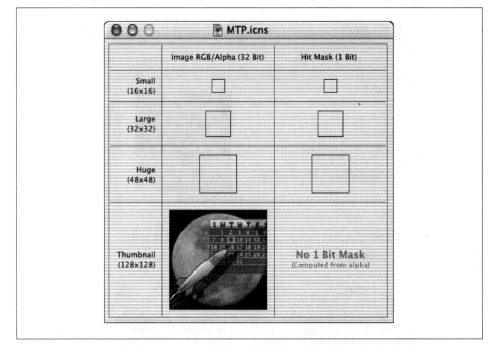

Figure 13-4. A thumbnail icon in an Icon Composer file

2. Add the file to the Moon Travel Planner project. Choose Add Files from the Project menu. In the sheet that appears, select the MTP.icns or MTPDoc.icns file and click Open. Then click Add. If you need to, drag the MTP.icns or MTP-Doc.icns file reference to the Resources group.

Register the Application Icon File

Now that you've added the MTP.icns file, you need to make the appropriate settings so the new icon replaces the generic one:

1. Open the Application Settings pane. Click the Targets tab, select Moon Travel Planner from the Targets list, and then click the Application Settings tab.

2. Enter **MTP** as the name of the file. Type **MTP** in the Icon File text field, as shown in Figure 13-5.

 Make sure you do not add the .icns extension; Project Builder does that for you automatically.

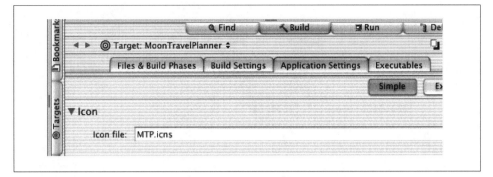

Figure 13-5. Entering the icon file name in the Application Settings pane

Add a Document Type

Now that you've created an Icon Composer file for a Moon Travel Planner document, and you've added it to your project, you need to set file type information. Follow these steps:

1. In the Application Settings tab, scroll until you can see the Type Information group box (as shown in Figure 13-6). You must add information for each document type your application will open or save. The Moon Travel Planner application will open a custom document type—iTin (an itinerary file).

 We've made up the itinerary file type just to show you how to add a custom file type. If you create your own application that uses a custom file type, you must also define the custom file format and write functions that allow your application to store and retrieve data of that format. The Moon Travel Planner itinerary file type is just a text file.

2. Enter a name for the file type. In the Name field type **Itinerary**.

 When you provide type information, you are actually assigning values to the CFBundleDocumentTypes property keys defined in Chapter 10. The Name field is the CFBundleTypeName property.

3. Enter extensions information. This is the CFBundleTypeExtensions property. Extensions can help the user distinguish between various types of document files. Entering extension information is optional. Leave the Extensions field blank; the Moon Travel Planner application does not add an extension to document filenames. If you provide an extension, your file-saving functions

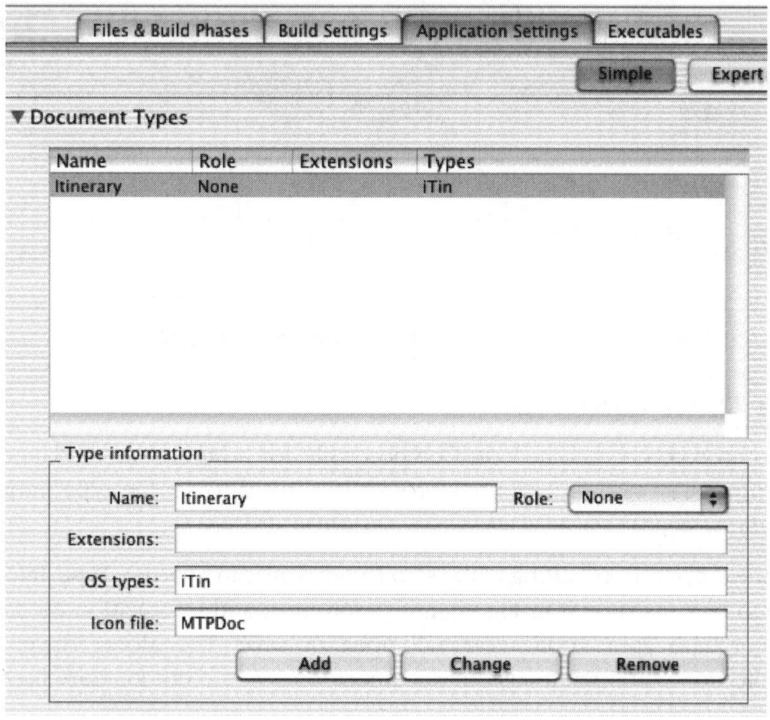

Figure 13-6. Adding document type information in Project Builder

should add the appropriate extension to the filename that the user enters in the Save dialog.

4. Enter an OS type. We're using the four-character code iTin to denote the itinerary file type. Type **iTin** in the "OS types" text field. This is the CFBundle-TypeOSTypes property.

5. Enter a filename for document icon file. Type **MTPDoc** in the "Icon file" text field. Make sure you do not add the .icns extension; that's done automatically. This is the CFBundleTypeIconFile property.

6. Click Add. The document type should appear in the Document Types list, as shown in Figure 13-6.

To add another file type, click in the blank area of the Document Types list to clear the Type Information fields. Then, repeat steps 2 through 6. The procedure for adding a generic type, such as 'TEXT', is the same as the one for adding a custom type.

Make Sure the Icons Display in the Finder

Let's make sure that the application and its documents use the icons you've added. You'll need to build and run the application, then check the icons in the Finder:

1. Click the Build button in the upper-left corner of the Moon Travel Planner project window.

2. Click the Run button in the upper-left corner of the project window. Look at the Dock as the Moon Travel Planner application launches. You should see the new icon as the application starts up.

3. Open an itinerary file. In the Moon Travel Planner application, choose Open Itinerary from the File menu, then select a file to open.

4. Save the itinerary file under a new name. Choose Save Itinerary As from the File menu and type a new filename.

5. In the Finder, navigate to the directory where you saved the itinerary file.

6. If you need to, click the icon view button. The saved itinerary file should appear with the custom document icon.

Recap

The Finder represents files and folders to the user through icons. You can add custom icons to your project to make it easier to identify your application and its associated document files. First you create the icons with a graphics program and store them in an icon file by using the Icon Composer application. Then you add the icon files to your project and add entries to the application's property list so that the icons will be recognized by the Finder.

By now you should have a complete, functioning Moon Travel Planner application with is own cool icon. We'll finish up in the next chapter by introducing a few advanced topics to whet your appetite to create you own application.

14

Beyond Moon Travel:
Advanced Topics

There are many more technologies in Carbon, and features in Apple's programming tools, than what we've covered in this book. You've learned about the core technologies and features that most applications need, and have had an opportunity to put into practice what you've learned by creating the Moon Travel Planner application. But what if you want to write a more advanced application?

You'll get a taste of three advanced topics that many developers have found useful:

- **Scriptable applications.** An application that is scriptable is capable of responding to high-level events sent by scripts, other applications, or the Mac OS itself.

- **Threads and multiprocessing.** These are useful technologies for applications that need to do more than one task at a time.

- **Tab controls.** A tab control used along with a user pane provides a compact way to present information to the user.

We'll provide an overview of each topic and give you enough information to get you started implementing each of these features.

Scriptable Applications

AppleScript is a scripting system that lets users control applications in the Mac OS without using a keyboard, mouse, or other input device. Think of it as plotting your course to the moon, then sitting back while the computer does all the work. An application is scriptable if it can perform actions in response to commands it receives. The biggest advantage of making your application scriptable is the flexibility it provides to users, who can write scripts consisting of simple, English-like statements, to:

- Automate repetitive tasks

- Use multiple applications to control complex workflows

- Exercise application features with a creativity even the application's designer may not have anticipated

Scripting power is multiplied because many parts of the Mac OS are scriptable. For example, you can write scripts that use:

- The Finder to perform many kinds of operations on windows, files, folders, and other desktop objects

- Sherlock to perform complex searches

- QuickTime to manipulate movies and other media

- ColorSync to control your color management environment

- Desktop Printing to create and control desktop printers and automate the printing process

You can even streamline your development effort by writing scripts to automate QA testing for your application.

The following sections provide a brief overview of how AppleScript works and how to make your application scriptable.

How Scripting Works

Mac OS X supports the *Open Scripting Architecture* (OSA), a standard mechanism from Apple Computer to support scriptable applications. Two key parts of the OSA are Apple events and the AppleScript scripting language.

An *Apple event* is a type of high-level message an application can use to send commands or data to itself or to other applications. The *Apple Event Manager* supplies functions and data types that applications can use to create, send, and interpret Apple events.

The *AppleScript scripting language* provides a natural language terminology so that users can write scripts (or series of instructions) made up of simple, English-like sentences. The *AppleScript component* implements this scripting language. When an application calls an Apple Event Manager function to execute a script, the AppleScript component converts script statements into Apple events to send to the appropriate applications. Mac OS X includes the *Script Editor*, an application that works with the AppleScript component to let users write, compile, test, and store scripts. The Script Editor is located in /Applications/AppleScript.

The Open Scripting Architecture supports multiple scripting languages with the same application interface. Any interested party can write a scripting component to support another scripting language, such as JavaScript. Also available are third party AppleScript script editors that supply additional features not found in Apple's Script Editor application.

H ere is an example of how a script can perform the same operations a user would perform to control an application. The Apple System Profiler is a scriptable Mac OS X application, located at /Applications/Utilities, that provides information about your computing environment. Figure 14-1 shows a user closing an Apple System Profiler window titled "ASP report 2-17-01" by using the mouse to choose the Close command from the File menu.

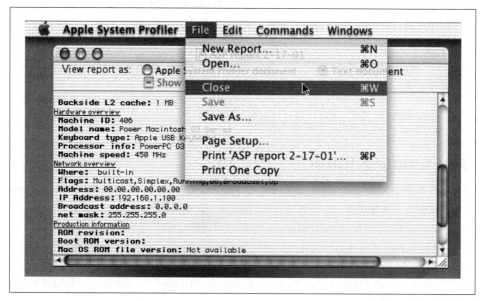

Figure 14-1. Closing an application window with the mouse

Example 14-1 shows a simple AppleScript script to close the same window.

Example 14-1: A Script that Closes an Application Window

```
tell application "Apple System Profiler"
    close window "ASP report 2-17-01"
end tell
```

You'll look at how this script works below, but first you'll need some additional information about AppleScript.

The *Apple event object model* provides a classification system that specifies items in a computing environment. Objects can range from a computer to a hard drive, an application, a window, or a word in a document. Each object belongs to a containment hierarchy. For example, the statement:

```
the third word in the first paragraph in the document MyReport
```

shows the containment for an object representing a specific word in a word-processing document.

A script can manipulate an object by sending commands to an application to get or set the object's data or perform other operations on it. A scriptable application includes a *scripting dictionary*, which specifies English-language terms for the objects and commands it understands. Example 14-2 shows the scripting dictionary for the Apple System Profiler application.

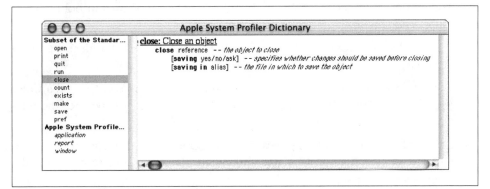

Figure 14-2. The Apple System Profiler application's scripting dictionary

You can display an application's scripting dictionary, if it has one, by dragging the application icon onto the Script Editor icon or by using the Script Editor's Open Dictionary command.

To put the whole picture together, let's look again at the script to close a window. Figure 14-3 shows a Script Editor window containing the previously shown script.

Here are some of the actions and interactions that allow the script to work:

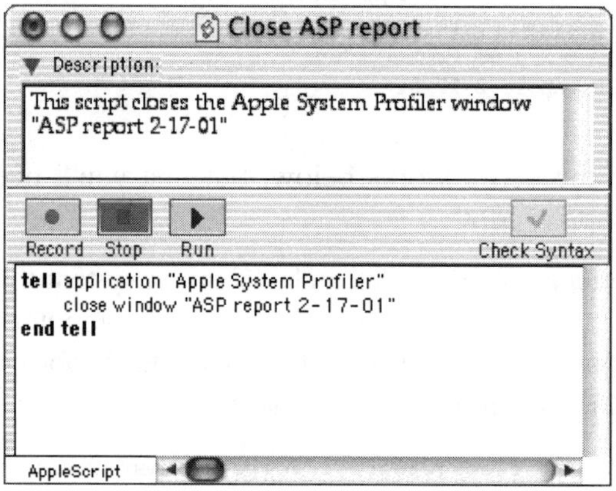

Figure 14-3. A Script Editor window

1. The user types the script into a Script Editor window and clicks the Run button.

2. The Script Editor calls on the AppleScript component to compile and execute the script. Note that a user can perform these steps separately by clicking the Check Syntax button to compile the script, then the Run button to execute it. AppleScript key words, such as `tell` and `end tell`, are shown in bold when a script is compiled.

3. The AppleScript component accesses the Apple System Profiler's scripting dictionary.

4. The AppleScript component calls on the Apple Event Manager to send a Close Apple event to the Apple System Profiler. Data in the event specifies the window object `ASP report 2-17-01`.

5. The Apple System Profiler application calls Apple Event Manager functions to help it examine the Apple event and obtain the command (Close) and the object (the `ASP report 2-17-01` window).

6. The application closes the window.

7. For some commands, an application may need to send an Apple event response. For example, if a word-processing application is told to get the third word in a document, it returns an Apple event containing that word.

8. If there is a response, the AppleScript component interprets it and sends the result to the Script Editor.

9. The user can display the result, if any, by opening the Script Editor's Result window.

For these steps to work as described, the target application must support the specified commands and objects. As shown in Figure 14-2, the dictionary for the Apple System Profiler does in fact include both the Close command and the Window object.

Here's another simple example of what an AppleScript script can accomplish. The script in Example 14-2 sets the `numFiles` variable to the count of the files in the system folder on the startup disk. The line that starts with -- is a comment and shows where you could add statements to process each of the files in the folder. The phrases `system folder` and `startup disk` represent two of several special folder and disk names the Finder understands.

Example 14-2: A Script that Counts the Files in a Folder

```
tell application "Finder"
    set numFiles to (count the files in the system folder of the startup disk)
    -- Perform some operation on the files.
end tell
```

AppleScript scripts can perform much more complex operations than those shown here. For example, a script could extract information from a database application, insert it into a spreadsheet document, and print a graph of the inserted data. Or you can write scripts to automate web site or network administration tasks.

AppleScript gets most of its power from the commands that applications implement, not from its own commands. A scriptable spreadsheet application knows all about spreadsheets, but AppleScript has no specific knowledge of spreadsheets (and doesn't need any).

AppleScript, in fact, contains only a handful of built-in commands (Copy, Count, Get, Set, and Run), but defines many additional commands that applications can, or in some cases must, support. Table 14-1 shows the required commands and some of the more commonly supported optional commands. All applications that are good Mac OS X citizens must support the required commands, even if they add no additional scripting support.

Scripting additions are files that extend AppleScript by providing additional commands or coercions you can use in scripts. A *coercion* converts a value from one class to another, such as from an integer value to a real value. Many standard coercions are built into Apple-Script.

Each scripting addition can contain one or more commands. If a scripting addition is located in the /System/Library/ScriptingAdditions directory in Mac OS X, its commands are available to any script targeting an application on that computer.

A scripting addition is sometimes referred to as an *osax*, based on its file type of `'osax'`. Mac OS X includes standard scripting additions that support actions ranging from working with URLs to speaking text.

Table 14-1. Required and Commonly Used AppleScript Commands

AppleScript Command	Description
Must Be Supported by All Applications	
Launch	Launches an application without invoking its standard startup procedures.
Run	Launches an application and invokes its standard startup procedures.
Open	Opens one or more files.
Reopen	Brings an already open application to the front and re-invokes its standard startup procedures.
Print	Prints one or more objects.
Quit	Terminates an application.
Commonly Supported by Scriptable Applications	
Get	Returns the value of an object.
Set	Assigns a value to an object.
Close	Closes one or more objects.
Save	Saves an object to a file.
Exists	Determines if an object exists.
Count	Counts elements of a particular class in an object.

Table 14-1. Required and Commonly Used AppleScript Commands (continued)

AppleScript Command	Description
Delete	Deletes one or more objects.
Duplicate	Copies an object or objects to a new location.
Make	Creates a new object.
Move	Moves an object or objects.

One of the advantages of the Apple event object model is that applications don't need to create a large universe of commands, because the same command can work on many objects. For example, your word-processing application should not define a get word command and a get paragraph command. Instead, it should support the get command for any objects a user would reasonably want to get, which might include words, paragraphs, and other objects.

See *AppleScript in a Nutshell* by O'Reilly & Associates for documentation covering the AppleScript language and information on scriptable control panels, extensions, and applications in Mac OS 9 and Mac OS X.

The *AppleScript Language Guide*, available in Carbon Help in the Project Builder Help menu, provides a comprehensive description of the commands, objects, expressions, control statements, and other components of the AppleScript Language.

You can also find lots of scripting information in AppleScript Help, available in the Help Center (in the Finder Help menu).

Making Your Application Scriptable

In previous sections, you saw some of the powerful advantages users can gain from scriptable applications and got an overview of how scripting works in Mac OS X. Traveling to the moon generally involves rockets, but making your application scriptable isn't rocket science, although it can be somewhat complex. The following sections provide a brief description of the key steps you take to create a scriptable application.

1. Design scripting in from the beginning

2. Identify the objects and commands your application will support

3. Create an 'aete' resource to describe your application's scripting support

4. Write handlers for the Apple events you support

5. Install your Apple event handlers

6. Process incoming Apple events

As you may have noticed, there are many similarities in working with Apple events and Carbon events. The following sections will point out some of these similarities.

Design scripting in from the beginning

Good scripting support starts with good application design. Before you've written a line of code, you need to think about the ways a user might want to control your application with scripts. You should design for the user first and work out the implementation details later.

As part of your design, work to separate program actions from user interface items. A scripter wants to accomplish a result (open the document "MyFile"), not necessarily perform the user interface actions they would use in the application (open the File menu; choose Open . . . ; navigate to the file; and so on).

 If you're already following the traditional model/view/controller paradigm in designing your application, you're well on your way to making it scriptable. Model/view/controller is an established design methodology that has the goal of separating an application into a model (the application's objects and data), the view (the user interface, or how the data is presented), and the controller (the component that handles physical manipulation of the view, but knows nothing of the underlying data).

The next section describes some concrete steps to help determine the Apple event objects and commands your application will work with.

Identify the objects and commands you will support

Similar to the process you used for Carbon events in Chapter 6, *Carbon Events*, you need to identify the Apple events your application will support (in addition to the required commands shown in Table 14-1). To do that, you'll identify the objects and commands a scripter could use to control your application. The following steps can help with that task:

- Write some simple sentence fragments (or better yet, have users write them) that describe what your application does. Turn the sentences into command statements. You should start to see patterns of common usage for objects and commands, with nouns typically representing objects and verbs representing commands your application can use:

```
open a TCP/IP connection
scale a shape
create a new customer record

tell the front window to scale the first oval by 25 percent
```

- Identify properties of the objects in your application. A customer has a name and address; a shape may have a color and a list of points; and so on.

- Identify the kinds of objects each command can operate on. The *rotate* command works on a shape, not a window. The *set* command may work with many objects (and many properties).

- Examine the relationships of the objects you've identified and start laying out your object model. Remember that the object model should reflect the containment relationships of the objects (`the third oval in the window "MyShapes"`).

You may have to work through these steps many times before you're satisfied with your collection of objects and commands. Again, remember that you're designing for users, so get their input as early as you can. Once you're satisfied, you're ready to incorporate the information into an `'aete'` resource for your application.

Create an 'aete' resource that describes your scripting support

Every scriptable application must include an Apple event terminology extension, or `'aete'`, resource. The `'aete'` resource is the scripting dictionary for your application. It describes the Apple events that your application supports and the user terminology that corresponds to those events. The `'aete'` resource allows the AppleScript scripting component to interpret scripts correctly and send the appropriate Apple events to your application during script execution.

Apple events contain data in the form of attributes and parameters, stored as Apple event descriptors, an opaque data type. Every Apple event has at least two attributes, an event class and an event ID, which together specify the type of event. The information in an `'aete'` resource associates the English language terms a scripter will understand with the event class and event ID values your application and AppleScript work with.

You can find constants for many standard event classes and event IDs, as well as for the scripting terminology used by AppleScript itself, in the header files `AERegistry.r`, `ASRegistry.r`, and `AppleEvents.r`. When you build your `'aete'` resource, you use constant values from these header files to identify standard commands and objects. For application-specific objects and commands, you define your own event class and event ID values.

You can work with an `'aete'` resource as a text file that you edit with any word processor, or as a compiled resource you edit with a resource editing application. Apple and third parties provide resource editors. One way to get started is to use a resource editor application to grab an existing `'aete'` from one of Mac OS X's scriptable applications, such as Apple System Profiler, then use the editor to modify it for your application.

Write handlers for the Apple events you support

As with Carbon events and the Carbon Event Manager, scriptable applications rely on a callback mechanism that dispatches Apple events to handler functions. You'll need to write a handler for each type of Apple event your application handles. In this section and the following section you'll learn how to add support for one of the required Apple events described previously, the Open Documents event to the Moon Travel Planner application.

Example 14-3 shows the format for an Apple event handler.

Example 14-3: An Apple Event Handler Callback Declaration

```
OSErr MyAEEventHandlerCallback (
    const AppleEvent *theAppleEvent,
    AppleEvent *reply,
    UInt32 handlerRefcon);
```

The first parameter is a pointer to the Apple event to handle, the second parameter is a pointer to the default reply Apple event provided by the Apple Event Manager, and the third parameter is a reference constant your application can use to supply additional information to your handler. The reference constant can be a simple four-byte value, a pointer to a block of data, or it can be NULL if you don't need it.

Example 14-4 shows how the Moon Travel Planner might implement an Open Documents event handler. The reason all well-behaved Mac OS X applications should support the Open Documents Apple event is that when a user selects one or more of an application's documents in the Finder and double-clicks, the Finder sends the application an Apple event describing a list of files that it should open. To respond properly to this Apple event, your application extracts the file descriptions from the Apple event and opens the documents.

Example 14-4: An Open Documents Apple Event Handler for the Moon Travel Planner

```
OSStatus MTPHandleOpenAppleEvent(const AppleEvent * appleEvt,
        AppleEvent * reply, SInt32 refcon)
{
    AEDesc fileList = {typeNull, NULL};                          // 1
    OSErr err;
    SInt32 itemsInList;
    FSRef fileToOpen;
    HFSUniStr255 theFileName;
    CFStringRef fileNameCFString;
    WindowRef newWindow;

    err = AEGetParamDesc(appleEvt, keyDirectObject,             // 2
                    typeAEList, &fileList);
    if (err == noErr)
    {
        err = AECountItems(&fileList, &itemsInList);            // 3
        if (err == noErr && itemsInList > 0)
        {
            OSType    keyword;
            OSType    returnedType;
            Size    actualSize;
            short i;
            for (i = 1; i <= itemsInList; i++)                  // 4
            {
                err = AEGetNthPtr(&fileList, i, typeFSRef, &keyword,  // 5
                        &returnedType, &fileToOpen,
                        sizeof(FSRef), &actualSize);

                if (err == noErr)
                {
                    err = FSGetCatalogInfo(&fileToOpen, kFSCatInfoNone,  // 6
                            NULL, &theFileName, NULL, NULL);
                    fileNameCFString =  CFStringCreateWithCharacters (   // 7
                                        NULL,
                                        theFileName.unicode,
                                        theFileName.length);

                    newWindow = MTPDoNewItinerary( fileNameCFString);    // 8

                    ShowWindow(newWindow);                               // 9

                    err  = MTPReadFile(&fileToOpen, newWindow);          // 10
                }
            }
        }
    }
    return err;
}
```

Here's how the MTPHandleOpenAppleEvent function works:

1. It initializes an Apple event descriptor record to hold the list of references to files to open. This line shows the approved style for initializing a descriptor record.

 Though an apple event descriptor is just an opaque data structure of some type, descriptors have traditionally been known as descriptor records.

---

2. It calls the Apple Event Manager function AEGetParamDesc, to extract a list of descriptor records (one for each file to be opened). It passes the values keyDirectObject and typeAEList to tell the function what kind of information to look for, and the parameter fileList to return the list.

3. If no error occurs, it calls the Apple Event Manager function AECountItems, to count the number of file descriptor records in the list.

4. If no error occurs, it sets up a loop to iterate over each item in the list.

5. It calls the Apple Event Manager function AEGetNthPtr, to extract an FSRef record that describes the current file to be opened. It passes the value typeFS-Ref to indicate the type of information it is expecting, and the address of a variable of type FSRef for the returned value. If the specified record in the file list contains an FSRef for a file to open or any value that can be coerced (converted) to an FSRef, the MTPHandleOpenAppleEvent function automatically returns the desired type. This handler could examine the returnedType parameter to verify that the returned value is indeed the expected type, but it's a trusting little function and may end up lost in space someday.

6. If no error occurs, it calls the File Manager function FSGetCatalogInfo to get the name of the file to be opened as a Unicode string.

7. It calls the Core Foundation function CFStringCreateWithCharacters to get the file name as a CFStringRef.

8. It calls the function MTPDoNewItinerary, shown in Chapter 11, *Files*, to create a new itinerary window.

9. It calls the Carbon function ShowWindow to make the window visible.

10. It calls the function MTPReadFile, shown in Chapter 11, to read the itinerary information from the file and display it in the window.

Your application can implement a Print Documents event handler with much of the same code shown in Example 14-4. As with the Open Documents event, the Apple event contains a list of one or more references to files that your application should print. To do so, you extract the file references as shown here, do any preparation you might need for printing, then call the `MTPDoPrint` function to display the Print dialog.

Most Apple event handlers call Apple Event Manager functions to extract parameter and attribute information from the event. Parameters and attributes in Apple events are not the same as parameters to C function calls. Every Apple event parameter is an Apple event descriptor, a self-typed data structure that can represent files, aliases, numbers, strings, URLs, enumerated constants, and many other values. The underlying data type for the Apple event descriptor is the `AEDesc` structure. The event descriptor is an opaque type, but the Apple Event Manager provides functions for accessing its data.

Apple events can have a variable number of parameters, some of which are optional and some of which can contain additional nested descriptors. But the Apple Event Manager doesn't define a large number of function calls with varying parameter lists to supply Apple event parameter values. Instead, your event handler routines extract Apple event parameters from an event by calling the `AEGetKeyDesc` function, which copies the parameter (if present) into an `AEDesc` structure. You use the `AEGetDescData` function to extract data from a descriptor structure.

When a parameter consists of an object specifier record (an Apple event descriptor that specifies an Apple event model object), your handler should call the `AEResolve` function to start the process of resolving the object specifier. For example, the specifier created from the statement:

`third word in the second paragraph in the document "MyReport"`

resolves to an Apple event descriptor that identifies the specified word.

Resolving object specifiers is a detailed process that's beyond the scope of this book. Apple supplies two helper libraries, the Object Support Library (OSL) and MoreOSL, that can help your application handle object specifier resolution. See the Apple Event Manager documentation in Carbon Help (available in the Project Builder Help menu) for more information on the Object Support Library. For information on MoreOSL, see the Sample Code area in the Apple developer web site (listed in Appendix A, *Additional Resources*).

Install your Apple event handlers

As you do with Carbon events, your application must install its Apple event handlers. You do so by calling the function `AEInstallEventHandler`. Example 14-5 shows how to install the Open Documents event handler described previously.

Example 14-5: Installing an Open Documents Event Handler

```
OSErr err;
err = AEInstallEventHandler(
        kCoreEventClass,
        kAEOpenDocuments,
        NewAEEventHandlerUPP((AEEventHandlerProcPtr) MTPHandleOpenAppleEvent),
        NULL,
        false);
```

The first two parameters specify an event class and event ID that identify the type of Apple event. The third parameter is a pointer to your event handler. You create this pointer by calling the function `NewAEEventHandlerUPP`. The fourth parameter has the value `NULL`, indicating that this event handler doesn't need any information passed to it in its `refcon` parameter. And the final parameter has the value `false`, indicating that this handler is an application handler, not a special type of handler.

Process incoming Apple events

If your application uses the Carbon event model, as the Moon Travel Planner application does, and calls `RunApplicationEventLoop`, you won't need to do anything special to receive Apple events. The Carbon Event Manager will automatically direct Apple events sent to your application to the Apple event handlers you have installed. Your handlers then perform the necessary operations to handle the events they receive.

In addition, applications that use the Carbon event model don't need to write handlers for the required Run or Quit Apple events, because they're handled automatically.

AppleScript is a mature and powerful scripting language that lets users streamline application tasks and allows applications to communicate with each other using Apple events. The Apple Event Manager allows your application to create and interpret Apple events, and you can use various third-party applications to help you to create and debug scripts. Most important commercial applications are AppleScript-savvy, so yours should be no exception.

When you're ready to add scripting support, you'll find documentation for AppleScript and the Apple Event Manager in the Interapplication Communication documentation in Carbon Help (available in the Project Builder Help menu).

Threads and Multiprocessing

Simple applications tend to be very focused, concentrating on one task at a time. However, as your programs get more complex or sophisticated, you may want your application to start doing multiple things at once. Say you have any application that, among other things, periodically downloads information off a network and updates a window with the new information. For the best user experience, you would like the information retrieval to be independent of any other actions the application can take. Otherwise, the retrieval process will "lock up" your application for the duration, and your user will be left twiddling thumbs (or, more likely, cursing, as shown in Figure 14-4) until the download is complete. The best way to do this is to create a separate thread to handle the download.

Threads, which are sometimes called *tasks,* are independent execution paths within your application. They have their own stack and function almost like mini-applications. However, they share the same address space as the main application, which means they can share memory. This makes it easy to pass information between the thread and the main application. For example, if an application wants to spawn a thread to process an image in the background, it can simply pass a pointer to the image rather than copying the image itself.

Typically you create threads to perform background processing that doesn't require interaction from the user. For example, time-intensive calculations or file transfers are good candidates for background threads. Saving a file, however, may not be, as you probably don't want the user to be able to continue modifying a file while it is being saved. In some cases, it's advantageous to have your main application thread handle only the user interface and delegate all other actions to background threads.

Most asynchronous communication between the thread and the main application (or between multiple threads) occurs by sending simple messages. For example, a thread may set a particular bit high to indicate "Okay, I'm ready for your data." After it receives the data, it resets the bit and begins processing. When it finishes, it may set a different bit that indicates "Data is processed. Come pick it up." Things can quickly get more sophisticated than that, but the general idea is the same.

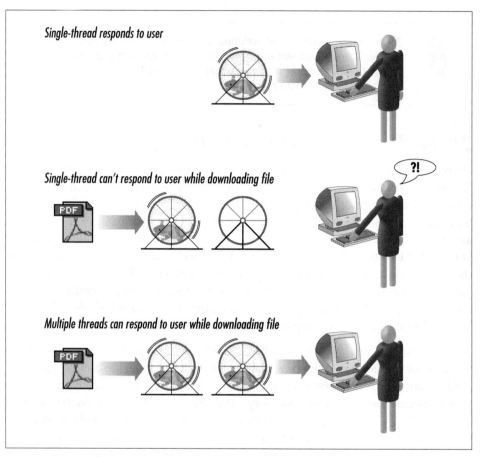

Single-thread responds to user

Single-thread can't respond to user while downloading file

Multiple threads can respond to user while downloading file

Figure 14-4. Single-threaded versus multithreaded applications

Carbon has two programming interfaces that let you create independent threads:

- Multiprocessing Services lets you create preemptively scheduled threads (called tasks in Apple's documentation). These threads are given processor time just as if they were separate processes in the system. Better yet, if you are running on a multiprocessor Macintosh, threads created with Multiprocessing Services automatically take advantage of the extra processors. This is the interface of choice for most threaded applications. The only restriction is that some system software calls are not reentrant (that is, they cannot be called by multiple threads at the same time) and therefore cannot be called directly from a preemptive thread. (You can, however, use a callback mechanism called a remote procedure call to call nonreentrant functions.)

- The Thread Manager lets you create cooperatively scheduled threads. Just as in a cooperative-tasking runtime environment (as used in older Mac OS operating systems), each thread must voluntarily cede processor time to the main application (and other threads). While not as flexible as Multiprocessing Services, the Thread Manager is a good tool to use if you need more control over when your threads are running.

Multiprocessing Services in a Peanut Shell

Let's see how you'd go about using Multiprocessing Services to create a thread that handles a lengthy calculation in the background. You would need to create the thread, pass it the data to be processed, then wait for it to complete. We'll take a closer look at each step.

 The Multiprocessing Services documentation in Carbon Help refers to preemptive threads as tasks, mostly to distinguish them from the Thread Manager's cooperative threads. However, because most programmers are more familiar with the term thread, this book will adhere to that term instead.

First, you need to create the thread. You do so by calling the Multiprocessing Services function `MPCreateTask`. You pass a number of parameters indicating such items as the desired stack size for the thread and a queue to notify when the thread terminates. The latter is important because the thread is not synchronized to your main application; it could terminate the thread (by calling `MPTerminateTask`), but it has no way of knowing if the thread is actually terminated unless it receives confirmation of some kind.

You can think of the preemptively scheduled thread as being a field agent for some spy organization. The spy works independently and is essentially out of reach of headquarters. If headquarters wants some mission accomplished, it places a message (or a signal) at some prearranged location. After sending this notice, headquarters must monitor another prearranged location for a response message, which the spy sends when the task is accomplished.

The thread itself is just defined as a function, which may or may not take any parameters. Typically, the parameters define information useful over the life of the thread, such as the locations of "dropboxes" for messages to and from the main application. These dropboxes are called *notification methods* in multitasking parlance. Two common notification methods are message queues and semaphores:

- Message queue. A first-in-first-out stack for messages, which are 96 bits long. A message can contain any sort of information, such as a pointer to the data to process or computation instructions. A message queue is analogous to a specific drop site where the spy can pick up an envelope of instructions.

- Semaphore. A simple state variable that can be incremented from one to some specified maximum value. For example, setting a binary semaphore (that is, a semaphore with two states, zero and one) to a value of one could indicate that the data is ready for the thread to process. Semaphores cannot communicate as much information as message queues, but they incur less processing overhead.

Typically, your application sets up two queues or semaphores for a thread: one to send notifications and one to receive them. However, it's possible for more than one thread to use the same queue. This arrangement can be useful for distributing work in multiprocessor systems: you can create multiple instances of the same function, one for each available processor.

Implementing a notification method is fairly straightforward. Each particular method has its own creation, termination, signaling, and waiting functions. For example, message queues use the following Multiprocessing Services functions:

- `MPCreateQueue`. Creates a message queue and gives you a pointer to the queue object.

- `MPTerminateQueue`. Removes a queue object. Typically you do this after you terminate the associated thread.

- `MPNotifyQueue`. Places a 96-bit message on the specified queue.

- `MPWaitOnQueue`. Stops execution of the thread that calls it and waits for a message on the specified queue. When a message appears (or if one was already present when the function was called), it removes the message from the queue and lets the thread continue execution.

Multiprocessing Services threads are usually written as an endless loop, waiting for an appropriate signal, executing the task when the signal arrives, sending a response signal, and then waiting again. This implementation ensures that no processor time is wasted; if there is nothing for the thread to do, it does nothing.

Similarly, after signaling the thread, your main application must wait for a "task completed" notification so it knows the task is done processing. However, most likely your application can't afford to just wait, as it may be interacting with the user, updating windows, or even signaling another thread.

One solution is to poll the queue periodically by calling `MPWaitOnQueue` with a zero timeout (that is, by passing `kDurationImmediate` as the timeout constant). However, polling on preemptive multitasking systems is generally regarded as a bad thing, because it means that your application can use up valuable processor time doing essentially nothing. Fortunately, the Carbon Event Manager comes to the rescue by allowing you to send yourself a custom event instead of polling.

In addition to all the event kinds defined by the Carbon Event Manager, you can define your own. Doing so can be a useful way of notifying yourself that some special event has occurred. For example, your thread can send an event to the main application to say, "there's a message on the result queue." On the application end, you need to register an event handler to handle your custom event. This handler can call MPWaitOnQueue with a wait time of kDurationImmediate (because it knows that a message exists) and then process the message appropriately. To implement this mechanism, you will need the following Carbon Event Manager functions:

- CreateEvent. Creates a custom event. You must specify an event class and kind, as well as any attributes (if desired). On return, you get an event reference that defines the event.

- GetMainEventQueue. Returns a pointer to the main application event queue. This is the queue that contains all events your application wants to process.

- PostEventToQueue. Places an event on the specified queue.

Figure 14-5 illustrates the basic operation sequence for working with a Multiprocessing Services thread:

- First, you perform any application initialization, create the In and Out message queues, and create the custom event. You register your custom event handler as you would any other, by calling InstallEventHandler. The event reference target can be arbitrary, as you will be controlling who sends the event. Your application calls MPCreateTask when it needs to spawn the preemptive thread.

- If your application has work for the thread to do, it signals the thread by calling MPNotifyQueue to place a message in the In message queue.

- When your thread has finished processing, it places a message in the Out message queue. Then it calls GetMainEventQueue to get the main event queue and PostEventToQueue to place your custom event on the queue. After placing the event on the queue, the thread returns to its MPWaitOnQueue function, remaining blocked until a new message appears in the In queue.

- Back in the main application thread, when the Carbon Event Manager pulls the custom event off the queue, your event handler gets called. It can then call MPWaitOnQueue to get the message on the Out message queue and take any additional actions.

Note that one advantage of using Carbon events for communicating with your main application is that you don't need to worry about interrupting actions that shouldn't be interrupted. For example, you wouldn't want your application to start processing data it received from the thread while the user was pulling down a menu.

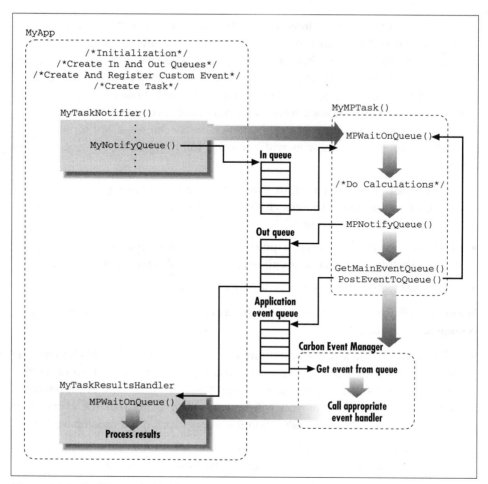

Figure 14-5. Working with a Multiprocessing Services thread.

If you want your application to do several different tasks simultaneously, you should consider creating independent execution threads. You can use either the Thread Manager or Multiprocessing Services to create your threads, but in most cases you will want to use the latter. Multiprocessing Services threads are preemptively scheduled, and they can automatically take advantage of multiple processors.

Tab Controls

The *tab control* provides a convenient way to present information in a multipage format. Figure 14-6 shows two tabs centered horizontally in a window. The content area below a tab is called a *pane*. Panes are often used to organize settings for a utility program or control panel. When panes are used in combination with tabs, users can see, at a glance, all the categories of settings or features available. Tabs allow users to quickly switch from one pane to another with a single click.

As shown in the figure, you can use other controls, such as push buttons, radio buttons, and text fields, in a tabbed window. The controls can be *global*—affecting the settings of all panes—or specific to an individual pane. Make it clear through labeling and placement (within or outside of a tab pane's boundary, for example) whether a control affects one pane or all panes. In the figure shown, the Quit button is outside the pane area, so it's available regardless of which pane is visible.

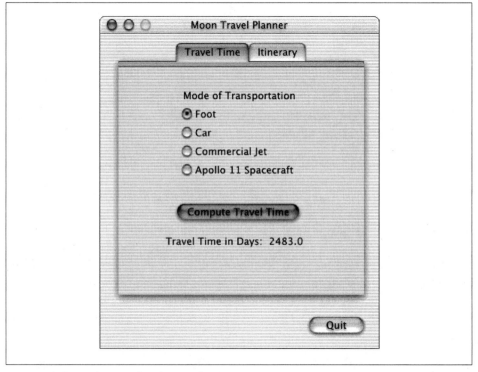

Figure 14-6. A tab control with two tabs

When the user clicks a tab, the pane should switch appropriately. For example, when the user clicks the Itinerary tab, the Travel Time pane should disappear and the Itinerary pane should appear, as shown in Figure 14-7. Although it appears to the user as if the pane and the tab are one, you must implement this illusion in your code, because the tab and the pane operate independently. Each tab must be paired with a pane. When the user clicks a tab, your code must switch the tab view, make the appropriate pane visible, and make sure all other panes are hidden. (You'll see how to do this in the section "Write a Handler for the Tab Controls and Panes.")

Figure 14-7. The Itinerary pane appears when the user click the Itinerary tab

Besides coordinating tabs with panes, the other tricky aspect of tab controls is adding items to a pane. When you add items, you need to make sure you are actually adding them to the appropriate pane. It's easy to either add the items to the wrong pane or simply add an item to the window, but not associate the item with a pane. If you do either of these, when you run your application you'll see misplaced items or items that persist from pane to pane. We'll show you how to avoid this in the example that follows.

You'll add tabs to an interface by doing the following:

1. Add a tab control to a window

2. Add controls to a user pane

3. Write a handler for a tab control and panes

Add a Tab Control to a Window

Adding a tab control using Interface Builder is fairly straightforward. You'll start with a window and add a tab data view that has two tabs. You can add more if you'd like, but we'll stick to two for the purpose of showing you how to do it:

1. Drag a tab control (shown in Figure 14-8) from the DataViews palette in Interface Builder to a window.

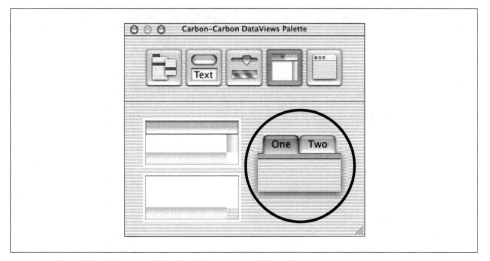

Figure 14-8. The tab control on the DataViews palette

2. Resize the tab control by dragging its corner until it fits the Aqua guides, as shown in Figure 14-9.

3. Use the Show Info window to set the number of tabs and tab orientation. Click the middle of the tab view, then choose Show Info from the Tools menu. The Tab Info window should open. You'll keep the default values: 2 as the number of tabs, and North as the tab direction.

4. Assign the tab control an ID and a signature. The ID must be an 8-bit value; use the application's creator code as the signature. You'll need these when you write a handler to switch tabs. Choose Control from the pop-up menu. In the Control ID box, type **MTPP** for the signature and 128 for the ID.

5. Double-click the tab labeled One to make the tab and its pane editable. The Info window should now be titled Tab Item Info and you should see a thick line around the pane, as shown in Figure 14-10.

6. Use the Attributes pane of the Tab Item Info window to name the tabs. For each tab, type the name in the Label text field, as shown in the example for the Travel Time tab in Figure 14-10. Type **Travel Time** for tab One and **Itinerary** for tab Two.

7. Assign a User Pane Signature and User Pane ID to each tab item. The User Pane Signature for each tab item should be the same as that assigned to the tab—the application's creator code. Type **MTPP** in the User Pane Signature text field. The IDs should be sequentially assigned, using the ID you assigned

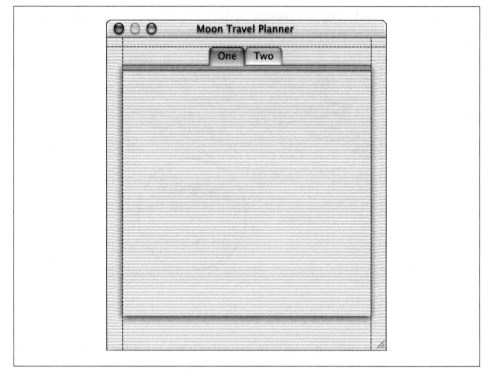

Figure 14-9. Use the Aqua guides to size the tab control

to the tab (128) as the basis. Type **129** in the User Pane ID field for the Travel Time tab item and **130** for the Itinerary tab item.

Add Controls to a User Pane

The procedures for adding controls to a user pane are the same as those you used in Chapter 5, *Interface Builder: Tools and Controls*, to add controls to a window. The only difference is that you must make sure the pane to which you want to add controls is in edit mode and is in front of the other panes.

Before you add a control, double-click the tab associated with the pane to which you want to add a control. Make sure the user pane is editable—the tab you clicked should be active and a thick line should appear around the pane. Then, you can drag controls to the pane as you would to a window.

Write a Handler for the Tab Controls and Panes

You need to write a handler that switches the frontmost tab in response to a user click on a tab and then shows the appropriate pane while hiding the others. First, you'll need to declare the constant that represents the IDs you assigned to the tab

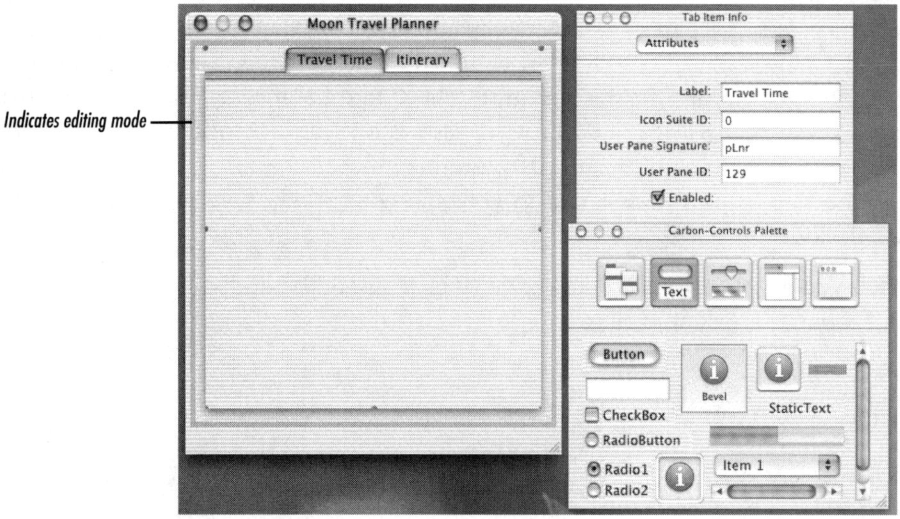

Figure 14-10. The thick line indicates you are editing the pane and tab shown

control and tab items when you set them up in Interface Builder. First, define constants to represent the tab ID:

```
#define    TAB_ID    128;
```

Next, set up an array—a tab list—to specify the number of tabs and the ID of each tab. The first item in the array is 2 because you set up two tab items. Recall you assigned 129 and 130 as the tab item IDs. The variable `lastTabIndex` is a housekeeping variable you'll use to keep track of the last tab chosen by the user. You'll set the starting value at 1:

```
int    tabList[] = {2, 129, 130};
int    lastTabIndex = 1;
```

You'll need to declare the tab handler (`MyTabEventHandler`) and the function (`MySwitchItemOfTabControl`) that switches from one pane to another. Here are the function declarations for each:

```
pascal OSStatus MyTabEventHandler (EventHandlerCallRef inHandlerRef,
                        EventRef inEvent, void *inUserData);
void MySwitchItemOfTabControl (int index, ControlRef tabControl);
```

In your main function, you install an event handler for the tab control. You'll use the `InstallEventHandler` function we discussed in Chapter 6. As you recall, this function requires an event target as its first parameter. The event target is the tab control, but you need to pass a parameter of type `EventTargetRef`. The Carbon Event Manager has a function, `GetControlEventTarget`, that takes a control as a parameter and returns an `EventTargetRef` for that control. But `GetControlEvent-Target` takes a `ControlRef` as a parameter. You know what the ID and signature of the tab control are, so you'll need to use those to get the `ControlRef` associated with our tab control's ID and signature. The Control Manager has a function, `GetControlByID`, that will get a `ControlRef` associated with a window reference and a `ControlID` data type. A `ControlID` is a structure that contains a signature and an ID—the two items you assigned to your tab control when you set it up in Interface Builder.

When you put it all together, the code (which should be added to your main function) looks like Example 14-6.

Example 14-6: Code to Install the Tab Control Event Handler

```
ControlID            controlID;
controlID.signature  = TAB_SIGNATURE;
controlID.id         = TAB_ID;
GetControlByID (MyWindow, &controlID, &tabControl);
eventTypeSpec        controlSpec = {

InstallEventHandler (GetControlEventTarget (tabControl),
                     NewEventHandlerUPP (MyTabEventHandler),
                     2,
                     &controlSpec,
                     0,
                     NULL);
```

You need to assure that when your application launches, the tab control displays properly. To do so, put the following code in your main function to select the first tab item when the application launches:

```
MySwitchItemOfTabControl (1,tabControl);
```

Now, you are ready to add the actual tab handler shown in Example 14-7. The handle switches tabs only if the tab value has changed. If the user clicks the active tab, nothing happens.

Example 14-7: The Tab Event Handler

```
pascal OSStatus MyTabEventHandler (EventHandlerCallRef inHandlerRef,
                                   EventRef inEvent, void *inUserData)
{
    ControlRef  tabControl;
    ControlID   controlID;
    OSStatus    result;
    controlID.signature = TAB_SIGNATURE;
    controlID.id        = TAB_ID;

    GetControlByID (MyWindow, &controlID, &tabControl);          // 1
    if (GetControlValue (tabControl) == lastTabIndex)            // 2
    {
```

Example 14-7: The Tab Event Handler (continued)

```
                   result = eventNotHandledErr;
   }
   else {                                                              // 3
       MySwitchItemOfTabControl (GetControlValue (tabControl), tabControl);
       result = noErr;
       }
   return result;
}
```

Here is what the function does:

1. You need to get the `ControlRef` associated with the tab control so you can check its value. As you saw in Chapter 6, the Control Manager function `GetControlById` will do just that.

2. You use `GetControlValue` to get the value of the pane setting and compare it with the last known value to see if the tab value has changed. If it hasn't changed, you pass back `eventNotHandledErr` to give the Carbon Event Manager a chance to let another handler take care of the event.

3. Otherwise, the value has changed, so you need to call your function (`MySwitchItemOfTabControl`) to switch the pane associated with the tab and then redraw the tab control.

You'll need to add the function called by your tab handler, as shown in Example 14-8, to switch to the pane associated with the tab.

Example 14-8: A Function to Switch Panes

```
void MySwitchItemOfTabControl (int currentTabIndex,
                               ControlRef tabControl)
{
    ControlRef userPane;
    ControlRef selectedPane = NULL;
    ControlID controlID;
    UInt16 i;

    lastTabIndex = currentTabIndex;
    controlID.signature = TAB_SIGNATURE;

    for (i = 1; i < tabList[0] + 1; i++)
    {
        controlID.id = tabList[i];
        GetControlByID (MyWindow, &controlID, &userPane);          // 1

        if (i == currentTabIndex)                                  // 2
            selectedPane = userPane;
        else
            SetControlVisibility (userPane,false,true);            // 3
    }
    if (selectedPane)
```

Example 14-8: A Function to Switch Panes (continued)

```
        SetControlVisibility (selectedPane,true,true);              // 4

    Draw1Control (tabControl);                                      // 5
}
```

Here is what the function does:

1. Call the Control Manager function `GetControlByID` to get the control reference for the pane associated with a tab control.

2. If the current tab index has the same value as the pane you're checking, then set the selected pane to the pane you're checking.

3. If the selected pane is not the same as the pane you're checking, then call the Control Manager function `SetControlVisibility` to set the visibility for the pane to `false` (don't show it) and update the display (indicated by `true`).

4. If the selected pane is the same as the pane you're checking, call the function `SetControlVisibility` to make the pane visible and update the display.

5. The Control Manager function `Draw1Control` updates the tab control so the correct tab is active.

Notice that none of the code you've added handles controls in the pane. How could you handle them? Let's say your tabbed window has a pane identical to the Travel Time pane shown earlier, in Figure 14-6. You would use the same window event handler and compute travel time functions you wrote in Chapter 6. You let your tab handler take care of switching the view while your window event handler and compute travel time functions respond to user interaction in the actual pane.

Instead of displaying content in multiple windows, tab controls let your application display the content as a stack of panes in a single window. To use tabs, you must add tab controls to your application and then write a handler that switches from one pane to another when the user clicks a tab. As an exercise, you can modify the Moon Travel Planner application to use multiple panes instead of multiple windows.

Epilogue

A trip to the moon may still be a way off for you, but your Carbon application development foray is well under way. Throughout the course of this book, you've created a fairly substantial Carbon application—the Moon Travel Planner—with which you should be pleased.

The application has most of the features users expect from a Mac OS X application:

- Its own icon

- The slick new Aqua interface

- Printing

- File handling

- Help using Apple's two help facilities: the Carbon Help Manager for help tags and the Apple Help Manager for help books

- An application-specific menu (the Moon menu)

- An About window

Moon Travel Planner is ready for localization because Project Builder provided a language-specific folder to which you added a localizable strings file. You also put user-readable properties into the InfoPlist.strings file so they can be translated and added to the appropriate language-specific folders.

In this chapter, we've tempted you with a few advanced topics. If you've enjoyed what you've done so far, you might try to expand the Moon Travel Planner application by using some of the ideas we covered. Revise the application so it uses tabs and user panes instead of windows. Make the application scriptable. Add some computationally intensive functions (such as computing travel time by taking into account earth and moon gravitational effects and other physical phenomena) that benefit from adding multiprocessing capabilities to the application.

To start creating your own application, you can supplement the basic knowledge you've gained with information available in Carbon Help and from the resources in Appendix A. Don't forget the overview of Carbon programming interfaces in Chapter 1, *Introduction to Carbon*. The overview is a great place to start if you know what you want your application to do, but you are not sure which Carbon technology or service supports the functionality you want.

A

Additional Resources

If your mission is to produce commercial quality software for Mac OS X, *Learning Carbon* has provided a great lift-off. But your journey to market still has a fair distance to go. This appendix lists information about the documents referred to in this book and points you to other resources that can further help you in your Carbon application development. These resources include:

- Carbon and Mac OS X books aimed at the general programmer audience
- Articles and postings about particular Carbon programming topics
- Sample code
- Carbon developer mailing lists and newsgroups
- Partnership programs with Apple Computer

Your first source of additional information pertaining to the material presented in this book is the book's own web site, located at:

http://www.oreilly.com/catalog/learncarbon/

At this site, you'll find the book's sample code available for downloading, as well as any errata and plans for future editions.

Read further to learn how to locate other development resources.

Building Your Mac OS X Library

There are some books that every Carbon programmer should keep on the bookshelf, if only on the "virtual" bookshelf. If you installed Project Builder from the Mac OS X Developer CD, you already have PDF versions of the books listed in this section. To access them from the main Carbon Help page, choose Carbon Help from the Project Builder Help menu.

If you prefer print over PDF, you can order printed, bound copies of these and other selected documents from Apple's print-on-demand provider, *Fatbrain.com*:

http://www1.fatbrain.com/documentation/apple/

Inside Mac OS X: System Overview

This overview of Mac OS X is valuable for anyone doing software development with Carbon. You should read *Inside Mac OS X: System Overview* to familiarize yourself with the architecture of Mac OS X and how to best take advantage of its design. This guide not only describes the features and capabilities of the operating system, but also describes concepts, facilities, and conventions common to the system's Carbon, Cocoa, Java, and BSD application environments.

Inside Mac OS X: Aqua Human Interface Guidelines

This book describes how to design your application for the Mac OS X user interface, known as Aqua. *Inside Mac OS X: Aqua Human Interface Guidelines* is primarily intended for Carbon and Cocoa developers—but is also applicable for Java developers—who want their applications to look right and behave correctly in Mac OS X. This guide provides examples of how to use such Aqua interface elements as windows, controls, dialogs, and icons so that the users of your Carbon application will be familiar and comfortable with your product the moment they double-click its icon.

Inside Carbon: Carbon Porting Guide

Perhaps you've been assigned the job of porting an existing Macintosh application to Mac OS X, and being unfamiliar with the Mac OS, you read *Learning Carbon* to introduce yourself to the Carbon environment. If you're updating a Mac application for Mac OS X, you should read *Inside Carbon: Carbon Porting Guide*. This guide tells you how an older application can benefit from Mac OS X, and it contains all the basic information required to begin porting that application to Carbon.

Discovering QuickTime

If you want to add QuickTime to your application, this book is a must have. You'll get a step-by-step introduction to QuickTime programming, from movies and animation to streaming video on the Internet. The CD-ROM included with the book provides working applications, sample code, and the essential programming resources you need to get started. Morgan Kaufmann publishes this and several other books about QuickTime. For more information, go to:

http://developer.apple.com/quicktime/quicktimeintro/docs.html

Tapping the Carbon Developer Community

The Carbon developer community is one of its own best resources. There are several vehicles for you to learn from this community and, in turn, to share your own growing knowledge and expertise.

Mac DevCenter

Affiliated with O'Reilly & Associates books, the O'Reilly Network hosts Mac DevCenter, a hub site that offers news, FAQs, original articles, and other technical information for Mac OS X developers:

http://www.oreillynet.com/mac/

MacTech Magazine

MacTech magazine is a monthly print journal that presents programming articles and news about Macintosh technology and development. For subscription information, go to:

http://www.mactech.com/

This MacTech web site also contains a lot of downloadable source code and a web version of *MacTech Online*, a monthly column from the magazine that provides online technologies and resources. These resources include links to web pages, shareware archives, newsgroups, mailing lists, and castanet channels aimed at Macintosh programmers.

The MacDev-1 Email List

Cosponsored by MacTech Magazine, Developer Depot (a retailer of programming tools), and Apple, MacDev-1 is a source of news, information, updates, and special offers for the Mac programmer community. The goals of the MacDev-1 list are to make developers more aware of available programming resources and to provide vendors of Mac development tools with an efficient channel through which to spread the word about product releases.

This list is moderated by the MacTech Magazine staff. For information on how to participate in MacDev-1, go to:

http://www.mactech.com/macdev-1/index.html

Carbon Development Email List

Apple moderates an email list focused exclusively on Carbon development issues. For information on how to subscribe to this mail list, go to:

http://lists.apple.com/mailman/listinfo/carbon-development

Although Apple restricts this list to discussions about creating or porting Carbon applications, Apple welcomes any non-development feedback you might offer. You can send these comments to *carbon@apple.com.*

Keeping Current

Apple uses the Developer Documentation area of its web site to post new documents and update existing ones on a daily basis. You might want to check the Carbon documentation site for more recent versions of the documents provided on the Mac OS X Developer CD:

http://developer.apple.com/techpubs/macosx/Carbon/carbon.html

You will instantly see that this page looks remarkably like the Carbon Developer Documentation page in Project Builder. That's because Apple takes a "snapshot" of this web site for distribution whenever it releases an update to the Mac OS X Developer CD. You can quickly see what documents have been added or updated by clicking the "New and updated documentation" link.

The web edition of this documentation makes searching easy through its Sherlock plug-in. Be sure to download this plug-in from the Carbon Developer Documentation site.

It's even easier to stay up-to-date by signing up for Apple's free Online Program offered by Apple Developer Connection (ADC). See the section "Partnering with Apple."

Getting Sample Code

Sometimes there is no better way to learn how to write code than to see working code written by someone else. Apple provides software development kits (SDKs) free of charge for most of Apple's key technologies. You'll find header files, libraries, sample code, and other useful tools and resources in each SDK. You can access a link to Apple's SDKs from this web site:

http://developer.apple.com/macosx/carbon/index.html

You'll also find links to Carbon Development Tips & Tricks, a page dedicated to sharing Carbon development, debugging, and porting information.

Registering Creator Codes

When you start developing a commercial application, you can register a unique creator code with Apple at this web site:

http://developer.apple.com/dev/cftype/

Partnering with Apple

Your success is Apple's success. Apple wants developers like you to create successful applications that make customers clamor for Apple computers.

You should tap into some of the programs, products, and services offered by Apple Developer Connection (ADC). Aimed at both large and small developers, the stated purpose of ADC is "to help you successfully develop, test, market, and distribute software and hardware products for Apple platforms and technologies."

In addition to publishing the Developer web site at *developer.apple.com* (which includes the Carbon Developer Documentation suite), hosting an annual Apple Worldwide Developers Conference, and championing developer needs to Apple's own development engineers, ADC offers several program packages useful to you and other developers.

You should become a member of one of these programs—at a minimum, sign up for the Online program. It's free! The Online program allows you to download up-to-date development tools, gain access to certain early software releases, and receive weekly technical updates via email.

If you'd rather have this type of information mailed to you, you can pay to become an ADC Mailing customer. You'll then receive the latest in development tools, system software, development kits, and reference materials via a CD series delivered to you monthly via snail mail.

A low-cost ADC Student Program is targeted at university students around the world. ADC Student developers receive special introductory tools, access to a student community of Mac programmers, and other educational opportunities, including the chance to win scholarships to the Worldwide Developers Conference.

The priciest ADC programs are called Select and Premier. These programs offer a multitude of plush products and services, including fat discounts on Apple hardware and third-party products and services and access to Apple's technical support engineers.

For information on signing up for any of these programs, go to:

http://developer.apple.com/membership/

B

Carbon Event Classes and Kinds

In order to handle events, you need to tell the Carbon Event Manager what kinds of events you want to be notified about. You do so by specifying the class and kind of each event you want to handle. Tables B-1 through B-9 list the most common event classes and kinds. After you've identified the event class (keyboard, mouse, and so forth) and the event kind (mouse up, mouse down, and so on) appropriate to your application's needs, you pass these to the Carbon Event Manager when installing your event handler. See Chapter 6, *Carbon Events*, for more information.

Table B-1. Event Kinds in the Application Event Class (kEventClassApplication)

Event Kind	Means
kEventAppActivated	This application brought to foreground
kEventAppDeactivated	This application sent to background
kEventAppFrontSwitched	Frontmost (active) application changed
kEventAppLaunched	Another application started up
kEventAppTerminated	Another application terminated
kEventAppQuit	This application about to be terminated

Table B-2. Event Kinds in the Command Event Class (kEventClassCommand)

Event Kind	Means
kEventCommandProcess	Menu item chosen or a control with a command that has been pressed
kEventCommandUpdateStatus	Determine enabled or disabled status of command

Table B-3. Event Kinds in the Control Event Class (kEventClassControl)

Event Kind	Means
kEventControlDefInitialize	Control created
kEventControlDefDispose	Control to be destroyed
kEventControlHit	Mouse button pressed in control
kEventControlSimulateHit	Sent when the control should simulate a hit in response to some other action (such as when the Return key is pressed to activate a default button)

Table B-4. Event Kinds in the Keyboard Event Class (kEventClassKeyboard)

Event Kind	Means
kEventRawKeyDown	Key pressed
kEventRawKeyRepeat	Keystroke repeated when key held down
kEventRawKeyUp	Key released
kEventRawKeyModifiersChanged	Modifier key pressed or released

Table B-5. Event Kinds in the Menu Event Class (kEventClassMenu)

Event Kind	Means
kEventMenuBeginTracking	Mouse button pressed in menu or menu bar
kEventMenuEndTracking	Mouse button released after press in menu or menu bar
kEventMenuOpening	Menu about to be displayed
kEventMenuClosed	Menu has been hidden
kEventMenuTargetItem	Cursor dragged over menu item
kEventMenuMatchKey	Match menu item with command event
kEventMenuEnableItems	Determine enabled or disabled status of menu items

Table B-6. Event Kinds in the Mouse Event Class (kEventClassMouse)

Event Kind	Means
kEventMouseDown	Mouse button pressed
kEventMouseUp	Mouse button released
kEventMouseMoved	Mouse position changed
kEventMouseDragged	Mouse position changed with button held down
kMouseWheelMoved	The mouse scroll wheel moved

Table B-7. Event Kinds in the Tablet Event Class (kEventClassTablet)

Event Kind	Means
kEventTabletPointer	Pen has touched the tablet
kEventTabletProximity	Pen has entered or exited the tablet's proximity region

Table B-8. Event Kinds in the Text Input Event Class (kEventClassTextInput)

Event Kind	Means
kEventUnicodeForKeyEvent	Text character typed from keyboard
kEventOffsetToPos	Map character index to screen position
kEventPosToOffset	Map screen position to character index
kEventGetSelectedText	Determine currently selected text
kEventUpdateActiveInputArea	Request to update the text input area
kEventShowHideBottomWindow	Request to show or hide a text input window

Table B-9. Event Kinds in the Window Event Class (kEventClassWindow)

Event Kind	Means
kEventWindowInit	Window created
kEventWindowDispose	Window to be destroyed
kEventWindowActivated	Window activated (brought to front)
kEventWindowDeactivated	Window deactivated (sent behind)
kEventWindowShown	Window made visible
kEventWindowHidden	Window made invisible
kEventWindowDrawContent	Draw window's contents on screen
kEventWindowCursorChange	Cursor moved into content region
kEventWindowClickContentRegion	Mouse click in content region
kEventWindowHandleContentClick	Mouse click occurred in content region, but the click did not occur in a control and it is not a contextual menu click
kEventWindowAcquired	Keyboard focus acquired
kEventWindowRelinquish	Keyboard focus to be relinquished
kEventWindowOriginChange	Window to be moved
kEventWindowOriginChanged	Window moved
kEventWindowSizeChange	Window to be resized
kEventWindowSizeChanged	Window resized
kEventWindowCollapse	Window to be minimized
kEventWindowCollapsed	Window minimized

Table B-9. Event Kinds in the Window Event Class (kEventClassWindow) (continued)

Event Kind	Means
kEventWindowCollapseAll	All windows to be minimized
kEventWindowExpand	Window to be expanded
kEventWindowExpanded	Window expanded
kEventWindowExpandAll	All windows to be expanded
kEventWindowZoom	Window to be zoomed
kEventWindowZoomed	Window zoomed
kEventWindowZoomAll	All windows to be zoomed
kEventWindowClose	Window to be closed
kEventWindowClosed	Window closed
kEventWindowCloseAll	All windows to be closed

C

Parameter Names and Types for Common Event Kinds

If you want to retrieve the value of a parameter associated with a Carbon event, you need to call `GetEventParameter` (discussed in Chapter 6, *Carbon Events*). However, while calling the function is fairly straightforward, the tricky part is figuring out the parameter names and types associated with the event; you can't retrieve the proper parameter unless you know how to specify it properly in your function call. This appendix provides a solution by listing the parameter names and types for most common events and for many of the uncommon ones as well. The parameter names and types are grouped by event class (command, menu, window, and so on) and then by event kind within each class (mouse up, mouse down, window closed, and so on).

Apple Events

The Apple Event Manager sends Apple events between applications on the same computer or between applications on remote computers. Applications typically use Apple events to request services and information from other applications or to provide services and information in response to such requests.

If you're curious, an Apple event conforms to the Apple Event Interprocess Messaging Protocol (AEIMP).

Table C-1. Parameter Names and Types for Apple Event Kinds

Event kind	Parameter name	Parameter type
kEventAppleEvent	kEventParamAEEventID	typeType

Control Events

Control events are generated from onscreen user interface objects-buttons, check-boxes, scroll bars, and so forth.

Table C-2. Required Parameter Names and Types for Control Event Kinds

Event kind	Parameter name	Parameter type
kEventControlInitialize	kEventParamDirectObject	typeControlRef
	kEventParamInitCollection	typeCollection
kEventControlDispose	kEventParamDirectObject	typeControlRef
kEventControlGetOptimal-Bounds	kEventParamDirectObject	typeControlRef
	kEventParamControlOptimalBounds	typeQDRectangle
kEventControlHit	kEventParamDirectObject	typeControlRef
	kEventParamControlPart	typeControlPartCode
	kEventParamKeyModifiers	typeUInt32
kEventControlSimulateHit	kEventParamDirectObject	typeControlRef
kEventControlHitTest	kEventParamDirectObject	typeControlRef
	kEventParamMouseLocation	typeQDPoint
	kEventParamControlPart	typeControlPartCode
kEventControlDraw	kEventParamDirectObject	typeControlRef
kEventControlApplyText-Color	kEventParamDirectObject	typeControlRef
	kEventParamControlSubControl	typeControlRef
	kEventParamControlDrawDepth	typeShortInteger
	kEventParamControlDrawInColor	typeBoolean
kEventControlSetFocusPart	kEventParamDirectObject	typeControlRef
	kEventParamControlPart	typeControlPartCode
kEventControlGetFocusPart	kEventParamDirectObject	typeControlRef
	kEventParamControlPart	typeControlPartCode
kEventControlActivate	kEventParamDirectObject	typeControlRef
kEventControlDeactivate	kEventParamDirectObject	typeControlRef

Table C-2. Required Parameter Names and Types for Control Event Kinds (continued)

Event kind	Parameter name	Parameter type
kEventControlSetCursor	kEventParamDirectObject	typeControlRef
	kEventParamMouseLocation	typeQDPoint
	kEventParamKeyModifiers	typeUInt32
kEventControlContextual-MenuClick	kEventParamDirectObject	typeControlRef
	kEventParamMouseLocation	typeQDPoint
kEventControlTrack	kEventParamDirectObject	typeControlRef
	kEventParamMouseLocation	typeQDPoint
	kEventParamKeyModifiers	typeUInt32
	kEventParamControlAction	typeControlActionUPP
	kEventParamControlPart	typeControlPartCode
kEventControlGetScrollTo-HereStartPoint	kEventParamDirectObject	typeControlRef
	kEventParamMouseLocation	typeQDPoint
	kEventParamKeyModifiers	typeUInt32
kEventControlGetIndica-torDragConstraint	kEventParamDirectObject	typeControlRef
	kEventParamMouseLocation	typeQDPoint
	kEventParamKeyModifiers	typeUInt32
	kEventParamControlIndicatorDrag-Constraint	typeIndicatorDrag-Constraint
kEventControlIndicator-Moved	kEventParamDirectObject	typeControlRef
	kEventParamControlIndicatorRegion	typeQDRgnHandle
	kEventParamControlIsGhosting	typeBoolean
kEventControlGhostingFin-ished	kEventParamDirectObject	typeControlRef
	kEventParamControlIndicatorOffset	typeQDPoint
kEventControlGetAction-ProcPart	kEventParamDirectObject	typeControlRef
	kEventParamKeyModifiers	typeUInt32
	kEventParamControlPart	typeControlPartCode
kEventControlGetPartRe-gion	kEventParamDirectObject	typeControlRef
	kEventParamControlPart	typeControlPartCode
	kEventParamControlRegion	typeQDRgnHandle

Table C-2. Required Parameter Names and Types for Control Event Kinds (continued)

Event kind	Parameter name	Parameter type
kEventControlGetPart-Bounds	kEventParamDirectObject	typeControlRef
	kEventParamControlPart	typeControlPartCode
	kEventParamControlBounds	typeQDRectangle
kEventControlSetData	kEventParamDirectObject	typeControlRef
	kEventParamControlPart	typeControlPartCode
	kEventParamControlDataTag	typeEnumeration
	kEventParamControlDataBuffer	typePtr
	kEventParamControlDataBufferSize	typeLongInteger
kEventControlGetData	kEventParamDirectObject	typeControlRef
	kEventParamControlPart	typeControlPartCode
	kEventParamControlDataTag	typeEnumeration
	kEventParamControlDataBuffer	typePtr
	kEventParamControlDataBufferSize	typeLongInteger
kEventControlValueField-Changed	kEventParamDirectObject	typeControlRef
kEventControlAddedSubControl	kEventParamDirectObject	typeControlRef
	kEventParamControlSubControl	typeControlRef
kEventControlRemovingSub-Control	kEventParamDirectObject	typeControlRef
	kEventParamControlSubControl	typeControlRef
kEventControlBoundsChanged	kEventParamDirectObject	typeControlRef
	kEventParamAttributes	typeUInt32
	kEventParamOriginalBounds	typeQDRectangle
	kEventParamPreviousBounds	typeQDRectangle
	kEventParamCurrentBounds	typeQDRectangle
kEventControlOwningWindowChanged	kEventParamDirectObject	typeControlRef
	kEventParamAttributes	typeUInt32
	kEventParamControlOriginalOwning-Window	typeWindowRef
	kEventParamControlCurrentOwning-Window	typeWindowRef

Table C-2. Required Parameter Names and Types for Control Event Kinds (continued)

Event kind	Parameter name	Parameter type
kEventControlArbi-traryMessage	kEventParamDirectObject	typeControlRef
	kEventParamControlMessage	typeShortInteger
	kEventParamControlParam	typeLongInteger
	kEventParamControlResult	typeLongInteger

Command Events

Command events are generated by selecting menu items or activating controls.

Table C-3. Parameter Names and Types for Command Event Kinds

Event kind	Parameter name	Parameter type
kEventCommandProcess	kEventParamDirectObject	typeHICommand
kEventCommandUpdateStatus	kEventParamDirectObject	typeHICommand

Menu Events

Menu events are generated when the user opens or closes a menu or when programmatic changes are made to the application (such as enabling a menu item).

Table C-4. Parameter Names and Types for Menu Event Kinds

Event kind	Parameter name	Parameter type
kEventMenuBeginTracking	kEventParamDirectObject	typeMenuRef
	kEventParamCurrentMenuTrackingMode	typeMenuTrackingMode
kEventMenuEndTracking	kEventParamDirectObject	typeMenuRef
kEventMenuOpening	kEventParamDirectObject	typeMenuRef
	kEventParamMenuFirstOpen	typeBoolean
kEventMenuClosed	kEventParamDirectObject	typeMenuRef
kEventMenuTargetItem	kEventParamDirectObject	typeMenuRef
	kEventParamMenuItemIndex	typeMenuItemIndex
	kEventParamMenuCommand	typeMenuCommand
kEventMenuMatchKey	kEventParamDirectObject	typeMenuRef
	kEventParamEventRef	typeEventRef
	kEventParamMenuEventOptions	typeMenuEventOptions
	kEventParamMenuItemIndex	typeMenuItemIndex

Table C-4. Parameter Names and Types for Menu Event Kinds (continued)

Event kind	Parameter name	Parameter type
kEventMenuEnableItems	kEventParamDirectObject	typeMenuRef
	kEventParamEnableMenuForKeyEvent	typeBoolean

Mouse Events

Mouse events are generated when the user manipulates the mouse (moving, clicking, dragging, and so on).

Table C-5. Parameter Names and Types for Mouse Event Kinds

Event kind	Parameter name	Parameter type
kEventMouseDown	kEventParamMouseLocation	typeQDPoint
	kEventParamKeyModifiers	typeUInt32
	kEventParamMouseButton	typeMouseButton
	kEventParamClickCount	typeUInt32
kEventMouseUp	kEventParamMouseLocation	typeQDPoint
	kEventParamKeyModifiers	typeUInt32
	kEventParamMouseButton	typeMouseButton
	kEventParamClickCount	typeUInt32
kEventMouseMoved	kEventParamMouseLocation	typeQDPoint
	kEventParamKeyModifiers	typeUInt32
kEventMouseDragged	kEventParamMouseLocation	typeQDPoint
	kEventParamKeyModifiers	typeUInt32
	kEventParamMouseButton	typeMouseButton
kEventMouseWheelMoved	kEventParamMouseLocation	typeQDPoint
	kEventParamKeyModifiers	typeUInt32
	kEventParamMouseWheelAxis	typeMouseWheelAxis
	kEventParamMouseWheelDelta	typeLongInteger

Text Input Events

Text input events are generated in response to text input handled by the Text Services Manager. These events typically correspond to actions taken by a text input method, rather than raw keystrokes, although some of the parameters allow you to extract individual characters.

Table C-6. Required Parameter Names and Types for Text Input Event Kinds

Event kind	Parameter name	Parameter type
kEventUpdateActiveIn-putArea	kEventParamTextInputSendCompo-nentInstance	typeComponentInstance
	kEventParamTextInputSendRefCon	typeLongInteger
	kEventParamTextInputSendSLRec	typeIntlWritingCode
	kEventParamTextInputSendFixLen	typeLongInteger
	kEventParamTextInputSendText	typeUnicodeText for a Unicode document; typeChar otherwise
kEventUnicode-ForKeyEvent	kEventParamTextInputSendCompo-nentInstance	typeComponentInstance
	kEventParamTextInputSendRefCon	typeLongInteger
	kEventParamTextInputSendSLRec	typeIntlWritingCode
	kEventParamTextInputSendText	typeUnicodeText
	kEventParamTextInputSendKey-boardEvent	typeEventRef
kEventOffsetToPos	kEventParamTextInputSendCompo-nentInstance	typeComponentInstance
	kEventParamTextInputSendRefCon	typeLongInteger
	kEventParamTextInputSend-TextOffset	typeLongInteger
	kEventParamTextInputReplyPoint	typeQDPoint
kEventPosToOffset	kEventParamTextInputSendCompo-nentInstance	typeComponentInstance
	kEventParamTextInputSendRefCon	typeLongInteger
	kEventParamTextInputSendCur-rentPoint	typeQDPoint
	kEventParamTextInputReplyRe-gionClass	typeLongInteger
	kEventParamTextInputReply-TextOffset	typeLongInteger
kEventShowHideBot-tomWindow	kEventParamTextInputSendCompo-nentInstance	typeComponentInstance
	kEventParamTextInputSendRefCon	typeLongInteger
kEventGetSelectedText	kEventParamTextInputSendCompo-nentInstance	typeComponentInstance
	kEventParamTextInputSendRefCon	typeLongInteger

Window Events

Windows generate a wide variety of events. This section is organized into separate tables for window refresh, activation, state change, cursor change, action, focus, and definition event kinds.

Table C-7. Parameter Names and Types for Window Refresh Event Kinds

Event kind	Parameter name	Parameter type
kEventWindowUpdate	kEventParamDirectObject	typeWindowRef
kEventWindowDrawContent	kEventParamDirectObject	typeWindowRef

Table C-8. Parameter Names and Types for Window Activation Event Kinds

Event kind	Parameter name	Parameter type
kEventWindowActivated	kEventParamDirectObject	typeWindowRef
kEventWindowDeactivated	kEventParamDirectObject	typeWindowRef
kEventWindowGetClickActi-vation	kEventParamDirectObject	typeWindowRef
	kEventParamMouseLocation	typeQDPoint
	kEventParamKeyModifiers	typeUInt32
	kEventParamClickActivation	typeClickActivationResult

Table C-9. Parameter Names and Types for Window State Change Event Kinds

Event kind	Parameter name	Parameter type
kEventWindowBoundsChanging	kEventParamDirectObject	typeWindowRef
	kEventParamAttributes	typeUInt32
	kEventParamOriginalBounds	typeQDRectangle
	kEventParamPreviousBounds	typeQDRectangle
	kEventParamCurrentBounds	typeQDRectangle
kEventWindowBoundsChanged	kEventParamDirectObject	typeWindowRef
	kEventParamAttributes	typeUInt32
	kEventParamOriginalBounds	typeQDRectangle
	kEventParamPreviousBounds	typeQDRectangle
	kEventParamCurrentBounds	typeQDRectangle
kEventWindowShown	kEventParamDirectObject	typeWindowRef
kEventWindowHidden	kEventParamDirectObject	typeWindowRef

Table C-10. Parameter Names and Types for Window Cursor Change Event Kinds

Event kind	Parameter name	Parameter type
kEventWindowCursorChange	kEventParamDirectObject	typeWindowRef
	kEventParamMouseLocation	typeQDPoint
	kEventParamKeyModifiers	typeUInt32

Table C-11. Parameter Names and Types for Window Action Event Kinds

Event kind	Parameter name	Parameter type
kEventWindowCollapse	kEventParamDirectObject	typeWindowRef
kEventWindowCollapsed	kEventParamDirectObject	typeWindowRef
kEventWindowCollapseAll	kEventParamDirectObject	typeWindowRef
kEventWindowExpand	kEventParamDirectObject	typeWindowRef
kEventWindowExpanded	kEventParamDirectObject	typeWindowRef
kEventWindowExpandAll	kEventParamDirectObject	typeWindowRef
kEventWindowClose	kEventParamDirectObject	typeWindowRef
kEventWindowClosed	kEventParamDirectObject	typeWindowRef
kEventWindowCloseAll	kEventParamDirectObject	typeWindowRef
kEventWindowZoom	kEventParamDirectObject	typeWindowRef
kEventWindowZoomed	kEventParamDirectObject	typeWindowRef
kEventWindowZoomAll	kEventParamDirectObject	typeWindowRef
kEventWindowContextualMenuSelect	kEventParamDirectObject	typeWindowRef
kEventWindowPathSelect	kEventParamDirectObject	typeWindowRef
kEventWindowGetIdealSize	kEventParamDirectObject	typeWindowRef
	kEventParamDimensions	typeQDPoint
kEventWindowGetMinimumSize	kEventParamDirectObject	typeWindowRef
	kEventParamDimensions	typeQDPoint
kEventWindowGetMaximumSize	kEventParamDirectObject	typeWindowRef
	kEventParamDimensions	typeQDPoint
kEventWindowProxyBeginDrag	kEventParamDirectObject	typeWindowRef
kEventWindowProxyEndDrag	kEventParamDirectObject	typeWindowRef

Table C-12. Parameter Names and Types for Window Focus Event Kinds

Event kind	Parameter name	Parameter type
kEventWindowFocusAcquire	kEventParamDirectObject	typeWindowRef
kEventWindowFocusRelinquish	kEventParamDirectObject	typeWindowRef

Table C-13. Parameter Names and Types for Window Definition Event Kinds

Event kind	Parameter name	Parameter type
kEventWindowDrawFrame	kEventParamDirectObject	typeWindowRef
kEventWindowDrawPart	kEventParamDirectObject	typeWindowRef
	kEventParamWindowDefPart	typeWindowDefPartCode
kEventWindowGetRegion	kEventParamDirectObject	typeWindowRef
	kEventParamWindowRegionCode	typeWindowRegionCode
	kEventParamRgnHandle	typeQDRgnHandle
kEventWindowHitTest	kEventParamDirectObject	typeWindowRef
	kEventParamMouseLocation	typeQDPoint
	kEventParamWindowDefPart	typeWindowDefPartCode
kEventWindowInit	kEventParamDirectObject	typeWindowRef
	kEventParamWindowFeatures	typeUInt32
kEventWindowDispose	kEventParamDirectObject	typeWindowRef
kEventWindowDragHilite	kEventParamDirectObject	typeWindowRef
	kEventParamWindowDragHiliteFlag	typeBoolean
kEventWindowModified	kEventParamDirectObject	typeWindowRef
	kEventParamWindowModifiedFlag	typeBoolean
kEventWindowSetupProxy-DragImage	kEventParamDirectObject	typeWindowRef
	kEventParamWindowProxyImageRgn	typeQDRgnHandle
	kEventParamWindowProxyOutlineRgn	typeQDRgnHandle
	kEventParamWindowProxyGWorlPtr	typeGWorldPtr
kEventWindowStateChanged	kEventParamDirectObject	typeWindowRef
	kEventParamWindowStateChangedFlags	typeUInt32
kEventWindowMeasureTitle	kEventParamDirectObject	typeWindowRef
	kEventParamWindowTitleFullWidth	typeSInt16
	kEventParamWindowTitleTextWidth	typeSInt16
kEventWindowDrawGrowBox	kEventParamDirectObject	typeWindowRef

Table C-13. Parameter Names and Types for Window Definition Event Kinds (continued)

Event kind	Parameter name	Parameter type
kEventWindowGetGrowImageRegion	kEventParamDirectObject	typeWindowRef
	kEventParamWindowGrowRect	typeQDRectangle
	kEventParamRgnHandle	typeQDRectangle
kEventWindowPaint	kEventParamDirectObject	typeWindowRef

Index

Symbols

{ } (braces), writing strings for Localizable.strings file, 125
= (equal sign), writing strings for Localizable.strings file, 125
; (semicolon), writing strings for Localizable.strings file, 125
/ (slash) in file pathnames, 218, 220
~ (tilde) in file pathnames, 218, 220
" " (quotation marks), writing strings for Localizable.strings file, 125

Numbers

2D graphics, 7
3D graphics, 10

A

About menu item, 21
About window, 24, 186
    commands for, 113
    creating from nib files, 192
    event handlers for, 195-197
AboutWindowCommandHandler function, 193
access paths, 205
Acrobat Reader, viewing Developer Guides, 42
activate event in Receives option window, 56
AddEventTypesToHandler function, 94

additions (scripting), 283
Adobe Photoshop, adding PICT Resource files, 76
advanced topic in Carbon, 278-307
AECoerceDesc functon, 244
AECoersceDesc function, 233
AECountItems function, 290
AEDisposeDesc function, 234, 246
AEGetDescData function, 233, 244
AEGetNthPtr function, 290
AEInstallEventHandler function, 292
'aete' resource, 288
Alert window class, 53
Alias Manager, 8
    referencing files with, 204
Alignment
    palette, 68
    tools, 79
allocation blocks, 206
API (application programming interface), 95
AppDrawPage function, 143
Appearance Manager, 6
Apple Developer
    Technical Support, maintaining database of creator codes, 62
    webHelp Software Development Kit (SDK), 123
Apple Event Manager, 8
Apple events, 279

We'd like to hear your suggestions for improving our indexes. Send email to *index@oreilly.com.*

About the Author

Learning Carbon was created by the technical writers, engineers, support specialists, and other professionals at Apple Computer, Inc. who are committed to making Mac OS X a superior platform for innovation, productivity, and enjoyment. These professionals have diligently collected, compiled, and edited the information in this books to ensure that it is a useful resource for Mac OS X developers.

Colophon

Our look is the result of reader comments, our own experimentation, and feedback from distribution channels. Distinctive covers complement our distinctive approach to technical topics, breathing personality and life into potentially dry subjects. The animals on the cover of *Learning Carbon* are bloodhounds.

Sarah Jane Shangraw was the production editor and proofreader for *Learning Carbon*. Paulette Miley was the copyeditor. Catherine Morris and Claire Cloutier provided quality control. Ann Schirmer, Linley Dolby, and Matt Hutchinson worked on interior composition. Joe Wizda wrote the index.

Pam Spremulli designed the cover of this book, based on a series design by Edie Freedman. The cover image is a 19th-century engraving from the Dover Pictorial Archive. Emma Colby produced the cover mechanical with QuarkXPress 4.1 using Adobe's ITC Garamond font.

Melanie Wang designed the interior layout based on a series design by Nancy Priest. Jason McIntosh converted *Learning Carbon* into DocBook XML from Apple's native XML format and formatted the book with a program created by Norman Walsh, Lenny Muellner, and Erik Ray. The text and heading fonts are ITC Garamond Light and Garamond Book; the code font is Constant Willison. The illustrations that appear in the book were produced by Robert Romano and Jessamyn Read using Macromedia FreeHand 9 and Adobe Photoshop 6.

Whenever possible, our books use a durable and flexible lay-flat binding. If the page count exceeds this binding's limit, perfect binding is used.

Want To Know More About Mac OS X?

The Apple Developer Connection offers convenient and timely support for all your Mac OS X development needs.

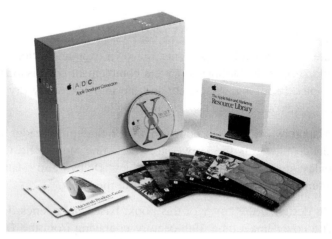

Developer Programs

The Apple Developer Connection (ADC) helps Macintosh developers build, test, market, and distribute software and hardware products for Mac OS X. ADC Programs provide direct, affordable access to Mac OS X software, along with many other products and services, including:

- Pre-release software seeds
- Apple hardware discounts
- Technical support
- Discounts on third-party services such as Mac OS X migration, Aqua and Cocoa integration, Carbon porting, quality assurance, and more.

Programs range in price from $0 (free) to US$3500 and are available worldwide.

Developer Documentation

The ADC web site has a wide variety of reference materials including in-depth articles, tutorials, sample code, FAQs, and technical notes such as "Moving Your Code to Mac OS X". Our electronic newsletter keeps members notified with up-to-the-minute information on new releases and documentation.

Developers and Mac OS X

ADC Program members are mailed advance copies of Mac OS X software and development tools such as Interface Builder and Project Builder. ADC also helps you tell the world about your Mac OS X products when they are ready to ship.

Join today!
Visit http://developer.apple.com/membership/

Apple Developer Connection

How to stay in touch with O'Reilly

1. Visit Our Award-Winning Web Site

http://www.oreilly.com/

★ "Top 100 Sites on the Web" —*PC Magazine*
★ "Top 5% Web sites" —*Point Communications*
★ "3-Star site" —*The McKinley Group*

Our web site contains a library of comprehensive product information (including book excerpts and tables of contents), downloadable software, background articles, interviews with technology leaders, links to relevant sites, book cover art, and more. File us in your Bookmarks or Hotlist!

2. Join Our Email Mailing Lists

New Product Releases

To receive automatic email with brief descriptions of all new O'Reilly products as they are released, send email to:
ora-news-subscribe@lists.oreilly.com
Put the following information in the first line of your message (*not* in the Subject field):
subscribe ora-news

O'Reilly Events

If you'd also like us to send information about trade show events, special promotions, and other O'Reilly events, send email to:
ora-news-subscribe@lists.oreilly.com
Put the following information in the first line of your message (*not* in the Subject field):
subscribe ora-events

3. Get Examples from Our Books via FTP

There are two ways to access an archive of example files from our books:

Regular FTP

- ftp to:
  ftp.oreilly.com
  (login: anonymous
  password: your email address)
- Point your web browser to:
  ftp://ftp.oreilly.com/

FTPMAIL

- Send an email message to:
  ftpmail@online.oreilly.com
  (Write "help" in the message body)

4. Contact Us via Email

order@oreilly.com
To place a book or software order online. Good for North American and international customers.

subscriptions@oreilly.com
To place an order for any of our newsletters or periodicals.

books@oreilly.com
General questions about any of our books.

software@oreilly.com
For general questions and product information about our software. Check out O'Reilly Software Online at **http://software.oreilly.com/** for software and technical support information. Registered O'Reilly software users send your questions to: **website-support@oreilly.com**

cs@oreilly.com
For answers to problems regarding your order or our products.

booktech@oreilly.com
For book content technical questions or corrections.

proposals@oreilly.com
To submit new book or software proposals to our editors and product managers.

international@oreilly.com
For information about our international distributors or translation queries. For a list of our distributors outside of North America check out:
http://www.oreilly.com/distributors.html

5. Work with Us

Check out our website for current employment opportunites:
http://jobs.oreilly.com/

O'Reilly & Associates, Inc.
101 Morris Street, Sebastopol, CA 95472 USA
TEL   707-829-0515 or 800-998-9938
       (6am to 5pm PST)
FAX   707-829-0104

International Distributors

http://international.oreilly.com/distributors.html

UK, EUROPE, MIDDLE EAST AND AFRICA (EXCEPT FRANCE, GERMANY, AUSTRIA, SWITZERLAND, LUXEMBOURG, AND LIECHTENSTEIN)

INQUIRIES
O'Reilly UK Limited
4 Castle Street
Farnham
Surrey, GU9 7HS
United Kingdom
Telephone: 44-1252-711776
Fax: 44-1252-734211
Email: information@oreilly.co.uk

ORDERS
Wiley Distribution Services Ltd.
1 Oldlands Way
Bognor Regis
West Sussex PO22 9SA
United Kingdom
Telephone: 44-1243-843294
UK Freephone: 0800-243207
Fax: 44-1243-843302 (Europe/EU orders)
or 44-1243-843274 (Middle East/Africa)
Email: cs-books@wiley.co.uk

FRANCE

INQUIRIES & ORDERS
Éditions O'Reilly
18 rue Séguier
75006 Paris, France
Tel: 1-40-51-71-89
Fax: 1-40-51-72-26
Email: france@oreilly.fr

GERMANY, SWITZERLAND, AUSTRIA, LUXEMBOURG, AND LIECHTENSTEIN

INQUIRIES & ORDERS
O'Reilly Verlag
Balthasarstr. 81
D-50670 Köln, Germany
Telephone: 49-221-973160-91
Fax: 49-221-973160-8
Email: anfragen@oreilly.de (inquiries)
Email: order@oreilly.de (orders)

CANADA (FRENCH LANGUAGE BOOKS)

Les Éditions Flammarion ltée
375, Avenue Laurier Ouest
Montréal (Québec) H2V 2K3
Tel: 00-1-514-277-8807
Fax: 00-1-514-278-2085
Email: info@flammarion.qc.ca

HONG KONG

City Discount Subscription Service, Ltd.
Unit A, 6th Floor, Yan's Tower
27 Wong Chuk Hang Road
Aberdeen, Hong Kong
Tel: 852-2580-3539
Fax: 852-2580-6463
Email: citydis@ppn.com.hk

KOREA

Hanbit Media, Inc.
Chungmu Bldg. 210
Yonnam-dong 568-33
Mapo-gu
Seoul, Korea
Tel: 822-325-0397
Fax: 822-325-9697
Email: hant93@chollian.dacom.co.kr

PHILIPPINES

Global Publishing
G/F Benavides Garden
1186 Benavides Street
Manila, Philippines
Tel: 632-254-8949/632-252-2582
Fax: 632-734-5060/632-252-2733
Email: globalp@pacific.net.ph

TAIWAN

O'Reilly Taiwan
1st Floor, No. 21, Lane 295
Section 1, Fu-Shing South Road
Taipei, 106 Taiwan
Tel: 886-2-27099669
Fax: 886-2-27038802
Email: mori@oreilly.com

INDIA

Shroff Publishers & Distributors Pvt. Ltd.
12, "Roseland", 2nd Floor
180, Waterfield Road, Bandra (West)
Mumbai 400 050
Tel: 91-22-641-1800/643-9910
Fax: 91-22-643-2422
Email: spd@vsnl.com

CHINA

O'Reilly Beijing
SIGMA Building, Suite B809
No. 49 Zhichun Road
Haidian District
Beijing, China PR 100080
Tel: 86-10-8809-7475
Fax: 86-10-8809-7463
Email: beijing@oreilly.com

JAPAN

O'Reilly Japan, Inc.
Yotsuya Y's Building
7 Banch 6, Honshio-cho
Shinjuku-ku
Tokyo 160-0003 Japan
Tel: 81-3-3356-5227
Fax: 81-3-3356-5261
Email: japan@oreilly.com

SINGAPORE, INDONESIA, MALAYSIA AND THAILAND

TransQuest Publishers Pte Ltd
30 Old Toh Tuck Road #05-02
Sembawang Kimtrans Logistics Centre
Singapore 597654
Tel: 65-4623112
Fax: 65-4625761
Email: wendiw@transquest.com.sg

ALL OTHER ASIAN COUNTRIES

O'Reilly & Associates, Inc.
101 Morris Street
Sebastopol, CA 95472 USA
Tel: 707-829-0515
Fax: 707-829-0104
Email: order@oreilly.com

AUSTRALIA

Woodslane Pty., Ltd.
7/5 Vuko Place
Warriewood NSW 2102
Australia
Tel: 61-2-9970-5111
Fax: 61-2-9970-5002
Email: info@woodslane.com.au

NEW ZEALAND

Woodslane New Zealand, Ltd.
21 Cooks Street (P.O. Box 575)
Waganui, New Zealand
Tel: 64-6-347-6543
Fax: 64-6-345-4840
Email: info@woodslane.com.au

ARGENTINA

Distribuidora Cuspide
Suipacha 764
1008 Buenos Aires
Argentina
Phone: 5411-4322-8868
Fax: 5411-4322-3456
Email: libros@cuspide.com

O'REILLY®

TO ORDER: **800-998-9938** • **order@oreilly.com** • **http://www.oreilly.com/**
OUR PRODUCTS ARE AVAILABLE AT A BOOKSTORE OR SOFTWARE STORE NEAR YOU.
FOR INFORMATION: **800-998-9938** • **707-829-0515** • **info@oreilly.com**